Contents

The English Garden · *Page 2*
Garden Designers · *Page 4*
Town Parks and Gardens · *Page 6*
The National Trust · *Page 8*
Entertainment in Gardens · *Page 10*
Victorian Roses and Rose Gardens · *Page 12*
Garden Features · *Page 14*
National Garden Festival, Stoke-on-Trent · *Page 24*
Notes on Garden Visiting · *Page 29*

The GARDENS *of* ENGLAND

Cumbria · *The County of Cumbria · Page 30*
East Anglia · *Cambridgeshire, Essex, Norfolk, Suffolk · Page 34*
East Midlands · *Derbyshire, Leicestershire, Lincolnshire, Northamptonshire, Nottinghamshire · Page 39*
Heart of England · *Gloucestershire, Hereford and Worcester, Shropshire, Staffordshire, Warwickshire, West Midlands · Page 44*
London · *Page 51*
Northumbria · *Cleveland, Durham, Northumberland, Tyne & Wear · Page 56*
North West · *Cheshire, Greater Manchester, Lancashire, Merseyside · Page 60*
South · *Hampshire, Eastern Dorset and the Isle of Wight · Page 65*
South East England · *East Sussex, Kent, Surrey, West Sussex · Page 70*
Thames and Chilterns · *Bedfordshire, Berkshire, Buckinghamshire, Hertfordshire, Oxfordshire · Page 77*
West Country · *Avon, Cornwall, Devon, Somerset, Western Dorset, Wiltshire and the Isles of Scilly · Page 83*
Yorkshire and Humberside · *North, South and West Yorkshire, Humberside · Page 92*

Gardens for Disabled People · *Page 97*
Garden Centres and Nurseries · *Page 100*
Hotels · *Page 103*
Garden Holidays and Tours · *Page 109*
Index · *Page 110*
Advertisers' Index · *Page 112*

The ENGLISH GARDEN

Gardening in England arrived with the Romans, nearly vanished in the Dark Ages (sustained largely by monks) and only scanty evidence survives of its resurgence in the Middle Ages. But we have just enough information from that time to suggest small, enclosed gardens featuring arbours, trellises festooned with trailing plants, and geometric beds containing roses, lilies and flowers from meadow and hedgerow.

A serious interest really began only in the Tudor and Elizabethan periods, when travellers returned from abroad with new species to augment the pretty but humble hardy natives. The typical Tudor garden, for viewing from the front windows of the house, was a formal square bounded by low walls or hedges. Most had two main alleys intersecting in the centre, where a flower-bed or fountain provided a focal point. There would be further paths – perhaps bounded by fruit trees – running parallel with the main alleys. In between were knots, small beds of dwarf plants or sand and gravel laid out in interwoven patterns that closely resembled those found in contemporary embroidery. Relief from this mathematical order was provided by topiary, statues, arbours, trellises, mazes, pavilions and fishponds, with a mount or raised perimeter terrace to give views of the surrounding countryside in some larger designs.

The basic square garden lasted well into the 17th century, especially in more modest schemes, but now tended to be sited at the rear of the house. Sometimes there were side gardens as well, so that the grounds of a large house consisted of a series of interconnected squares. But the fashionable trend – influenced by the French thinking exemplified by Versailles – was to expand outwards. In many schemes the knot gave way to a much larger, patterned terrace called a parterre. In the grandest gardens, broad, tree-lined avenues fanned outwards from a semi-circular patte d'oie (literally, goose's foot), drawing the eye towards fountains, statues, temples and other strategically sited features and on into the landscape beyond. Water was also employed – in canals and basins – to create similar vistas. This was gardening for royalty and nobility, and Hampton Court, Melbourne Hall and Bramham Park give us some idea of its scope for the spectacular.

At the end of the 17th century there was a brief dalliance with the far simpler, boxed-in Dutch style championed by William and Mary. It made great use of evergreens, canals were a major feature, and orange trees (housed, in the colder months, in elegant orangeries) were the very height of fashion.

Then came a far more radical change, one entirely English in invention. This was the landscape movement, whose practitioners disdained the formality of earlier styles, the obsessive concern for order and pattern. Nature, they claimed, should be the inspiration – but it was nature as seen by poets and painters (especially Italian ones) rather than the natural beauties of the English landscape. The landscape style evolved gradually. At first the garden – still somewhat formal – simply melted away into the landscape, with a sunken fence or ditch called a ha-ha

The formal style – orderly, patterned, harmonious. The enclosed garden became a world all of its own.

A Guide to English Gardens

Hardy's Cottage, Dorset

dividing the two. But by the second quarter of the 18th century, the landscape itself had become the garden. William Kent, the foremost arbiter of taste, devised flowing, Italian-style vistas of groves and glades, with scattered plantings of trees and shrubs and winding paths to lead the eye over contours dotted here and there with temples, pavilions and bridges in the Palladian style. Stourhead is the classic example of this style; it flirted with Chinese and Gothic notions and reached its zenith at Alton Towers, a phantasmagoria of decorative ideas not completed until a century later.

In the mid 18th century, the picturesque approach gave way to the idealised 'natural' landscape epitomised in the work of 'Capability' Brown at Blenheim, Bowood and elsewhere. Brown stripped the landscape down to its bare essentials, removing not only all formal plantings and decorations (and destroying much valuable earlier work in the process) but also the notion of the garden itself. The parkland came right up to the house; plants were of little consequence, except as aesthetic groupings to punctuate the sweep of the contours. He created lakes, flattened or raised hills, and restricted flowers to the confines of the kitchen garden. But his successor as leader of the landscape movement, Humphry Repton, reinstated the pleasure-garden notion, siting terraces and flower-beds near the house, clothing the walls with climbers and putting in conservatories and shrubberies to unify house and garden.

Plants themselves may have been almost irrelevant to 'Capability' Brown's way of thinking, but to the Victorian mind they were all-important. Their gardens were homes for plants as much as displays of the owner's wealth and taste. Collectors such as David Douglas, William Lobb, John Gould Veitch and Robert Fortune shipped home countless new species, while propagators and 'improvers' at home produced hybrids in ever-increasing numbers. To cater for these tender plants, huge heated greenhouses were constructed as shelters from the cold and damp of the English winter – such monuments in glass and iron became garden features in their own right.

After a brief interregnum in the early part of the 19th century, when the pretty, if rather prim 'gardenesque' style of John Claudius Loudon held sway, there was a return to sumptuous elaboration. Wide terraces, parterres, geometrically shaped beds and extensive herbaceous borders played host to massed ranks of exotics. They were bedded out in summer, in such displays of colour and form as had never before been seen in England. Urns, statues and other ornaments were

The sweeping expanse of the landscape garden – a sense of openness, of involvement with the countryside beyond.

Packwood House, Warwickshire

mass-produced in huge quantities and these too were crammed into the overflowing gardens of the genteel Victorians.

Towards the end of the century, the predictable reaction to this extravagance took place. William Robinson and Gertrude Jekyll in particular argued for a less ostentatious approach, strongly reminiscent of the cottage gardens they so much admired. And yet, the informal plants they favoured, with gentle drifts of colour and a harmonious interrelation between house and garden, demanded that nature be 'improved' by art, much as it had been with the landscapists. And so their gardens – Robinson's at Gravetye in Sussex, Miss Jekyll's at her Surrey home, Munstead Wood, and among others at Barrington Court and Hestercombe in Somerset – were masterpieces of sophistication, with each vista and plant grouping a picture carefully created with the eye of an artist.

The present century has seen a great diversity of styles, but if any two gardens could be singled out as its symbols the choice must surely fall on Hidcote Manor in Gloucestershire (begun in 1905 by Lawrence Johnston) and Sissinghurst Castle in Kent, the work of Vita Sackville-West and Harold Nicolson from the 1930s onwards. Both hark back to the 16th- and 17th-century notion of dividing the garden into separate sections, rather like the rooms of a house, both combine a formality of style with an effortless informality of planting (much use is made of 'old-fashioned' English flowers); both display a great variety in design and arrangement, and yet the parts are always subordinate to the whole. They sum up all that is best about the English garden – its long, cosmopolitan history of styles, its sensitivity towards colour, scent and form, its ability to encompass both the grand and the homely. The visitor knows that nowhere else in the world can such a diversity be enjoyed in such abundant splendour.

GARDEN DESIGNERS

Just as music, art and literature are susceptible to the vagaries of fashion and taste, garden design through the years has undergone some revolutionary changes of style. Since the eighteenth century, a succession of innovative designers have been responsible for changing the shape of the English garden. Examples of their original work, and wide-ranging influence, can be seen in many beautiful gardens throughout the country.

WILLIAM KENT
(1685–1748)

Something of a polymath (architect, designer and undistinguished painter), Kent was a Yorkshireman who fell in love with the mythical landscapes of classical Italy. The protégé of the Earl of Burlington, he was enamoured equally of Palladian architecture and the picturesque paintings of Claud Lorrain and Poussin of half a century earlier. When he turned his hand to garden design at Rousham House near Oxford, Stowe School and Chiswick House, London, these influences were strongly marked. The first true landscapist, he created idealised Italian scenes full of statuary, temples and arcades in the heart of English countryside, and succeeded in removing much of the stiffness and formality of earlier standards, injecting instead a fashionable note of romanticism.

LANCELOT 'CAPABILITY' BROWN
(1716–1783)

Northumberland-born, he worked from 1741 to 1751 in the great garden at Stowe designed by William Kent, and later took over his predecessor's mantle as leader of the landscape movement. From 1751 onwards he became a designer in his own right, and remodelled a great many famous gardens, among them those at Blenheim, Bowood, Chatsworth, Harewood House, Kew, Longleat, Luton Hoo and Sheffield Park. Entirely rejecting the formality of earlier styles and the neo-classical elaboration of Kent, his raw materials were contours and lakes rather than flowers and statues, though he made extensive use of clumps of hardwood trees to create simplified, natural-looking landscapes. His name comes from his habit of assuring anxious clients that their grounds had 'great capabilities' for improvement in the manner he envisaged: frequently this involved the wholesale demolition of existing features, the excavation of valleys and lakes, the flattening of hills and their re-siting elsewhere.

HUMPHRY REPTON
(1752–1815)

The leader of the third great phase of landscape gardening, following the death of 'Capability' Brown. Raised in Suffolk, he spent some of his formative years in Holland and was influenced by the neat, simple Dutch style. Though still a great believer in 'the genius of the place' – seeking largely to enhance the landscape's natural characteristics – he nevertheless increased the planting of the estate with trees and also reintroduced the formal garden surrounding the house. He was responsible for the gardens at Tatton Park, Cheshire and Sheringham Hall in Norfolk, among others, and in an entirely different vein also designed Russell Square, Bloomsbury Square and Cadogan Place in London's West End.

JOHN CLAUDIUS LOUDON
(1783–1843)

A very influential garden writer throughout the Victorian period, Loudon's phenomenal drive and thirst for knowledge led him – after the collapse of his own landscape gardening business – to produce a steady stream of garden literature. The *Gardener's Magazine*, which he founded in 1826, was the first of its kind devoted to the popular market. His 'gardenesque' style treated plants with respect – each was to be regarded as a specimen, each to be displayed to its best advantage. A Loudon garden was therefore never cluttered, and since he was a great

advocate of the use of rare and unusual plants had great educational as well as aesthetic value. His approach was widely adopted, from great country estates down to the most modest suburban villa.

GERTRUDE JEKYLL
(1843–1932)

A highly influential garden designer and writer from the 1890s onwards. Gertrude Jekyll (rhymes with 'treacle') was an artist of considerable ability and versatility. She was a close friend and colleague of William Robinson. When her eyesight began to fail in middle age, she turned from painting to gardening, and formed a productive partnership with the architect Edwin Lutyens, planning gardens around the houses he designed. Strongly influenced by the Arts and Crafts movement of William Morris, she championed the use of natural and traditional materials. Her plans for herbaceous borders were highly influential, with a sensitive use of colour and texture and careful planting to ensure continuity of display throughout the year. She is also notable for rediscovering many old-fashioned flowers which, during the great Victorian bedding craze, had been all but lost. Most of her books are still in print today, a tribute to the continued validity of her philosophy.

WILLIAM ROBINSON
(1893–1935)

Though Irish by birth, Robinson was responsible almost single-handedly for creating one of the most English of all horticultural styles – the 'natural' or 'wild' garden, an understandable reaction against the pomp and ostentation of Victorian fashion. Inspired by both the cottage garden and the wild flowers of meadow and woodland, he brought a slice of the English countryside into the domestic plot. Curiously, he dedicated *The Garden* – one of the numerous journals he founded and edited – to John Loudon, whose prim style he much admired. The leader of the so-called 'Surrey School', he was a close friend of Gertrude Jekyll; the effortlessly natural effect they both strived for was in fact the product of careful planning, a great knowledge of and love for plants, and a highly tuned artistic sensibility.

A GUIDE TO ENGLISH GARDENS

TOWN PARKS *and* GARDENS

by Ashley Stephenson
Bailiff of the Royal Parks

England's towns and cities boast a wealth of parks and gardens open to the public. These open spaces provide a welcome sanctuary, often only minutes from the busiest parts of our cities.

Amongst the many parks of Greater London are the Royal Parks. Some are of historic importance – areas which have changed little over the past hundred years; whilst others have been altered in response to a demand for more colour and variety. Hyde Park is probably the best-known park in the country, an oasis of 375 acres right in the heart of London. Whilst Hyde Park has only a few areas of horticultural interest, Regent's Park has at its centre Queen Mary's Rose Garden – one of the finest collections in the country. Also in central London is Holland Park with woodland and a fine parterre. Further out of London at Hampton Court, bedding can be seen at its very best and the Pond Garden and the Great Vine are also popular attractions. Peace and solitude can be found in the vast expanse of Richmond Park, where herds of Red and Fallow deer roam freely around 2,500 acres of parkland.

London doesn't hold a monopoly on parks; most cities have their fair share. Sheffield, for example, has no fewer than 52! Whirlow Brook Park, one of the grandest, was previously a private estate with landscaped grounds surrounding a water garden. Newcastle upon Tyne has an area of great beauty constructed in a natural valley at Jesmond Dene, and also Leazes Park, designed with curving paths and a large lake to supply movement to the scene.

Towns which do well in the 'Beautiful Britain' competition are always worth a visit. Cheltenham and Harrogate have much to offer, and Shrewsbury bursts into a riot of colour in the summer months. Bath is surely one of the prettiest cities where parks and open spaces add to the character of the city's fine old terraces. The keen gardener shouldn't miss a visit to Royal Victoria Park, close to Bath's Royal Crescent – it has one of the finest

A GUIDE TO ENGLISH GARDENS

collections of trees and shrubs to be found in a public park, as well as colourful flower gardens.

Seaside towns are well-known for their parks, which attract visitors throughout the year. Eastbourne has much to enjoy with colourful flower beds along its immaculate seafront; Brighton has many parks within its boundaries, many designed as areas where plants can grow as nature intended. Bournemouth's seafront is full of colour to regale those taking a stroll along the promenade. Southport, the first Victorian garden town, has wide tree-lined boulevards, and Scarborough, one of the first English seaside resorts, has Italian and rose gardens in Peasholm Park. Torquay is almost sub-tropical in its planting: majestic palms decorate the shore, and the town parks contain a rich variety of plants, many of them impossible to grow in colder parts of the country. Elsewhere in England botanic gardens provide a means of seeing exotic species of plants not normally found in this country. Botanic gardens are found in the heart of many of our cities and are well worth a visit at any time of year.

In 1984 Liverpool was the venue for the first of the Garden Festivals, and much of the Festival site has been left to form an area of open space and recreation. The city has other parks of merit, the most outstanding being Calderstones Park with its Japanese Garden and Rock Garden. Stoke-on-Trent is the venue for the 1986 National Garden Festival, constructed on a derelict site but with the intention of being handed over to the city to maintain. The importance of parks and gardens in our inner-city areas has been recognised and a long, healthy tradition of city parks and gardens is thus set to continue.

Left: Regent's Park, London
Above: Harrogate's Valley Gardens, N. Yorks.

The
NATIONAL TRUST

by John Sales, Gardens Adviser,
The National Trust

For centuries gardening has been a national obsession for the English and it remains by far our most popular leisure activity today. The richness and variety of gardens and parks in England is unparalleled elsewhere. Not only have we a talent for making gardens but, thanks to our social and political stability, we have also preserved them. Hence England can offer a feast to the hungry garden visitor, whatever his taste and however great his capacity.

Over the last 50 years The National Trust has acquired, preserved and restored an important cross-section including some of the greatest gardens ever made. In the number of gardens it owns (over 100) and in the unique collections of cultivated plants they contain, it has a position unequalled in the world. It plays a crucial part in the conservation of historic gardens and has led the way in their restoration and renewal.

At Westbury Court, Gloucestershire, the Trust has restored a unique 17th-century formal water garden showing Dutch influence, a remarkable survival through successive changes in garden style over nearly three centuries. Thanks to an engraving by Kip and the meticulously accurate accounts of its creator Maynard Colchester, the original layout and planting were precisely recorded. A similar approach was taken in the restoration of the garden at Ham House, Surrey, where access to the original plan and the absence of any later scheme of importance made it possible and appropriate to restore its original 17th-century appearance using, as at Westbury Court, only the trees, fruit and flowers available at the time.

But these are not typical because the history of gardens in England is one of constant innovation, addition and adjustment, a series of changes over-laying and enriching the original plan. At Blickling Hall in Norfolk the original early 17th-century garden has accommodated an 18th-century Park, Temple and Orangery, a Victorian formal garden and parterre in the 'French style', and a Gertrude Jekyll-style flower garden designed circa 1930, together with a great variety of plants. The result is a garden which rightly bears the rich imprint of successive generations of the owners, their tastes and the styles of the times in which they lived, a garden as interesting as it is beautiful.

Enthusiasm for the 18th-century English Landscape style led to many formal gardens being swept away, but since then the way of the English has been to alter, to adapt and to enrich, paying respect to the achievements of the past. This tradition can be observed at Cliveden in Buckinghamshire where a great variety of styles has been successfully brought together on this superb site above the Thames; also at Lanhydrock in Cornwall where the Gatehouse is Elizabethan, the park 18th-century and the garden principally Victorian, with a marvellous collection of Himalayan tree magnolias added in this century. It is true also at Wallington in Northumberland where traces of the formal 17th-century layout remain alongside an English Landscape Park in the style of Lancelot 'Capability' Brown (who walked four miles from Kirke Harle to attend school on the estate), as well as a charming Georgian walled garden where the former mixture of flowers and vegetables has given way to a rich and colourful array of flowers and shrubs.

The English Landscape style of the 18th century was a remarkable and truly English innovation and the idealised 'natural' landscapes of Kent, Brown and Repton have been copied throughout the world. The development of the style can be traced at Claremont in Surrey where the Trust has restored the unique grass amphitheatre of Charles Bridgeman's formal layout, William Kent's buildings and improvements and Lancelot Brown's further

Wallington House, Northumberland

A Guide to English Gardens

Scotney Castle, Kent

changes, while retaining some of the 19th-century minor additions. Studley Royal, in North Yorkshire, also illustrates this transition, John Aislabie's ambitious formal water garden of the early 18th century giving way gradually to the romantic style and the incomparable vista to Fountains Abbey. Stourhead, in Wiltshire, is the Trust's most famous and most complex 18th-century garden: here the carefully composed structure of buildings, water and trees designed by Henry Hoare has been modified and added to by successive generations of the family and enriched with exciting new species of trees and shrubs introduced from America and the Far East in the 19th and early 20th centuries.

One feature which distinguishes English gardens is the collections of plants that they contain. As a trading and seafaring nation the English were always well placed to collect exotics on their travels and our climate, although much maligned, is suitable for a vast range of plants from abroad – indeed they often grow better than at home. Superb collections of trees and shrubs have been assembled by landowners who could afford to indulge their hobby and sponsor plant hunting expeditions to the Americas, to China, Japan and Australia. Great gardens like Killerton in Devon, Nymans in West Sussex, Sheffield Park in East Sussex, and Trengwainton in Cornwall are the abiding legacy of this passion for new plants.

Through her work and her books Gertrude Jekyll was the catalyst through which the 20th-century English garden style was developed. This found its full expression at Hidcote in Gloucestershire, where Lawrence Johnston created a garden of contrast and variety in a firm structure of hedges. In the spaces thus formed he combined a vast range of plants, using colour schemes based on Gertrude Jekyll's principles. His style has been copied and developed in Britain and across the world and is rightly recognised, along with the Woodland Garden style of Knightshayes in Devon, as England's great contribution to gardening in this century.

Over a hundred gardens are opened to visitors by the National Trust, which depends on the voluntary support of the public and its members. *For further information and membership details, write to:*
The National Trust,
36 Queen Anne's Gate, London SW1H 9AS.

ENTERTAINMENT
in
GARDENS

'It has great capabilities'; thus spoke the great Lancelot Brown when viewing the estates of would-be patrons, but even he could not have known just what those capabilities would prove to be. He and other skilled artists created many of our most famous gardens as private pictures of paradise; time, whilst fulfilling the beauty of their original designs, has given them a livelier, more entertaining role.

The seeds of public popularity were sown in the 18th century, when revellers crossed the Thames by boat for an evening of glittering entertainment at Vauxhall Gardens. They listened to music, marvelled at fireworks and spectacles like the Grand Cascade, and there too, in elegant supper boxes, they dined off ham cut so thin they could see the plate through it, while 'young bloods' stalked the Dark Walk looking for amorous adventure. Ranelagh Gardens followed suit rounding off concerts with a masked ridotto, at which the company joined in the dance. In the nineteenth century, the select garden parties, pageants and village fêtes held in grounds belonging to the local gentry kept a foot in the door which the 20th century was to swing wide. For then, not only did many private gardens open their gates to the public, but they also began putting their space, their beauty and their versatility to a variety of popular uses.

The Tudors and Stuarts used gardens as a stage, to great effect. At Kenilworth in 1575, the Earl of Leicester dazzled his queen with a display in which a triton appeared from the waters of the moat sounding his trumpet, whereupon the Lady of the Lake and her nymphs floated across to pay their homage; under Charles I, the court took its pleasures in the form of elaborate masques devised by Inigo Jones. Without going quite that far, we have managed to preserve the elegance and enchantment of the English garden on a summer night, which lives again through the opera at Glyndebourne, concerts round the lake at Kenwood or in Shakespeare's immortal lines spoken in the fragrant twilight of the rose garden at Regent's Park. In recent years the National Trust

has taken this strain of magic and spun it into the highly enjoyable 'fêtes champêtres', at which participants dress up for an evening of music, dancing, spectacle, fireworks, eating and drinking amongst the floodlit trees and lakes of stately gardens.

But if such pictures fade with the dawn, there are plenty more to take their place. Out comes the sun, and with it the families eager to get to grips with all that gardens have to offer – entertainments which now go beyond the traditional maze or boat-ride on the lake to tackling an adventure

10

playground, following a nature trail or beating the bounds on a bicycle. And when these pleasures begin to pall, there is often something else of interest close at hand; collections of birds, butterflies or wild beasts have brought many parks and gardens a long way from the days of a pair of peacocks on the terrace. And in the summer months, as gardens really get into their stride with flower shows, horse trials, jousting tourneys, steam rallies and gatherings of hot-air balloons, in the parks the bands play on and Punch and Judy fight it out before yet another generation of delighted children.

Time marches on even in gardens, however, and with it a new phenomenon is emerging. It takes the shape of garden festivals dedicated to staging exciting events in a garden setting, and 1986 looks set to see Stoke-on-Trent match Liverpool's success in this line with an extravaganza of entertainment.

So thank you, Lancelot Brown and friends; those capabilities which you developed became the foundation of a popular and cherished part of our inheritance.

VICTORIAN ROSES
and
ROSE GARDENS

By Mark W. Mattock, Rosarian and Chairman of the Rose Growers' Association

Mme Isaac Pereire (Bourbon)

Each decade sees a resurgence of interest in the Old Garden roses. Many an 'expert' is quoted and hailed as the person who 'made old roses popular again'. The best varieties, however, have consistently appeared in the catalogues of old-established firms, in some cases since their introduction.

The Hybrid Perpetuals can be found in many of England's longer-established gardens, as well as the older roses such as the Centifolias (the hundred-leaved rose), the Gallicas (the French rose), both of which were such a feature of the paintings of Redouté, and the Moss Roses, often looked upon as the epitome of the Victorian era.

Despite being superseded in municipal gardens by the hybrid teas and floribundas of modern breeding, many of the historic roses hold their places as shrubs in their own right.

Rosa Centifolia Carnea by Pierre Joseph Redouté

Remontant (repeat-flowering) varieties evolved through chance seedlings of the tea-scented or Bengal roses, the China roses, and the Bourbon roses which were brought back by travellers on their return from China, India, and the Iles de Bourbon in the eighteenth and nineteenth centuries.

These new hybrids heralded the development of the rose as we know it today, introducing new colours such as the deep velvety-crimson colour so beloved nowadays. They excited so much interest that a whole new pattern of gardening evolved, and rose-growing became quite a cult. One story tells how a Mr. Kennedy, acting as agent for the Empress Josephine, travelled across the Channel, despite the state of war existing between England and France, carrying varieties of roses which the Empress had asked for.

The tea-scented roses were only half-hardy and in Britain were grown in the warmer southern counties, or in conservatories in colder areas. However, interest in the results of natural hybridisation led to hand pollination and the development of the hardy Hybrid Perpetuals, which could be said to be the real 'Victorian rose'. By the end of the century almost one thousand varieties were listed, but the world had to wait more than ten years into the present century before it saw true yellow or orange roses. By then, different species had been used in breeding and the heyday of the Hybrid Perpetual was coming to an end.

'Standard' roses in the Queen of Hearts' garden from 'Alice's Adventures in Wonderland': for many people their earliest impression of a Victorian Rose Garden.

In a few gardens today Hybrid Perpetuals can still be found treated in the Victorian manner. This involves pegging down the long shoots, thus forcing dormant buds all along the length and producing flowering shoots over the whole of the plant. In some cases a wire frame constructed a foot above the ground takes the place of individual pegs. 'Standard' roses were another Victorian favourite which appeared in Britain in 1813 when a Chelsea nurseryman imported the first consignment from France. They proved so popular that he was soon selling them at a guinea a plant!

The charm of these favourites of our grandparents may be seen in gardens throughout Britain. Many gardens listed in this publication mention 'shrub roses' and 'rose gardens'. They are all very well worth a visit, especially during June and July when roses of every shape and hue are at their best.

To select but a few of these gardens might be thought unfair to the many; however, a special mention must be made of The Gardens of the Rose at Chiswell Green, St. Albans, Hertfordshire, home of the Royal National Rose Society. The Society arose during the reign of Queen Victoria at the height of the interest generated by the appearance of the remontant roses.

The Gardens now contain 30,000 roses of some 1,700 different varieties, as well as the Trial Ground where roses from around the world are tested and judged for the Society's coveted awards. With a collection that ranges from Old Garden varieties to modern hybrids, the Gardens of the Rose are a living catalogue of roses past and present.

The Royal National Rose Society
Chiswell Green, St. Albans
Herts AL2 3NR
Tel (0727) 50461

Rosa gallica complicata

GARDEN FEATURES

by Anthony Huxley, former editor of *Amateur Gardening*, author of many books and articles, member of the Council of the RHS, and President of the Horticultural Club.

Alley A narrow walk, cut through dense woodland or formed by planting trees, trimmed on each side to give a wall-like effect. First used in France in the 16th century, several being laid out to radiate from a focal point.

Arbour A bower or retreat, either made of trained trees or plants such as ivy or vine grown on a framework, or an ornamental structure of metal or stone, round or square, with a dome.

Avenue A fairly wide road or walk planted with trees on either side; till the 17th century the word was used to denote roads or rides forming the approach to a house.

Bee Bole A niche in a wall, usually at ground level and arched at the top, around 3ft high and 2ft across, in which straw bee-skeps were placed in winter from Tudor times until the 19th century, when the square wooden hive was introduced.

Belvedere A place from which a 'fair sight' may be had; a look-out. Normally a roof-top or tower-top turret or 'lantern', but also describing any garden building which commands a view or a vista.

Bosket Derived from the French *bosquet*, a thicket or plantation of trees forming part of the design of park or garden, such as the backdrop to a parterre or the end-piece of an alley. The more elaborate boskets have paths and enclosures within, with fountains and statues.

Clair-Voyee Literally, a 'clear-view': an opening in a wall or hedge, sometimes protected with iron grilles or screens, which allows a garden vista to continue into the countryside beyond. Another type is a metal fence set between stone piers which replaced the original wall entirely.

Crinkle-Crankle Describing a wall built in serpentine fashion, the bays providing shelter for fruit trees.

Eye-Catcher Any feature in a landscape garden which creates a visual focal point – a temple, mock ruin, garden house, statue etc.

Folly A garden structure, usually bizarre, built to surprise but having no practical function. Follies include grottoes, mock ruins, castles, pinnacles, pyramids, stone circles, and extended, perhaps, to a few subterranean labyrinths.

Gazebo A place from which to gaze about: a turret or 'lantern' on a roof or tower, or a garden house, usually of two storeys, commanding a view.

Grotto A small cave; garden grottoes may take advantage of natural caves or be artificial, often above-ground constructions of tufa rock. Many are lined with shells, bones, pebbles, glass etc.

Ha-Ha A boundary between garden and park in the form of a deep, wide ditch, creating a barrier to farm animals while allowing uninterrupted views. The word is supposed to have arisen from the exclamation of surprise – 'Ah, ha!' – uttered by people first coming on a 'sunken fence'.

Indianesque The use of Indian features and ornamentation in gardens.

Italianate Apart from the enormous overall influence of Italian gardens on English formal garden design, this word refers specifically to deliberate copies of Italian gardens, filled with Roman statues, urns and sarcophagi acquired in Italy, made in England between 1830 and 1860.

Japanese Garden Attempts to reproduce Japanese garden style which typically result in arched bridges, stone lanterns, bronze cranes and stepping-stones across

Maze at Hever Castle, Kent

A GUIDE TO ENGLISH GARDENS

1	Rotunda	4	Clair-voyee	7	Arbour	10	Topiary	12	Stilt hedge	15	Grotto	17	Ha-Ha
2	Gazebo	5	Patte d'oie	8	Treillage	11	Pleached alley	13	Pergola	16	Palladian style bridge	18	Mount
3	Belvedere	6	Parterre	9	Canal			14	Pagoda			19	Eye-catcher

water among plants popular in Japan, but not in the meditative style of true Japanese gardening.

Knot A bed laid out in an intricate pattern made from low-clipped or naturally low-growing plants such as dwarfbox and cotton lavender; the area within the outline can be filled with seasonal plants or with inert coloured materials (sands, chalk, coal etc.). Knots originated in the 15th century and were designed to be seen from raised terraces of upstairs windows. *See also* Parterre.

Maze A word now generally used to denote a puzzle layout of paths, with dead ends, many alternatives and confusing turnings, enclosed in hedges. The true maze is of paths set in turf; the hedge maze is technically a labyrinth. Mazes originally had a religious or magical purpose but have long been popular garden features.

Moss House A Victorian wooden garden building of rustic appearance, the interior formed of wood slats between which were pressed pieces of moss.

Mount An artificial hill within a garden, built against an outer wall or free-standing, to allow views to the countryside beyond the garden in the early period when high walls were needed against marauders.

Orangery Precursors of the all-glass greenhouse, orangeries are typically tall buildings with long narrow windows in stone walls, and a solid roof, though some later examples

Temple at Studley Royal, North Yorks.

have glass lights in the roof. Most orangeries date from the 17th and 18th centuries.

Parterre A level garden area containing a number of flower-beds, usually rectangular, separated from the rest of the garden in a formal way, and with the beds often designed as knots of low clipped plants. The water parterre has a knot-like pattern of stonework in a shallow formal pool.

Patte d'Oie Literally, 'goose's foot': a number of alleys or vistas radiating in a fan pattern – like toes on a foot – from a central point.

Pavilion A garden house of some style, often decorated inside and with comfortable and heatable rooms.

Pergola A structure of uprights and horizontal beams enclosing a walk below and acting as a support for climbing plants. Pergolas of different styles form features in all kinds of gardens from grand to humble.

Potager In truth *jardin potager* simply means 'kitchen garden' in French, but *potager* has come to mean an ornamental kitchen garden, with vegetables, fruit and herbs, usually set in beds with low-clipped edgings like a parterre.

A Guide to English Gardens

Arley Hall, Cheshire

Root House A rustic garden house, occasionally created during the 19th century from the bases of tree trunks, and often thatched.

Ruins Mock ruins were often erected, from the 18th century on, as eye-catchers in landscapes; these follies are usually in Gothic style but sometimes in Roman.

Temple Replicas of classical temples, large and small, can be seen in many landscape gardens of the 18th and 19th centuries; mostly of stone, with imposing columns, they often feature statuary inside and out. They have a place in the design as eye-catchers to focus a view – by water, on hilltops or at the end of a valley.

Terrace There are several meanings to 'terrace'. One is a flat, paved area, usually enclosed with low walls or balustrades, forming a transition between house and garden, an open-air 'room' where guests can take the air and see the view. The second is where a steep slope has created the necessity for levelling, which often produces impressive layouts with walls and buttresses, and opportunities for statues, urns and pavilions. Finally a terrace can mean a flat walk on one level, following a contour line and hence often winding, with many opportunities for view-points, man-made vistas and vista-closers.

Topiary The art, and the results, of clipping or training evergreen shrubs and trees into shapes; it was invented by the Romans. Trimming the front privet hedge is elementary topiary but the word usually refers to free-standing specimens, geometric or fanciful forms, animal sculptures, and in modern times anything from locomotives to battleships. In Britain topiary is always the result of clipping; elsewhere, as in the US, it is sometimes created by training plants on wire frames.

Treillage Applied to structures created from trellis (light wooden or metal bars arranged to form a regular square or diamond-shaped pattern, fixed at each crossing point).

Trompe-l'Oeil Literally meaning 'deceive the eye'; there are many ways in which illusion is used in gardens. The ha-ha or sunken fence suggests the garden going indefinitely into the landscape. A curved inlet at the end of a lake can make it seem to continue beyond. Hedges can be made to look shorter or longer by increasing or decreasing their height towards their further end. Apparent length can be increased by setting straight hedges or borders to come slightly close together in the distance. In small gardens mirrors may be used to give an impression of more space, and trelliswork to suggest a receding vista instead of a wall.

Turf Seat A popular medieval feature in which a seat, built up with bricks or planking, is filled with soil on which grass grows. Modern examples usually use chamomile or dwarf thyme for the seat.

Urn A sculpted garden ornament modelled on classical originals (which were mostly funerary). Urns can be solid, with the top in the form of a cap, or open, when they can be used as plant containers. Large examples are often used as architectural incidents in landscape.

Vista A relatively confined view usually channelled by trees on either side, or along a valley.

Vista-Closer A building, obelisk or urn placed at the end of a vista as a focal end-point.

Many of England's privately-owned gardens are open regularly to the public.
The Historic Houses Association exists to represent their interests, supported by the 'Friends of the HHA'.

The Historic Houses Association
38 Ebury Street, London SW1W 0LU.

Hundreds of other private gardens not normally open to the public welcome visitors on certain days of the year in aid of charity, under the auspices of the National Gardens Scheme.

National Gardens Scheme
57 Lower Belgrave Street, London SW1W 0LR.
Tel. 01-730 0359

Keen amateur horticulturists and gardeners can benefit from membership of the Royal Horticultural Society. The Society aims to promote horticulture through its flower shows, lectures and library facilities.

The Royal Horticultural Society
80 Vincent Square, London SW1P 2PE.
Tel. 01-834 4333

Gardens worth seeing are gardens worth saving.

If you love gardens, the National Trust has so much to share with you: long-established gardens evolved over many generations, or faithfully reconstructed period pieces like Ham House or Moseley Old Hall. Perhaps you'll find a new plant you would like for your own garden, or an unexpected colour scheme or design. Or maybe you just like strolling in the open air, enjoying the colours and scents of the season.

With over 100 gardens in all parts of the country, the variety is endless. And by joining the National Trust, you can enjoy free admission to them all. Membership costs just £14.50 a year, and also admits you to all our historic buildings including many great houses with magnificent parks and gardens of their own.

Our 224 page Guide will tell you where to find them, plus some 500,000 acres of unspoilt coast and countryside.

Best of all, by joining the Trust, you'll be helping to keep the gardens you love blossoming intact for ever.

So join us now – there's no better time or season.

Join The National Trust.

To: The National Trust, FREEPOST, BECKENHAM, Kent BR3 4UN. (no stamp needed)   205

Name_____ Address_____

Please tick form of membership required:
TWELVE MONTH MEMBERSHIP:
☐ Individual: £14.50. Each additional member of the household: £8.50.
☐ Family Group: £28. One card admits parents and their children under 18.
☐ Under 23: £8. Please give date of birth

LIFE MEMBERSHIP:
☐ Individual: £300. ☐ Pensioner: (Men 60. Women 60): £200.
☐ Joint: £375 For husband and wife. ☐ Pensioner (Joint): £275.

I enclose cheque/PO for £_____ or please debit my Visa/Access/
American Express No._____
Signature_____

Or simply phone the National Trust on 01-658 8888 quoting your credit card no.

The National Trust

LEVENS HALL
World-Famous Topiary Garden

A really exciting and unusual place to visit, Levens Hall is a wonderland of topiary, the masterpiece of Monsieur Beaumont who laid out the garden in 1692. Magnificent tall trees clipped into fanciful shapes, vast beech hedges, colourful formal bedding and herbaceous borders.

Elizabethan mansion added to 13th C. pele tower contains superb panelling, plasterwork and furniture.
Steam Collection illustrating the power of steam from 1820-1920.

OPEN: Easter Sunday to 30th September

House, Garden, Gift Shop, Tearooms, Plant Centre, Picnic Area, Children's Play Area- Sun to Thurs. 11am. to 5pm. Steam Collection 2pm. to 5pm. Closed Friday & Saturday.
5 miles south of Kendal. Cumbria. on A6 (M6 exit 36). ☎ *Sedgwick (0448) 60321.*

GREAT DIXTER
Northiam, East Sussex.

Here is a series of gardens, not grand but almost cottage, designed by Sir Edwin Lutyens who restored and added to the 15th Century manor hall house. Laid out on the site of a farm yard, they are laced together by yew hedges, brick walls and the original barns and hovels. Tended by Christopher Lloyd V.M.H., is a wide variety of plants of great horticultural interest. Refreshing ideas can be found for mixing plants; noteworthy are the areas of naturalised meadow garden, the lowland equivalent of alpine meadows.

NEW SERVICE: Conducted tours of the gardens by qualified guides may be booked for groups of any number up to 25 by prior arrangement.

Telephone Northiam (07974) 3160 for more information.

Open every afternoon except ordinary Mondays from Easter to mid-October. 2pm to 5pm.

THE MAGIC OF ALTON TOWERS

"Britain's Most Outstanding Tourist Attraction"

It's no secret that Alton Towers is Europe's most successful leisure park. What is not so widely known is the other face of Alton Towers — the truly magnificent setting that takes the breath away from young and old alike.

For the 80 outstanding attractions, all free once you've paid to get in, are themed into 800 glorious acres. And the Great Gardens of Alton — created by the 15th Earl of Shrewsbury — remain today a splendid part of Britain's heritage.

1986 Admission £5.99; Coach Parties (12+) £4.99; Schools £3.99; OAPs £1.99; Children 3 & under FREE
Signposted from M6, J15 & J16; M1, J24 & J28.
Open 22nd March to 2nd November 1986. For details ring (0538) 702200, Alton Towers, Alton, Staffs.

TREWITHEN GARDENS,
Probus, Nr. Truro, Cornwall *(On A390 between Probus & Grampound)*

These gardens, covering some 20 acres created in the early years of this Century, are outstanding and internationally famous. Renowned for their magnificent collection of camellias, rhododendrons, magnolias and many rare trees and shrubs which are seldom found elsewhere in Britain. The extensive woodland gardens are surrounded by traditional parkland landscaped and planted in the 18th Century and include an enchanting Walled Garden — the original rose and herb garden — contemporary with the house and the early Water Gardens.

Open 1st March to 30th September, Monday to Saturday, 2-4.30p.m. Closed Sundays. Free car parking. A wide range of plants and shrubs always on sale in the Garden Centre. Dogs on leads. St. Austell (0726) 882418/882585. Head Gardener, St. Austell (0726) 882764. Wholesale orders welcomed.

Tatton Park
Knutsford, Cheshire

The complete country estate with 60 acres of magnificent gardens famed for spectacular rhododendrons and azaleas. Authentic Japanese and Italian gardens, a unique fernery, orangery, a fine arboretum, herbaceous borders, tree-lined paths and spacious lawns.

Ducks to feed on the Golden Brook and plants to buy in the Garden Centre.

Park and Gardens open all year, except Christmas Day. Mansion, Old Hall and Farm open April — October. Gift shop and restaurant. Ample coach and car parking. Reduced rates for parties of 12 or more.

For further information
tel. Knutsford (0565) 54722

Tatton Park

There's nowhere else like it in Britain

NESS GARDENS

University of Liverpool Botanic Gardens, Ness, Neston, South Wirral L64 4AY.

Extensive displays of trees and shrubs. Terraces and sweeping lawns. Rock, Rose, Herbaceous and Water Gardens. One of the best-known Heather gardens in the country. Fine views across the Dee Estuary to the Welsh hills. Visitor's Centre with slide sequences and exhibitions. Tea room and picnic area.

Open all year, daily exc. Christmas Day, 9am to dusk.
(Facilities for the disabled)

brackenwood nurseries
131 NORE ROAD
PORTISHEAD BRISTOL TEL 0272 843484

A beautiful **woodland garden** set in over 7 acres of mature woodland with magnificent views over the Bristol Channel. Masses of wild flowers, Rhododendrons, Camellias, Azaleas, Pieris, Japanese Maples, rare trees and shrubs; woodland pools with over 100 ducks, geese and swans from all over the world; aviaries containing exotic parrakeets. Adjoining is a unique **nursery and garden centre** offering a wide selection of rare and interesting plants — plus a full range of garden sundries. Only 3 miles from junction 19 on M.5 (Gordano interchange) and 10 miles from Bristol.

GRANADA

Your welcome to the motorways for fast and friendly service 24 hours a day 365 days a year

Petrol and diesel at competitive prices

Wholesome food freshly prepared and served

Take away food and beverages

Variety and value

Hotel accommodation at budget prices

M9/M80 Stirling
On Junction 9
Open Spring 1986

M6 Southwaite
Between Junctions 41 & 42

M6 Burton
Between Junctions 35 & 36
(Northbound only)

M62 Birch
Between Junctions 18 & 19

M5 Frankley
Between Junctions 3 & 4

M5 Exeter
On Junction 30

M4 Leigh Delamere
Between Junctions 17 & 18

M90 Kinross
On Junction 6

A1(M) Washington

M1 Woolley Edge
Between Junctions 38 & 39

M62/A1 Ferrybridge
On Junction 33

M1 Trowell
Between Junctions 25 & 26

M1 Toddington
Between Junctions 11 & 12

M4/A34 Newbury
On Junction 13
Open Summer 1986

M4 Heston
Between Junctions 2 & 3

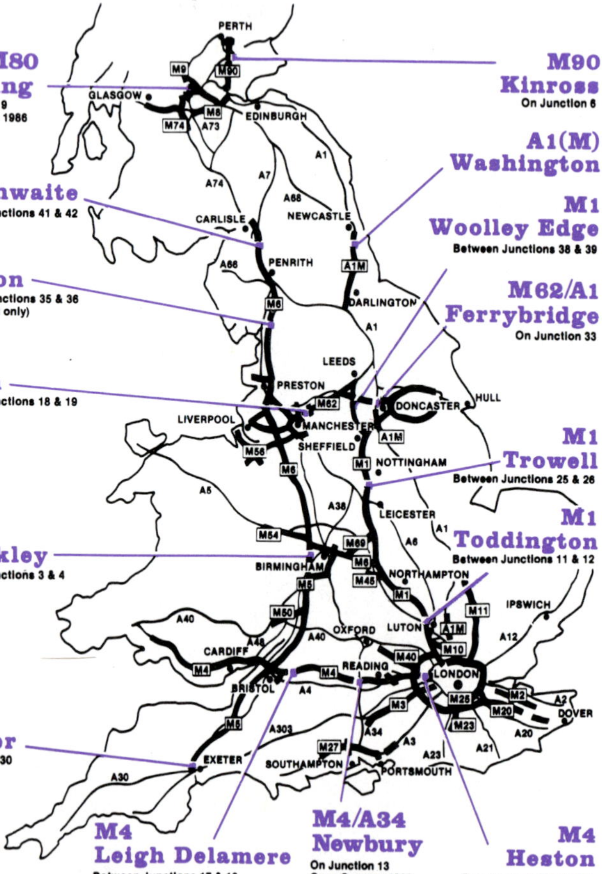

Wherever you are travelling, look out for Granada Motorway Service Areas. They offer a wide range of light refreshments, snacks, take-away food and full meals to suit all tastes and pockets. Shopping and petrol facilities are also available.

Granada Lodge hotels at Exeter and Stirling (both opening summer 1986) offer a high standard of accommodation at budget prices.

For further information call Sally Burton on Toddington (05255) 3881

THE GREATEST SHOW OF '86
FESTIVE · FLORAL · FANTASTIC FUN ·

Join in the fun with thousands of attractions for all the family, never mind the weather — more than 10 acres under cover.

Leaflets and tickets at post offices from April 1986 onwards or at the Festival entrances. There's so much going on, you'll want to visit again and again....

- CABLE-CARS, TRAIN RIDES
- LAKES, BRIDGES, CASCADES, FABULOUS LANDSCAPES
- FESTIVAL EXPO 86 — 20 changing exhibitions — from antiques to electronics
- SEE THE £1 MILLION GREENHOUSE 2000
- 80 COLOURFUL THEME GARDENS — THE FINEST YOU'VE EVER SEEN
- 50 CONTINUOUS HORTICULTURAL SHOWS IN THE GIANT FESTIVAL HALL
- VISIT THE FESTIVAL FARM, MARINA AND MARKET
- EUROPE'S MOST SPECTACULAR FESTIVAL
- Phone Festivaline (0782) 274777 NOW For recorded information

THE BIGGEST SPECTACULAR FESTIVAL IN EUROPE... RUNS FOR A WHOLE SIX MONTHS, FROM 1st MAY TO 26th OCTOBER

REAL VALUE FOR MONEY

Adults	£4·50
Children/OAP/Student/Unemployed	£3·00

CHILDREN UNDER 5 — FREE

Special discounts for groups and multi-visit tickets

SPECIAL PRICES

Fabulous Family 5 Ticket
2 CHILDREN FREE! 2 Adults and up to 3 Children — only £12 all in!
Ask at your Post Office for details.

NATIONAL GARDEN FESTIVAL
STOKE-ON-TRENT · STAFFORDSHIRE
OPEN EVERY DAY 10.00am–DUSK
1st MAY – 26th OCTOBER 1986

SEE YOU THERE!

PATRON HER MAJESTY THE QUEEN

EASY TO REACH

Situated midway between Birmingham and Manchester, the National Garden Festival is at the heart of the country's communication network. Easily accessible by road and rail, the M6 Motorway is a few minutes away and London is just a two-hour train journey. Parking couldn't be easier and there are special facilities for coach travellers.

80 GLORIOUS GARDENS

Every Garden an experience in itself. Take the traditional Pergola Walkway; discover the Chess Garden with its own giant pieces, see an ingenious sunken garden, stunning bedding displays and many, many more gardens of great beauty and interest.

Step from the past to the future and back again, from early Monastic Gardens through Tudor Times and right back up to date in a garden of Fun for the Eighties.

Sample the styles of China, Holland and Italy in the INTERNATIONAL AREA, or stay cool in the Hereford Cider Garden with its own bowling green. Themes abound, from a Kenyan Village to English Conservation — see them all.

NATIONAL GARDEN FESTIVAL
STOKE-ON-TRENT '86

Europe's largest horticultural and leisure event this year is the National Garden Festival, and more than three million people are expected to converge on the 180-acre site in Stoke-on-Trent. The Festival opens 1st May and will run until 26th October, 1986.

The nerve centre of the National Garden Festival's organisation is Etruria Hall, the former home of Josiah Wedgwood, who founded the world-famous pottery company. The house, built in 1769, has been restored to its former glory and stands proudly at the southern end of the site.

The National Garden Festival promises to provide the most spectacular blend of Theme Gardens and Horticultural Shows ever staged in the United Kingdom. But it will be much more than that with thousands of events taking place every day during the Festival's six months life, ranging from medieval jousting tournaments to one-man street theatre. Also included in the catalogue of events will be hot air balloon rallies and concerts covering the entire range of musical tastes. These events will be staged all over the site, both indoors and outside. An 800-seat Theatre in the shape of a Big Top will stage the larger indoor events while the Festival Arena will be the venue for the more athletic and energetic activities.

The aim of the festival is to provide a day out in Stoke which is Festive, Floral and Fun, with something for everyone, from the keenest gardener to the youngest fun-loving child. One of the major attractions will be the many Theme Gardens, some of which will be based on typically English scenes, including the Elizabethan Way, Sanctuary Garden and the Labyrinth. Other gardens will reflect a designer's own imagination using flowers as part of an overall concept. The gardens will provide the visitor with a different visual experience throughout the site. Although this year's Festival does not have International status, interest has been shown in the Festival from a number of countries, with the Dutch leading the way. Their Pavilion was one of the first buildings erected on site.

Specialist features bound to attract all the family will be the 200-feet high multi-coloured Butterfly Tower which will pierce the skyline from one of the highest points at the Festival. A two-and-a-half mile railway track is set to become a winner with old and young alike. The Festival Express train will snake its way around the site, calling at four stations along its route.

Catering outlets will be dotted strategically around the site, offering a wide range of food and drink from full 'à la carte' restaurants to ice cream stands. An eighty-berth marina has been specially carved into the side of the Trent and Mersey canal and a canal-side pub will provide an agreeable watering-hole for thirsty narrow-boat enthusiasts.

The Festival Hall will provide the venue for the numerous horticultural shows. They will include floral extravaganzas such as 'Grand Opening' and 'Harvest Festival' as well as specialist shows of alpines, flowering and foliage plants and society shows. Besides the horticultural shows, twenty major national exhibitions will take place on the site. They range from housing, gardens and homes, to sport, health and fitness and represent the most ambitious programme of events ever undertaken in a six-month period in Britain. The last and longest show, which will run for a month, will be linked to 1986 Industry Year. Other exhibitions will take place in the Festival's largest building – Greenhouse 2000 structure, a £1 million multi-bay glass house covering 68,000 square feet. This will feature a continuous programme of exhibitions based on a garden theme.

A 150-stall covered market will offer a wide variety of goods for visitors to buy. These will range from locally manufactured pottery, to herbs and heathers, jewellery and a full range of homes and gardens literature, as well as a variety of souvenirs.

The Festival naturally has its own Mascot, a mischievous cartoon mouse character called Festival Freddie Stilton. A life-size Freddie will wander around the site when the Festival opens and is bound to be a big attraction for the younger visitors.

The Festival is sited in the heart of the country and easily accessible by either road or rail. Linked to the national motorway network by the M6, there will be 8,000 car parking spaces and 300 coach spaces available. While

Part of the 180-acre Festival site

Park, Cannock Chase, Churnet Valley – and a wealth of historic houses and parks including the magnificent Shugborough Hall and Alton Towers with its pleasure grounds and landscaped garden.

The Festival at Stoke does not have the commercial restraints imposed on the Liverpool Festival in 1984 which was controlled by International Garden Festival rules. This has given many high street names the opportunity to take part in what is seen as Europe's biggest window this year. Education will also play a part in the overall scenario, with nature trails, woodland walks and adventure playgrounds.

Basically, a day out at the National Garden Festival will be Festive, Floral and Fun. Admission charges and opening times are listed below.

you're in the area, why not spend a few days exploring? Stoke offers excellent entertainment and shopping facilities, besides several museums and the famous ceramics factories to visit. Beyond the city there is a range of spectacular countryside – Derbyshire Peak District National

For further information ring the Festivaline 0782-274777.
Open daily 10am–dusk
Admission: Adults £4.50 (£2.00 after 5pm)
Reduced rate £3.00 (£1.50 after 5pm)
Children under 5 free
15% reduction for groups of 20+
Family tickets, multi-visit tickets and season tickets available.

DISCOVER THE MOORLANDS

Fresh air. Beautiful unspoilt countryside. Magnificent vistas in the Southern Peak District and Churnet Valley. Farm and country accommodation, potteries, historic houses, mill seconds shop, craft demonstrations and antique centres in market towns and villages. Alton Towers Gardens and Britain's National Garden Festival close by.

Details of all these are available from:
E.G. English, Tourist Information Centre, Stockwell Street, Leek, ST13 6HQ.
☎ 0538 385181 or 381000.

STAFFORDSHIRE MOORLANDS

STAFFORDSHIRE '86   HAVE THE TIME OF YOUR LIFE

Just make a date to see Europe's biggest Festival of flowers and fun - the **NATIONAL GARDEN FESTIVAL** at Stoke-on-Trent - and nearby take in **ALTON TOWERS**, Staffordshire's world class leisure experience.

Link them with a stay on a farm or friendly hotel, an exciting activity holiday, or a canal cruise. You'll find remote moorland villages, bustling market towns, castles, stately homes the worlds most famous potteries and star award winning industrial museums. For more information write to:

Tourist Information/Accommodation
Staffordshire Pavilion
N.G.F. '86
ETRURIA
Stoke-on-Trent
Staffordshire
ST1 5BQ
(Tel) (0782) 286 688

HOLIDAYS IN STAFFORDSHIRE ARE REALLY FANTASTIC

BARGAIN BREAKAWAYS

To NATIONAL GARDEN FESTIVAL FROM ONLY £44

- Includes one nights dinner, bed & breakfast hotel accommodation.
- Includes coach travel to Stoke-on-Trent and admission to festival.
- Travel any day.
- Supplementary extra nights if required.
- Reductions for senior citizens and children.

FOR FREE BROCHURE 'phone **021-455 9333** or post coupon.

To: National Express, 1 Vernon Road, Edgbaston, Birmingham B16 9SJ.
Please send me a 'Bargain Breakaways brochure.

Name _____

Address _____

NATIONAL EXPRESS »   SCOTTISH CITYLINK COACHES

EG

STOKE-ON-TRENT A Creative City.

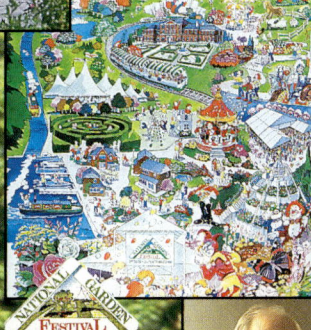

The City is known and admired as a forerunner in reclamation, particularly for its Hanley Forest Park reclamation scheme, and now hosts the National Garden Festival 1986, the largest event of its kind in Europe.

Generations of skills employed in the making of fine china and allied crafts can be seen in many museums and craft centres throughout the district, making the City an ideal visitor centre.

Stoke-on-Trent and its surrounding countryside now has a wide industrial base with the stability, friendship and warmth of this family of towns.

Our City is at the heart of the motorway and rail networks. Both Manchester and Birmingham airports are within one hour's drive.

STOKE-ON-TRENT · A fun place to live, work and play.

AS USUAL, WE'RE IN THE RIGHT PLACE WITH THE RIGHT CHOICE.

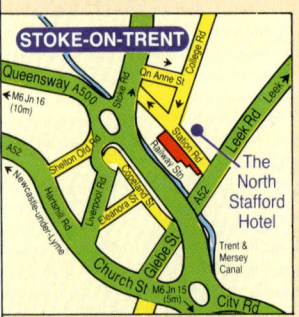

The North Stafford is an imposing hotel built in the style of a Jacobean manor house.
Its position alone, (a few minutes walk from the centre of Stoke-on-Trent and close to the railway station) will make it popular during the festival period. But, in the case of the North Stafford 'popular' does not mean crowded.
The Six Towns Restaurant can accommodate up to 90 diners in luxurious (but intimate) comfort.
The North Stafford is a popular base for tourists where guests enjoy the atmosphere, facilities and service expected of an international hotel.
The Post House Hotel Newcastle-under-Lyme is the perfect location for families who wish to spend more than one day at the festival. With ample parking space and 126 modern bedrooms all with private bath, colour TV, radio, telephone and tea/coffee making facilities, the attractions are obvious. Children are always welcome and there are special amenities like cots, high chairs, baby listening service and play area.
The restaurant has excellent lunch and dinner menus (the special 'Hungry Bear' menu for children is a firm favourite) and for less formal eating the Coffee Shop has a varied all-day menu. And all this is available at specially reduced 'Leisure Break' rates.

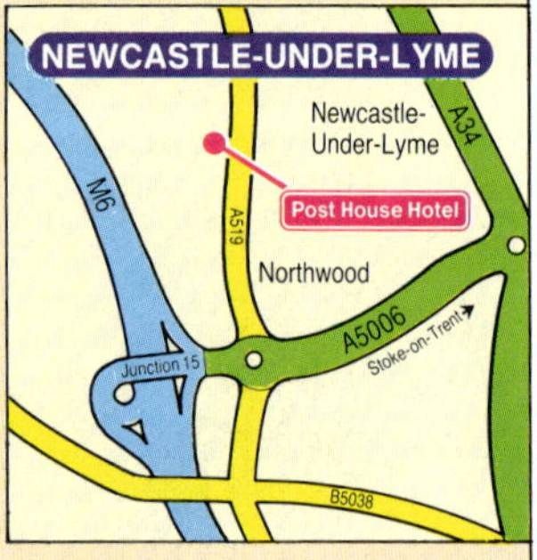

AND IF THAT'S NOT ENOUGH....

There are six other Trusthouse Forte hotels (listed below) all within easy reach of the M6 Motorway and the festival activities.

The North Stafford
STOKE-ON-TRENT
Station Road, Stoke-on-Trent, Staffs
ST4 2AE Tel: 0782 48501

Post House Hotel
NEWCASTLE-UNDER-LYME
Clayton Road, Newcastle-under-Lyme, Staffs ST5 4DL Tel: 0782 625151

THE GRAND MANCHESTER 061 236 9559	POST HOUSE MANCHESTER 061 998 7090	EXCELSIOR BIRMINGHAM 021 743 8141
EXCELSIOR (MANCHESTER AIRPORT) 061 437 5811	THE ALBANY BIRMINGHAM 021 643 8171	POST HOUSE BIRMINGHAM 021 357 7444

 Trusthouse Forte Hotels

A Guide to English Gardens

Notes on Garden Visiting

These entries have been compiled from information supplied by the gardens and were correct at the time of going to press (November 1985). However, opening times can be subject to sudden change, often because of uncontrollable factors such as the weather. We advise you to telephone the garden to check before setting out – check the admission charges, too. Those given in the entries do not always include admission to the house or other facilities in addition to the garden. Some of the gardens are willing to allow visitors by prior appointment at other times apart from their normal opening days. Where dogs are allowed in a garden, they should always be kept on a lead. NT ※ denotes gardens belonging to the National Trust – see also pages 8–9. The ♿ symbol shows which gardens are accessible to physically handicapped visitors – see also page 97.

Follow *the* Garden Code

To enable everybody to enjoy English gardens as they are supposed to be enjoyed, the Royal Horticultural Society asks you to observe the following DOs and DON'Ts.

DO
Be careful where you are walking – keep to the paths and don't step on the flower beds. Guard against risk of fire through casually dropped matches, cigarette ends or pipe ash.
Make sure your children are well-behaved and learn to respect a garden for its beauty as well as its recreational value.
Leave your dog at home – unless he's a guide dog for the blind.
By all means ask questions of the gardening staff, but do not delay them with lengthy conversations.

DON'T
Do not remove any plants or take cuttings.
Do not pick the flowers or the fruit.
Do not leave litter lying around – put it in a wastepaper bin or, even better, take it home with you.
Do not picnic just anywhere in the garden – ask first if it is permitted.
Do not play transistor radios or tape recorders.

Countryside Commission: illustrations by John Lawrence.

A Guide to English Gardens Promotions Co-ordinator: Harriet Dean. Managing Editor: Geraldine Rogers. Assistant Editor: Christine Davis. Designed by Carroll & Dempsey Ltd. Editorial contributors: Jean Ashton, Charmian Swengley. Illustrations: Andrew Davidson, Mary Evans Picture Library The Mansell Collection. Photography: Britain on View Photographic Library, Glyn Williams, Harry Smith Horticultural Photographic Collection, Peter Beales Roses. Cartography: Line & Line based upon Ordnance Survey Mapping with the permission of the Controller of Her Majesty's Stationery Office. Filmset by Metro Filmsetting. Printed in Great Britain by Pennington Litho Ltd. Advertisement Dept: James of Fleet Street Ltd, 184 Fleet Street, London EC4A 2HD. Tel: 01-242 0101/0330. Distributed in the UK by the Automobile Association, Fanum House, Basingstoke RG21 2EA. Tel (0256) 62929. Distributed overseas by the British Tourist Authority.

THE ENGLISH TOURIST BOARD Thames Tower, Black's Road, London W6 9EL. The English Tourist Board is a statutory body created by the Development of Tourism Act, 1969, to develop and market England's tourism. Its main objectives are to provide a welcome for people visiting England, to encourage people living in England to take their holidays there, and to encourage the provision and improvement of tourist amenities and facilities in England. The Board has a statutory duty to advise the Government on tourism matters relating to England and administers the Government's grant and loan schemes for hotels and other tourist attractions.

Important The information contained in this guide is given in good faith on the basis of information submitted to the English Tourist Board by the promoters of the activities and premises listed. The English Tourist Board cannot guarantee the accuracy of the information in this guide and accepts no responsibility for any errors or misrepresentation. All liability for loss, disappointment, negligence or other damage caused by the reliance on the information contained in this Guide, or in the event of the bankruptcy or liquidation of any company, individual or firm mentioned, or in the event of any company, individual or firm ceasing to trade, is hereby excluded.

© English Tourist Board 1986. Internal Reference Number: ETB/143/86 P&E/949/50M/1/86 ISBN: 0 84143 120 0

A GUIDE TO ENGLISH GARDENS

CUMBRIA

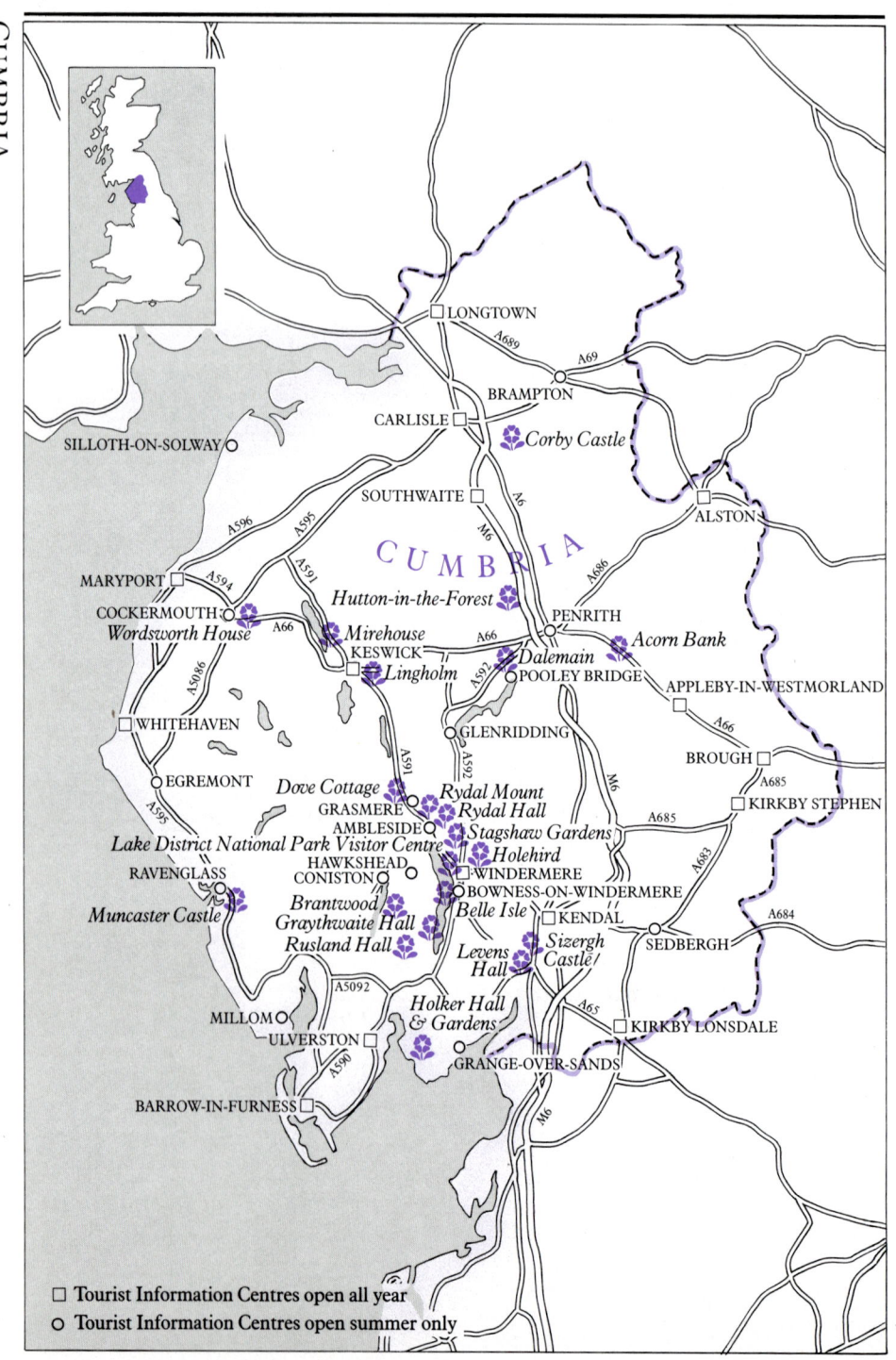

CUMBRIA

*C*umbria's gardens reflect the beauty which is a hallmark of this outstandingly lovely region. Its superb scenery of lakes and fells, sheltered valleys and solitary coasts inspired many notable poets and writers such as Wordsworth and John Ruskin. Now in turn, their own gardens have taken their place amongst the acknowledged beauties of Lakeland: Rydal Mount with its rare trees and shrubs, Cockermouth where bluebells and daffodils grow in abundance and Brantwood, set by the peaceful shores of Coniston water. Other gardens provide the ideal viewpoint from which to admire the drama of their Cumbrian settings: Holehird and Lingholm set their sights on towering mountain peaks; sandstone Muncaster Castle, famous for its collection of azaleas and rhododendrons, gazes over Eskdale from a lofty hilltop site, while the formal grounds and deer park at Holker Hall lie on the fringe of Morecambe's vast and sandy bay. Cumbria has its own Garden of Eden in the grounds of Corby Castle, which run along the wooded banks of the River Eden within a short drive of ancient Carlisle, and there are more woodland walks amongst magnificent specimen trees in the appropriately-named garden of Hutton-in-the-Forest near Penrith. You'll come across some unusual trees on your way around the region; Rusland Hall offers gingko and sequoia, while at Levens Hall in the tranquil valley of the River Kent, yew and box have been fashioned into fantastic topiary shapes in a style dating back to the 17th century. As you might expect in the Lake District, water plays a special part in many gardens. The many attractions at Brockhole, the Lake District National Park Visitor Centre, include boat trips and a Beatrix Potter Grotto, a favourite with children (and adults) of all ages. Mirehouse has a lakeside walk and a Norman lakeside church; lakes, pools and waterfalls glitter in the grounds of Sizergh Castle near Kendal, and Belle Isle actually is, as its name suggests, an island garden surrounded by the calm waters of Lake Windermere.

JANUARY

Botanic gardens provide an enjoyable introduction to the gardening year. Safe from the elements, their greenhouse collections are oases of tender things – orchids, ferns, cacti, succulents, palms and other trees and shrubs, all willing to share their haven of warmth with winter visitors. Each garden develops its own speciality, cultivating as many of that species as possible, and giving priority to any which are rare or endangered in the wild. Botanic gardens evolved from the physic garden, where plants were grown for medicinal purposes, but today their role in teaching and research has been extended to include attractive landscaping, with plenty of ideas for the home gardener.

Fern Alpine polypodium

ALPINE LADY'S MANTLE

Cumbria's fells provide the appropriate conditions for many mountain flowers, which are attracted in particular to the moister places. One of the most prolific is the alpine lady's mantle, which can tolerate life at a wide range of altitudes. Its sprays of miniature, greenish-yellow flowers display the sort of delicate detail so often associated with rock plants. Higher up the slopes comes the less-common purple saxifrage, whose purple and magenta flowers get a firm toe-hold on rocky crevices, while the large, pale-yellow globe flower prefers the company of damp mountain grass. All three species flower in June, and like many other alpines, they thrive under cultivation to make a colourful and undemanding addition to rock gardens all around the country.

Alchemilla alpina

For more information contact the
Cumbria Tourist Board,
Ashleigh, Holly Road, Windermere,
Cumbria LA23 2AQ ☎ (096 62) 4444
(written enquiries only).

A GUIDE TO ENGLISH GARDENS

CUMBRIA

Acorn Bank
Temple Sowerby, Cumbria
Charming garden full of spring bulbs; herb and walled gardens; colourful herbaceous borders; fruit trees and wild garden.
Open Mar to Oct, daily, 10am–5.30pm. Admission 60p adults, 30p children. No dogs except guide dogs.
☎ *Ambleside (0966) 33883. NT*

Belle Isle
Bowness-on-Windermere, Cumbria
38 acre island with gardens by Thomas White. Unique round house, new animated 'Below Stairs' exhibition. Picnic area, adventure playground, nature trail, arboretum. Cafeteria, shop.
Open mid-May to mid-Sept, Sun–Thur, 10.15am–4.45pm. Admission £2 adults, £1 children (includes boat trip and other attractions); parties by arrangement.
☎ *(096 62) 3353.*

Brantwood
Coniston, Cumbria
Home of John Ruskin, 1872–1900. Beautifully situated with magnificent mountain views across Coniston Water. Exciting new 15-acre woodland garden now being created. 3-mile nature trail.
Open mid-Mar to mid-Nov, daily 11am–5.30pm; Wed to Sun in winter 11am–4pm. Admission Grounds 50p adults, 35p children; House & Grounds £1.25 adults, 75p children.
☎ *(0966) 41396*

Corby Castle
Great Corby, Carlisle, Cumbria
River walks in castle grounds. Peace and quiet, fine trees and shrubs found in these lovely grounds; woodland walks along banks of River Eden.
Open 1 Apr to 30 Sept, daily, 2pm–5pm. Admission 30p adults, children free; parties by arrangement. Free car park.
☎ *Wetheral (0228) 60246.*

Dalemain
nr Penrith, Cumbria
On A592, Penrith-Ullswater road. Ancient house and estate park landscaped by Switzer in 1740s. Historic gardens with rare trees and plants; Elizabethan knot garden; walled and wild gardens with spring bulbs and blossom; terraced herbaceous walk. Plants for sale. Picnic area, adventure playground, museums.
Open 30 Mar to 12 Oct, Sun–Thur, 11.15am–5pm. Admission Grounds £1 adults, children free; House & Grounds £1.80 adults, £1 children; parties by arrangement.
☎ *Pooley Bridge (085 36) 450.*

Dove Cottage
Grasmere, Cumbria
William and Dorothy Wordsworth's garden developed from their arrival in 1799 and faithfully maintained. Wordsworth Museum displaying manuscripts, books, personnalia.

Periodic special exhibitions. Book and gift shop.
Open 1 Mar to 31 Oct and 8 Dec to 4 Jan 1987 daily, Apr to Sept 9.30am–5.30pm (Sun 11am–5.30pm), Mar and Oct 10am–4.30pm (Sun 11am–4.30pm), winter as in Oct. Admission Cottage & Museum £2 adults, £1 children; £1.60 adults, 80p children for parties 15+.
☎ *(096 65) 544.*

Graythwaite Hall
Ulverston, Cumbria
Seven acres of landscaped gardens. Rhododendrons, azaleas and other shrubs.
Open 1 Apr to 30 June, daily, 10am–6pm. Admission 75p adults, children free.
☎ *Newby Bridge (0448) 31248.*

Holehird (Lakeland Horticultural Society)
Windermere, Cumbria
Panoramic views of lakeland peaks; walks among unusual trees, shrubs and plants.
Open all year, daily, 9am–dusk. Admission free.

Holker Hall and Gardens
Cark-in-Cartmel, nr Grange-over-Sands, Cumbria
22 acres of formal and woodland gardens with many rare shrubs and trees, rhododendrons, azaleas, magnolias. Plus 122 acres deer park. Craft and countryside exhibition, adventure playground, baby animals. Cafeteria, gift shop.
Open 30 Mar to 26 Oct, daily exc Sat, 10.30am–6pm, last entry 4.30pm. Admission: Grounds, Garden & Exhibition £1.65 adults, £1 children; Hall extra; reduction for parties 20+.
☎ *Flookburgh (044 853) 328.*

Hutton-in-the-Forest
Penrith, Cumbria
14th-century Pele Tower with gardens and terraces dating from 17th century; walled garden and dovecote. Woodland Walk through outstanding specimen trees.
Gardens open all year, daily, dawn to dusk. Admission £1 adults, 50p children.
☎ *Skelton (085 34) 500.*

Levens Hall, Cumbria

CUMBRIA

Lake District National Park Visitor Centre
Brockhole, Windermere, Cumbria
30 acres of gardens by lake shore; formal gardens, rose terraces, azaleas, rhododendrons; fine bedding schemes and herbaceous borders. Designed by Thomas Hayton Mawson. Boat trips, putting green, Beatrix Potter Grotto. 'Living Lakeland' audio-visual. Cafeteria. Day courses on horticulture, garden tours May to Sept.
Open 20 Mar to 2 Nov, daily, from 10am and by special arrangement for parties. Admission £1.20 adults, 60p children, £1 per person for parties.
☎ *(096 62) 2231.*

Levens Hall
nr Kendal, Cumbria
Elizabethan house with famous topiary garden laid out in 1692; steam engine collection; plant centre; play and picnic areas.
Open 30 Mar to 30 Sept, daily exc Fri & Sat, 11am–5pm. Admission to House & Grounds £2.20 adults, £1.10 children, £2 OAPs; parties £1.80 adult, 90p children. No dogs.
☎ *Sedgwick (0448) 60321.* &

Lingholm
Keswick, Cumbria
Rhododendrons, azaleas and other shrubs in woodland and formal gardens with exceptional mountain views.
Open 1 Apr to 31 Oct, daily, 10am–5pm. Admission £1.25 adults, children free; discount for parties of 30+. No dogs.
☎ *(0596) 72003.* &

Mirehouse
Keswick, Cumbria
Woodland shrub garden containing rhododendrons, azaleas, daffodils, hydrangeas, eucryphias and buddleias and parkland along the shore of Bassenthwaite Lake. Three woodland play areas.
Open 1 Apr to 31 Oct, daily, 10.30am–5.30pm. Admission 50p adults, 35p children; discount for parties.
☎ *(0596) 72287 and 74317.* &

Muncaster Castle
Ravenglass, Cumbria
Famous collection of rhododendrons and azaleas; superb views over Esk Valley.
Open 28 Mar to 30 Sept, Tue to Sun, Bank Hol. Mon, garden 12 noon–5pm; house 1.30pm–4.30pm. Admission Grounds £1.30 adults, 70p children; House & Grounds £2.20 adults, £1.10 children. Special combined tickets for parties and schools.
☎ *(065 77) 614 or 203.* &

Rusland Hall
Rusland, Newby Bridge, Cumbria
18th-century classic gardens with mature specimen trees including cedar, gingko, sequoia, bamboo and wisteria; fountains; magnificent views. Rare white peafowl.
Open Apr to Sept, daily exc Fri & Sat,

Brantwood, Cumbria
11am–5.30pm. Admission House & Grounds £1 adults, 50p children.
☎ *Satterthwaite (022 984) 276.* &

Rydal Hall
Ambleside, Cumbria
Formal garden with double terrace and rose garden by Thomas Mawson. Restored 17th-century grotto and waterfall. 18th-century landscape garden.
Open all year, Wed and Sat, 9am–9pm. Admission free, donations welcome.
☎ *(0966) 32050*

Rydal Mount
Ambleside, Cumbria
The 4½-acre garden of Wordsworth's home contains rare trees and shrubs and has been described as 'one of the most interesting small gardens in England'.
Open 1 Mar to 31 Oct, daily, 10am–5.30pm; 1 Nov to mid-Jan, daily exc. Tue, 10am–12 noon, 2pm–4pm. Admission £1 adults, 50p children; parties 90p adults, 40p children.
☎ *(0966) 33002.*

Sizergh Castle
Sizergh, Cumbria
Fine, mainly 18th-century grounds

with lakes and pools. Exceptional rock garden with internationally famous collection of ferns and dwarf conifers.
Open 30 Mar to 31 Oct, Mon, Wed, Thur, Sun, 12.30pm–5.45pm. Admission 60p adults, 30p children.
☎ *Sedgwick (0448) 60070. NT* ❦

Stagshaw Gardens
Ambleside, Cumbria
Woodland garden with fine collection of rhododendrons and azaleas planted under thinned oaks up hillside. Many other ericaceous trees and shrubs, including magnolias, camellias and embothriums.
Open Apr to June, daily, 10am–6.30pm. Admission 60p adults, 30p children.
☎ *(0966) 33265. NT* ❦

Wordsworth House
Cockermouth, Cumbria
Birthplace of Wordsworth in 1770. Poet's childhood garden with terraced walk by River Derwent; interesting ferns, bluebells and daffodils.
Open 26 Mar to 2 Nov, daily exc. Thur, 11am–5pm (Sun 2pm–5pm). Admission House & Grounds £1.30 adults, 65p children; parties by arrangement. Guide dogs only.
☎ *(0900) 824805. NT* ❦

NOTES ON GARDEN VISITING

These entries have been compiled from information supplied by the gardens and were correct at the time of going to press (November 1985). However, opening times can be subject to sudden change, often because of uncontrollable factors such as the weather. We advise you to telephone the garden to check before setting out – check the admission charges, too. Those given in the entries do not always include admission to the house or other facilities in addition to the garden. Some of the gardens are willing to allow visitors by prior appointment at other times apart from their normal opening days. Where dogs are allowed in a garden, they should always be kept on a lead. NT ❦ denotes gardens belonging to the National Trust – see also pages 8–9. The & symbol shows which gardens are accessible to physically handicapped visitors – see also page 97.

A Guide to English Gardens

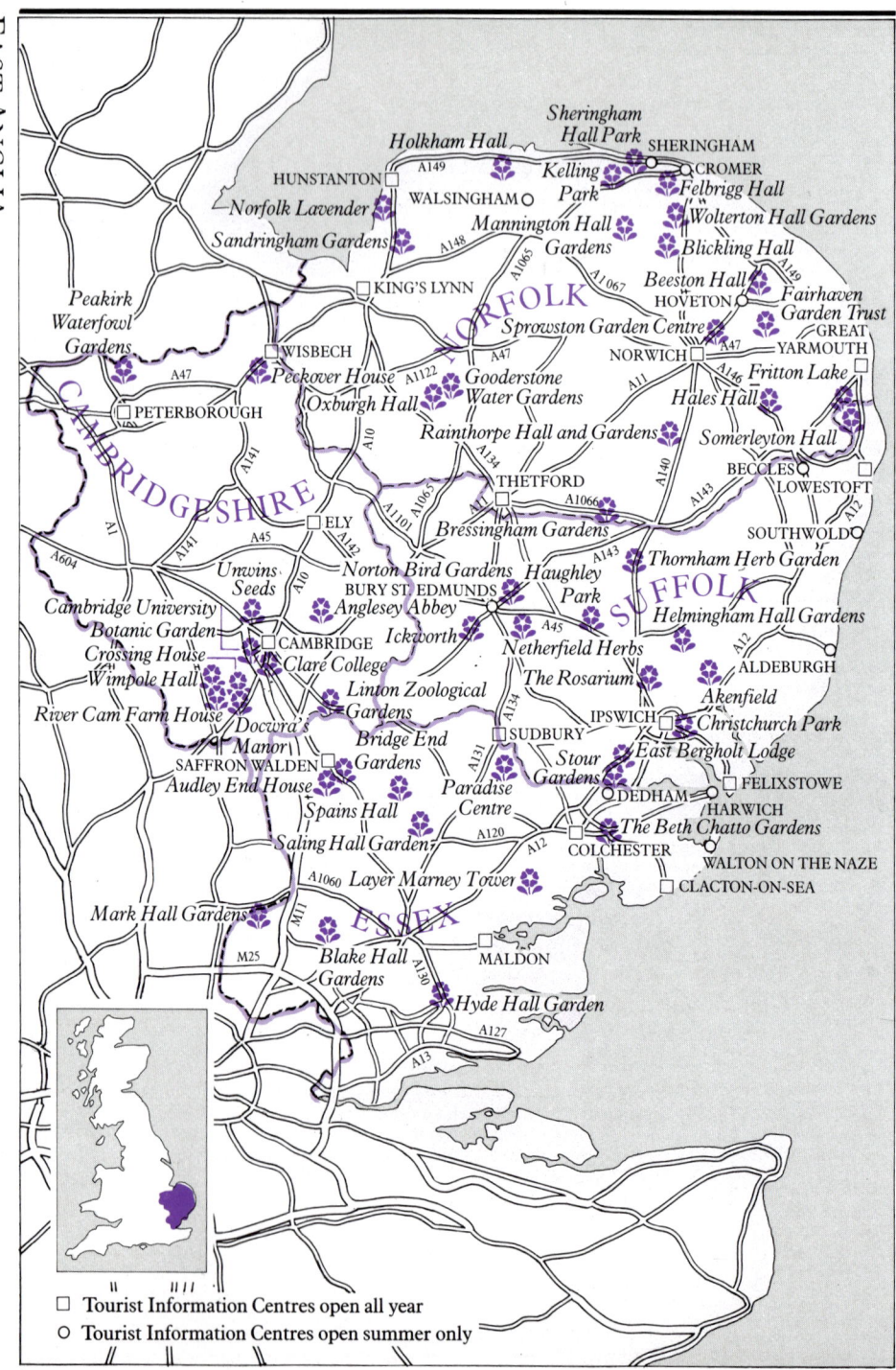

EAST ANGLIA

*B*etween them the gardens of East Anglia offer 'something of everything' from the real 'gardeners' gardens' to pleasant parkland settings for a family day out. It has its share of grandeur in the gardens and grounds of places like Audley End, landscaped by Capability Brown, in the formal gardens and woodlands of Jacobean Blickling Hall, in the great 18th-century landscapes of Holkham Hall, spectacular Wimpole Hall with its intriguing folly, or in the Queen's own home at Sandringham. But, grand as they are, such places are still happy to offer the popular touch in the form of pottery centres, miniature railways, motor museums, picnic areas or the welcome cup of tea. Some gardens make their impact with specialist displays – azaleas and rhododendrons at Somerleyton Hall; dahlias, hyacinths and daffodils at Anglesey Abbey or over 500 varieties of roses grown on the limey soil of The Rosarium near Ipswich. Others, like the Stour Gardens overlooking the Stour valley, the grounds of moated Oxburgh Hall, Helmingham Hall or Hales Hall, revel in the outstanding beauty of their settings. The styles of centuries are also well represented in East Anglia with Elizabethan, Georgian and Victorian gardens culminating in the 20th-century ideas put into practice in Clare College Gardens and others. Some impressive plant collections are also to be found here. There is a wide variety of hardy plants at Bressingham Gardens, rare woody plants at Cambridge's Botanic Garden, trees and shrubs at East Bergholt, heather at Sprowston Garden Centre, herbs at Rougham (Netherfield Herbs) and a fruity mixture of oranges, lemons, vines, figs and mulberries at Loddon (Hales Hall). Enthusiastic gardeners will find much to impress them in even the smaller gardens – Docwra's Manor's two acres contain an important collection of choice plants, and the Beth Chatto Gardens near Colchester are a treasure trove of unusual things for dry and damp gardens.

FEBRUARY

Flowers that put a brave face on the winter months are warmly welcomed for the cheerful touch they bring to the coldest corners. It is the hardy plants that are in bloom now, such as the grape hyacinth, the sturdy houseleek, the clear, yellow winter aconite or the pure white Christmas rose with its fuzzy yellow centre. Many trees and shrubs add their lively contributions – in the blossom of daphne mezereum and wintersweet, in the bright berries of skimmia japonica or the red flash of pyracantha. But February really belongs to the snowdrop. Legend has it that the first of these pure white flowers was a gift given by the angels, created from a snowflake to comfort Eve as she wept in her barren garden for the loss of Eden.

Snowdrop

LAVENDER

Lavender is believed to have been introduced into England by the Romans who used it to perfume their bath water, and from whose word 'lavo' – meaning I wash – its name developed. The Romans used it too for medicinal purposes, and its popularity has never faltered as the sweet-smelling garden herb which retains its scent longer than any other. The production of Norfolk Lavender was established in the 1930s at Heacham, where founder Linneaus Chilvers planted hybrids of the true Lavender (*Lavendula vera*) producing only the finest oils. Besides providing the basis of many perfumed products, today's six oil-bearing varieties also stage a magnificent display of fragrant flowers, caught at their best just before harvesting in July or August.

Lavender

For more information contact the
East Anglia Tourist Board,
Toppesfield Hall, Hadleigh,
Suffolk IP7 5DN
☎ (0473) 822922.

EAST ANGLIA

A GUIDE TO ENGLISH GARDENS

Botanic Garden, Cambridge

'Akenfield'
Charsfield, nr Woodbridge, Suffolk
Fine example of self-sufficient gardening, featuring 600 varieties of flowers, vegetables; ponds. As seen on BBC TV's 'Gardeners' World'.
Open 18 May to 28 Sept, daily, 10am–7pm. Admission 30p adults. No dogs.
☎ (047 337) 402. &

Anglesey Abbey
Lode, Cambridgeshire
Outstanding in scale and variety; marvellous displays of dahlias, hyacinths and daffodils.
Open Abbey & Gardens 29 Mar to 27 Apr, Sat, Sun & Easter Mon; 30 Apr to 12 Oct, Wed to Sun & Bank Hol Mon, 1.30pm–5.30pm. Garden only 2 Apr to 25 Apr, Wed–Fri, 5 May to 7 Oct, Mon & Tue, 1.30pm–5.30pm. Admission: Abbey & Garden £2 adults, £1 children, parties £1.50 adults. Garden only £1 adults, 50p children, parties 80p adults. No dogs.
☎ Cambridge (0223) 811200. NT ✿ &

Audley End House
Saffron Walden, Essex
Historic house in superb grounds landscaped by 'Capability' Brown; lake and river.
Open 1 Apr to 30 Sept, daily exc Mon (open Bank Hol Mon), House 1pm–6pm, Grounds 12noon–6.30pm. Admission £1.80 adults, 90p children/OAPs; 10% discount parties 11+.
☎ (0799) 22399. &

Beeston Hall
Beeston St Lawrence, nr Wroxham, Norfolk
Georgian Gothic mansion set in attractive gardens with fine views of lake and countryside. Tearoom in Orangery.
Open 30 Mar to 14 Sept, Fri, Sun, Bank Hols, 2pm–5.30pm. Admission 50p adults, children free; parties by arrangement. No dogs.
☎ Horning (0692) 630771. &

Blake Hall Gardens
Bobbingworth, nr Ongar, Essex
25 acres of grounds including rose gardens, herbaceous borders, Japanese garden, wild garden and new Tropical House with exotic plants and cacti. Original ice house. Trees, plants and flowers for sale.
Open all year, daily, 10am–6pm (5pm in winter). Admission £1 adults, 50p children; parties by appt.
☎ (0277) 362502. &

Blickling Hall
Aylsham, Norfolk
Fascinating gardens of Jacobean house; formal garden dating from 1729; lake; Temple; Orangery.
Open 30 Mar to 26 Oct, daily exc Mon & Thur, 12 noon–5pm. Admission £1.40 adults, 70p children. No dogs.
☎ (0263) 733084. NT ✿ &

Bressingham Gardens
nr Diss, Norfolk
Six acres of famous informal gardens with 5,000 kinds of hardy plants. Steam railway rides and museum.
Open Sun, 4 May to 28 Sept; Thur, 5 June to 4 Sept; also Wed in Aug, plus Spring and Summer Bank Hol Mons and weekend 6/7 Sept; 11.30am–5.30pm. Admission (1985 prices) £1.20 adults, 70p OAPs, 50p children.
☎ (0379 88)386. &

Bridge End Gardens
Saffron Walden, Essex
Important 18th/19th-century gardens containing recently restored pavilions, lawns; Dutch Garden and old-fashioned Rose Garden. Maze under restoration.
Open all year, daily. Admission free.
☎ Great Dunmow (0371) 5411. &

Cambridge University Botanic Garden
Cambridge, Cambridgeshire
Notable collection of rare woody plants, limestone rock garden, scented and winter gardens, herbaceous borders, glasshouses.
Open all year, Mon to Sat, 8am–6.30pm or dusk. Closed 25 & 26 Dec. Admission free. No dogs.
☎ (0223) 350101. &

The Beth Chatto Gardens
Elmstead Market, nr Colchester, Essex
A 'gardener's garden', set in a hollow with many unusual plants for both dry and damp gardens; adjoining nursery.
Open all year, 1 Mar to 31 Oct, Mon to Sat, 9am–5pm; 1 Nov to 28 Feb, 9am–4pm. Admission 50p adults, children free. No dogs.
☎ Wivenhoe (020 622) 2007. &

Christchurch Park
Ipswich, Suffolk
Beautiful parkland setting of Christchurch Mansion. Diverse tree species, formal gardens, ponds and ornamental wildfowl.
Open all year, daily, 9am–dusk; Mansion, Mon to Sat 10am–5pm (dusk in winter),

Sun 2.30pm–4.30pm or dusk.
Admission free.
☎ (0473) 211211 (Parks Dept.), 53246 (Mansion). &

Clare College
Cambridge, Cambridgeshire
Delightful 2-acre garden portraying many 20th-century ideas in English gardening. Designed for all-year use, although peak season is in summer.
Open all year, Mon to Fri (exc Bank Hols), 2.30pm–4.45pm. Admission free. No dogs.
☎ (0223) 358681. &

Crossing House
Meldreth Road, Shepreth, Cambridgeshire
Small cottage garden with many old-fashioned plants grown in mixed beds with modern varieties; shrubs, bulbs, alpines.
Open all year, daily. Admission free.
☎ Royston (0763) 61071. &

Docwra's Manor
Shepreth, Cambridgeshire
Two-acre garden containing a fascinating plant collection in a series of enclosed gardens. Plants for sale.
Open 1 Apr to 10 Oct, Wed, 10am–5pm; also 1st Sun in those months, 2pm–6pm. Admission £1 adults, 50p OAPs, children free. No dogs.
☎ Royston (0763) 60235/61473. &

East Bergholt Lodge
East Bergholt, nr Colchester, Suffolk
Woodland garden with over 350 different varieties of trees and shrubs, and over 140 varieties of rose. Rhododendrons and camellias. Home-grown plants for sale.
Open May & June, Sat, Sun, Bank Hols, 12noon–6pm; also Apr to Oct by appt. Admission 50p adults, 25p OAPs, children under 12 free.
☎ (0206) 298278.

Fairhaven Garden Trust
South Walsham, nr Norwich, Norfolk
Beech walk with primroses and spring bulbs. Private Broad. Massed display of candelabra primulas by waterways, spanned by small bridges. Azaleas, rhododendrons and many rare shrubs and plants. King oak reputedly over 900 years old. Bird sanctuary (by prior arrangement).
Open 28 Mar to 28 Sept, Sun & Bank Hols; 16 May to 7 Sept, Wed to Sun, 2pm–6pm. Admission 80p adults, 50p children & OAPs.
☎ (060 549) 449. &

Felbrigg Hall
nr Cromer, Norfolk
17th-century house with mature landscaped park and woodland. Formal gardens; walled garden with restored dovecote; fine display of camellias in orangery.
Open 29 Mar to 26 Oct, daily exc Tue & Fri, 11am–5.30pm. Admission £1.70 adults, 85p children, £1.30 parties (Tue, Wed, Thur); Gardens only 40p. No dogs.
☎ West Runton (026 375) 444. NT ✿ &

36

EAST ANGLIA

Fritton Lake
nr Great Yarmouth, Norfolk
Lakeside gardens; woodland walks; picnic and children's play area; pitch and putt; wildfowl collection; pony rides; windsurfing school.
Open 30 Mar to end Sept, daily, 9am–7pm. Admission £1 adults. No dogs.
☎ Fritton (049 379) 208. &

Gooderstone Water Gardens
Crow Hall Farm, Gooderstone, nr King's Lynn, Norfolk
Landscaped garden with flowers, shrubs, grassy walks, lake, pools and bridges. Refreshments served only on Sundays when open for charities.
Open daily 1 June to 27 Sept, 1.30pm–6pm. Admission 50p adults, 30p OAPs, 20p children; parties by arrangement. No dogs.
☎ (036 621) 645. &

Hales Hall
Loddon, Norfolk
Moated garden under restoration. Many unusual plants for sale including orange and lemon trees, vines, figs and mulberries. 15th-century Great Barn with superb roof.
Open Easter to end Sept, Sun, Bank Hol Mon, 2.30pm–5.30pm. Admission £1.50 adults, 50p children. No dogs.
☎ Raveningham (050 846) 395. &

Haughley Park
nr Stowmarket, Suffolk
Jacobean manor house with gardens, park and flowering woods.
Open May to Sept, Tue, 3pm–6pm; also Sun 11 and 18 May. Admission £1 adults, 50p children. No dogs.
☎ Elmswell (0359) 40205. &

Helmingham Hall Gardens
Helmingham, nr Stowmarket, Suffolk
The garden stands within a moat next to a Tudor mansion where drawbridges are raised each night. Herbaceous borders; walled garden. Deer park and picnic area. Stable shop.
Open 4 May to 28 Sept, Sun, 2pm–6pm. Admission £1.20 adults, 90p OAPs/students, 70p children; parties £1.
☎ (047 339) 363. &

Holkham Hall
Wells-next-the-Sea, Norfolk
Fine Palladian house beside lake set in beautiful parkland; terraces and fountains.
Open Spring & Summer Bank Hol Mons; 26 May to 29 Sept, Mon & Thur; also Wed in July & Aug; 1.30pm–5pm. Admission £1.30 adults, £1 OAPs, 50p children.
☎ Fakenham (0328) 710227. &

Hyde Hall Garden
Rettendon, Essex
Garden with interest throughout the year. Bulbs, flowering shrubs, trees, many roses, greenhouses. Light refreshments (Sundays only), plant stall.
Open 2 Apr to 24 Sept, Wed, 11am–5pm; also Sun 20 Apr, 25 May, 29 June, 17 Aug, 2pm–7pm. Admission Garden only 75p adults, 25p children, parties of 20+ 65p.
☎ Chelmsford (0245) 400256. &

Ickworth
nr Bury St Edmunds, Suffolk
Interesting house surrounded by formal gardens with herbaceous borders; orangery and woodland walks.
Open 1 Apr–13 Oct, daily exc Mon & Fri (open Bank Hol Mons) 1.30pm–6pm. Admission £1.70 adults (£2 weekends & Bank Hols), children half price. No dogs.
☎ Horringer (028 488) 270. NT

Kelling Park
Holt, Norfolk
Garden of rhododendrons, azaleas, camellias and roses; 150 different varieties can be seen. Award-winning Water Garden with Westmorland stone and waterfalls. Tropical bird aviaries.
Open all year, daily, 10am–8pm. Admission £1 adults, 75p OAPs, 50p children. No dogs.
☎ (026 371) 2235. &

Layer Marney Tower
nr Colchester, Essex
Tudor house with formal Tudor-style garden, yew hedges, 400 hybrid tea roses, and lawns.
Open 1 Apr to 1 Oct, Thur & Sun, 2pm–6pm. Admission £1 adults, 30p children.
☎ (0206) 330202. &

Linton Zoological Gardens
Linton, Cambridgeshire
10-acre zoo with flower-beds, shrubberies and exotic trees providing added botanical interest.
Open all year, daily exc 25 Dec, 10am–7pm or dusk. Admission (1985 prices) £1.75 adults, £1:20 OAPs, 90p children; reduced rates for parties 20+. No dogs.
☎ Cambridge (0223) 891308. &

Mannington Hall Gardens
Saxthorpe, Norfolk
Heritage rose garden, scented garden, chapel garden, walled garden, nature trail. 20 acres of parkland, wood, lake.
Open May to Sept, Sun 2pm–5pm, also Jun, Jul, Aug, Wed, Thur, Fri 11am–6pm. Admission £1 adults, 75p OAPs/students, 60p pre-booked parties. No dogs exc guide dogs.
☎ (0263 87) 284. &

Mark Hall Gardens
Muskham Road, off First Avenue, Harlow, Essex
Three walled gardens being developed as an unusual fruit garden, a 17th-century garden with parterre and a large walled garden which demonstrates a number of gardening styles and techniques. Opened May 1984.
Open all year, daily, 25 & 26 Dec, Apr to Sept 10am–5pm; Oct to Mar 10am–4pm. Admission free. No dogs exc guide dogs.
☎ (0279) 446416. &

Netherfield Herbs
Rougham, nr Bury St Edmunds, Suffolk
Lovely herb garden featuring two small knot gardens, chamomile seat, scented arbour, alpine herbs, 16th-century salad and medicinal herb beds, flowering cherry walk. 200 varieties of herbs, wild flowers and cottage flowers for sale.
Open all year, daily, 10.30am–6.30pm. Admission free; parties by arrangement with guided lecture tour of herbs for up to 25 persons £7.50. No dogs.
☎ Beyton (0359) 70452. &

Norfolk Lavender Ltd
Caley Mill, Heacham, Norfolk
Largest growers and distillers of lavender in Britain. Harvest mid-July to mid-August. Herb and rose gardens.
Open Jan to end Mar, 1 Oct –31 Dec, Mon to Fri, 9am–4pm; 1 Apr to 30 Sept, daily 9.30am–5.30pm. Admission free.
☎ (0485) 70384. &

Norton Bird Gardens
Norton, nr Bury St Edmunds, Suffolk
Collection of foreign birds set in 4-acre garden with flowering bulbs, roses, herbaceous beds, shrubs and trees. Tropical House.
Open all year, daily, 11am–6pm or dusk. Admission (1985 prices) £1.25 adults, £1 OAPs, 70p children; reduction for parties. No dogs.
☎ Pakenham (0359) 30957. &

GROWING BETTER FOR YOU IN EAST ANGLIA

Bypass NURSERIES

As one of Europe's leading growers of glasshouse flower seed, Bypass Nurseries have the specialist knowledge and facilities to offer an exceptionally wide range of both indoor and outdoor plants. Their fifty years of growing experience also enables them to offer truly professional service, help and advice to their customers.

Ipswich Road, Colchester, Essex CO1 2YF. Tel: (0206) 865500
A12 Road, Capel St. Mary, Ipswich IPN 2JR. Tel: (0473) 310604

EAST ANGLIA

Oxburgh Hall
Oxborough, King's Lynn, Norfolk
12 acres of garden include notable French parterre on east side of 15th-century moated house.
Open May to Sept, Sat to Wed, 1.30pm–5.30pm; also 29 Mar to 27 Apr, 4 Oct to 19 Oct, Sat & Sun, 1.30pm–5.30pm. Admission £1.80 adults, 90p children; parties £1.40 & 70p. No dogs.
☎ *Gooderstone (036 621) 258. NT* ✠ &

Paradise Centre
Lamarsh, nr Bures, Suffolk
Five-acre landscaped garden with unusual shrubs, bulbs, alpine plants; ponds with shade, bog and water plants. Animal paddock, picnic and play area with pets and aviary. Plants and pets for sale. Refreshments.
Open 6 Mar to 4 Nov, daily exc Mon (open Bank Hol Mon), 10am–5pm. Admission 75p adults, 60p OAPs, 45p children; parties 60p, 40p & 30p. No dogs.
☎ *Twinstead (078 729) 449.*

Peakirk Waterfowl Gardens
nr Peterborough, Cambridgeshire
Marvellous collection of ducks, geese, swans and flamingos in a garden setting.
Open all year, daily exc 24 & 25 Dec, 9.30am–5.30pm or dusk. Admission (1985 prices) £1.50 adults, £1.10 OAPs, 75p children; parties £1.10, 70p, 65p. No dogs.
☎ *(0733) 252271.* &

Peckover House
Wisbech, Cambridgeshire
Victorian garden containing rare trees and colourful flower borders; orange trees under glass.
Open 29 Mar to 12 Oct, Sat, Sun & Bank Hol Mon; May to Sept, Sat to Wed; 2pm–5.30pm. Admission £1.20 adults, 60p children/OAPs; parties 90p. No dogs.
☎ *(0945) 583463. NT* ✠ &

Rainthorpe Hall and Gardens
Tasburgh, nr Norwich, Norfolk
Elizabethan manor house set in large gardens on River Tas. Trees, bamboos, plants for sale.
Open 4 May to 7 Sept, Sun & Bank Hol Mons, 2pm–5pm. Admission £1 adults, 50p OAPs/children. (House extra, by appt only.)
☎ *Swainsthorpe (0508) 470618.* &

River Cam Farm House
Wimpole, Cambridgeshire
9 miles SW of Cambridge on south side of A603. 2-acre garden landscaped for shelter. Herbaceous borders, lawns, pond, many unusual plants and trees. Fine art gallery and studio.
Open Apr to Oct, daily exc Mon & Fri, 10.30am–5.30pm. Admission £1 adults, accompanied children free, 50p OAPs/students; parties by arrangement. No dogs.
☎ *Cambridge (0223) 207750.* &

The Rosarium
Claydon, nr Ipswich, Suffolk
More than 500 varieties of roses, many very rare or often thought to be extinct. Grounds also feature 18th-century lime kiln.
Open 15 May to 31 July, daily, 2pm–7pm. Admission 75p.
☎ *(0473) 830334.*

Saling Hall Garden
Great Saling, nr Braintree, Essex
12-acre garden; wall-garden dated 1698; small park with fine trees; extensive new collection of unusual plants; water gardens.
Open 14 May to 1 Aug and 3 Sept to 17 Oct, Wed, Thur, Fri, 2pm–5pm. Admission £1 adults, children free; parties by arrangement. No dogs.
☎ *Great Dunmow (0371) 850243.* &

Sandringham Gardens
nr King's Lynn, Norfolk
Beautiful royal gardens full of interest: lakes, flower gardens, shrub gardens; peaceful walks.
Open 30 Mar to 25 Sept, Mon to Thur 10.30am–5pm, Sun 11.30am–5pm. House closed 21 July to 9 Aug incl; Grounds closed 25 July to 6 Aug incl. Admission £1.30 adults, £1 OAPs, 70p children. House extra. No dogs.
☎ *(0553) 772675.* &

Sheringham Hall Park
Upper Sheringham, nr Sheringham, Norfolk
Rhododendron woods and landscaped park by Humphry Repton in 1812. Repton-designed temple built in park in 1975.
Open 1 May to 30 June, daily exc Sun, 10am–1pm and 2pm–6pm. Admission £1 adults, 50p children.
☎ *(0263) 823074.* &

Somerleyton Hall
nr Lowestoft, Suffolk
12 acres of gardens surrounding splendid Hall; magnificent specimen trees, azaleas, rhododendrons, statuary, glasshouses, maze, miniature railway.
Open 30 Mar to 30 Sept, Sun, Thur & Bank Hol Mon; also Tue & Wed in July & Aug, 2pm–5.30pm. Gardens only 30 Mar to 30 Sept, daily exc Sat, 2pm–5.30pm. Admission £1.80 adults, £1.30 OAPs, 90p children; parties £1.30 & 70p. No dogs.
☎ *(0502) 730224.* &

Spains Hall
Finchingfield, nr Braintree, Essex
Elizabethan manor house with beautiful grounds including flower and kitchen gardens and large Cedar of Lebanon tree planted in 1670.
Open May to July, Sun & Bank Hol Mons, 2pm–5pm. Admission 75p adults, 40p children.
☎ *Great Dunmow (0371) 810266.* &

Sprowston Garden Centre
Sprowston, Norwich, Norfolk
Show gardens which include heather

garden planted in 1977, lawns and shrubs already established and a further 2 acres of garden under construction with a huge houseplant greenhouse.
Open all year, daily, Mon to Sat 8.30am–5.30pm, Sun 10.30am–5pm. Admission free.
☎ *(0603) 412239.* &

Stour Gardens
Stour, nr East Bergholt, Suffolk
Attractive gardens affording excellent views over the lovely Stour Valley. Home of the late Randolf Churchill.
Open all year, daily, 10.30am–6pm (1985 times). Admission 50p adults, 25p children.
☎ *Colchester (0206) 298363.* &

Thornham Herb Garden
Thornham Magna, nr Eye, Suffolk
18th-century walled garden, with herb knot garden. Garden under reconstruction. Herbalist shop; plants for sale.
Open all year, daily, 9am–6.30pm. Admission free.
☎ *Mellis (037 983) 779.* &

Unwins Seeds Ltd
Histon, nr Cambridge, Cambridgeshire
Trial garden featuring 30,000 flowers including 100 varieties of marigold; dazzling colour displays. Included in the 4-acre trial garden are over 1,000 varieties of vegetables.
Open mid-July to mid-Sept, daily, dawn to dusk. Admission 25p adults (for local charities), children free. No dogs.
☎ *(022 023) 2270.* &

Wimpole Hall
Arrington, Cambridgeshire
Spectacular mansion set in beautiful landscaped park featuring a grand folly and Chinese bridge. Working farm with rare breeds of domestic animals.
Hall & Farm open 29 Mar to 26 Oct, daily exc Mon & Fri, 10.30am–6pm (Farm 10.30am–5pm); Park open all year, daily, dawn to dusk. Admission £1.90 adults (£2.20 Sat & Sun), 95p children (£1.10 Sat & Sun), £1.50 parties; Farm extra. No dogs.
☎ *Cambridge (0223) 207257. NT* ✠ &

Wolterton Hall Gardens
Erpingham, nr Aylsham, Norfolk
Rose garden, herbaceous borders, many flowering shrubs, Rhododendrons, azalias; interesting walled kitchen garden. Lake and parkland views landscaped by Repton.
Open June to Aug, Wed, 2pm–5pm. Admission 50p adults, children free; parties by arrangement. No dogs.
☎ *Cromer (0263) 761210.* &

BEFORE SETTING OUT it's always best to 'phone and check garden details. Opening times and prices may be subject to change at short notice!

EAST MIDLANDS

When Tennyson wrote 'Come into the garden Maud', he had the English Shires in mind – or Harrington Hall, to be precise. Today, with so many splendid examples to choose from, it's still a pleasure to follow his advice. Over the centuries this varied region of picturesque places – the White Peak, the Lincolnshire Wolds, the Vale of Belvoir and the Vale of Trent, Sherwood Forest and other woodlands – has seen the development of some ambitious estates whose grounds are now open to the public. At 3,800 acres Clumber Park is the largest survivor of the Dukeries, a group of grand houses and parks in North Nottinghamshire once owned by the nobility. Though most houses of the Dukeries have not survived the years, plenty in neighbouring counties have. Best known of them all is Chatsworth, the 'Palace of the Peak' whose parkland was laid out by Capability Brown around gardens featuring a now-famous staircase of waterfalls, the Great Cascade. But Derbyshire also produces real rivals to Chatsworth: nearby Haddon Hall must be one of the loveliest medieval manorial homes in England; Hardwick Hall, a supreme example of Elizabethan architecture, was actually designed by its owner 'Bess', Countess of Shrewsbury; Kedleston Hall is probably the finest Robert Adam house in England – and each has a garden well worthy of the house. Newstead Abbey and Melbourne Hall make a charming pair; the former was the home of Lord Byron, and the latter was owned by his good friend Lady Caroline Lamb. Some gardens bring particularly intriguing things to light – at Elvaston Castle Country Park it's a working estate museum, at Gunby Hall a Ghost Walk, at Newstead Abbey a Japanese garden and at Rockingham Castle an elephant hedge and a tilting-lawn. Others spring their surprises with sudden splashes of colour: look out for the displays of autumn leaves in town parks and wooded gardens, of azaleas and rhododendrons at Lea near Matlock and of bulbs at Doddington Hall and Springfields.

MARCH

Spring is well and truly on the way, heralded by the brighter, stronger colours of early flowers. As the sunshine hours increase, a widening variety of trees and shrubs are tempted into bloom producing bold sprays of forsythia, Japanese quince or fragrant flowering currant, and delicate-looking flowers on the witch hazel and ornamental plum. Borders and rock gardens come to life with small varieties of tulips, irises and narcissi, with old favourites like polyanthus which always put on a good show, or with less common plants such as bergenia or 'bear's ears'. Above all March is the month for crocuses; year after year, right on cue, they splash their distinctive purples, yellows and whites across rockeries and lawns in vivid patches of colour.

Spring Crocus

THE TULIP

Every April, glorious displays of tulips, daffodils and other bulbs transform Lincolnshire's 'Little Holland' into a glowing carpet of colour. Single, double, pink or purple, striped or frilly, the versatile tulip – that most Dutch of flowers – has made itself at home in nearly every English garden. Tulips were introduced into Britain in 1577, but they remained expensive and exclusive until the 19th century when they became a flower for 'shopkeepers and workers'. The first really cheap bulbs were imported from America, but today the area around Spalding is the centre of Britain's own thriving bulb industry. In early May thousands of tulip heads removed to promote the growth of sturdy bulbs are used to decorate floats for the spectacular Spalding Flower Parade.

Tulip

For more information contact the
East Midlands Tourist Board,
Exchequergate, Lincoln, Lincolnshire
LN2 1PZ ☎ (0522) 31521/3 (written and telephone enquiries only).

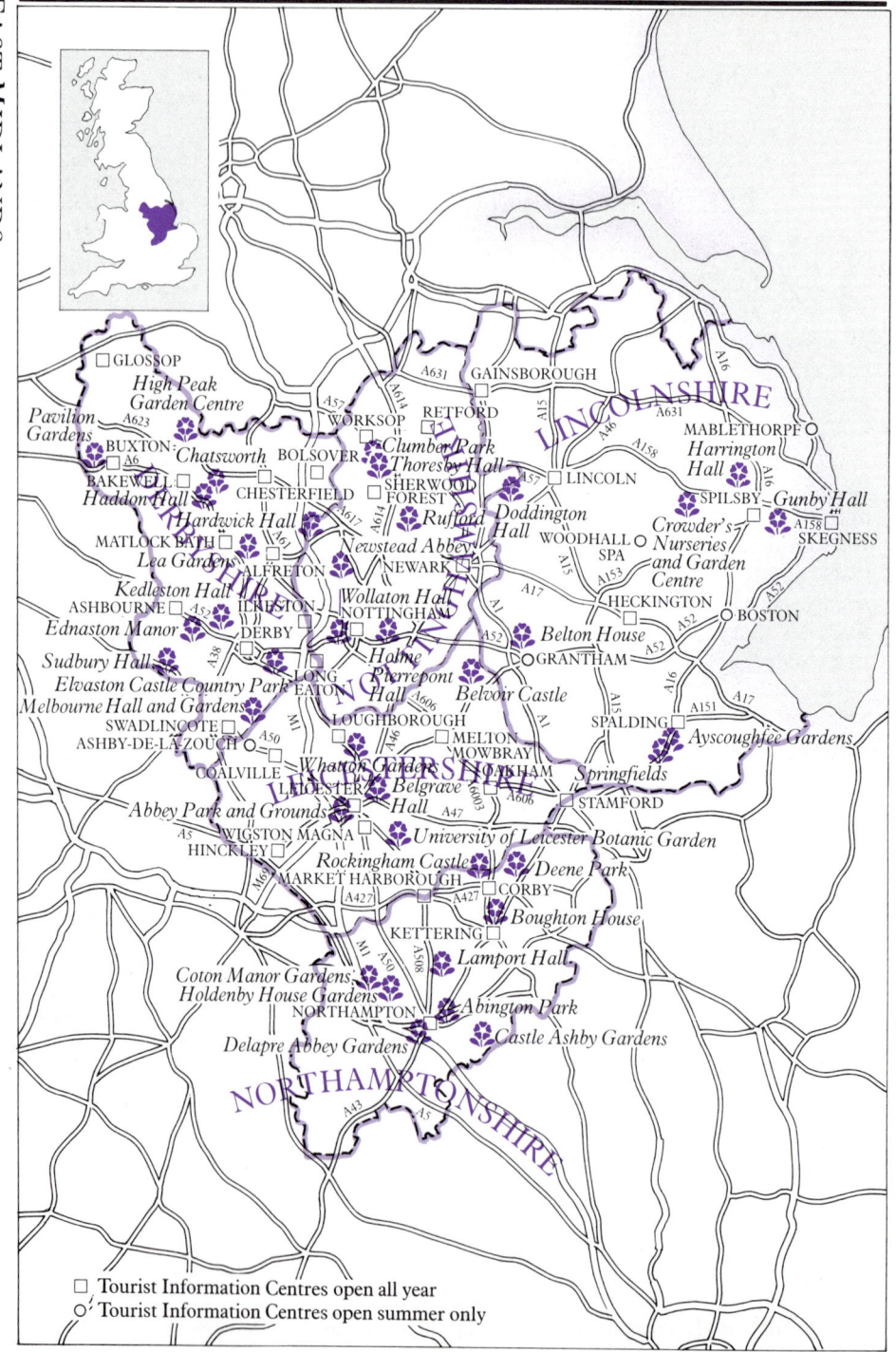

A Guide to English Gardens

EAST MIDLANDS

- GLOSSOP
- High Peak Garden Centre
- Pavilion Gardens
- BUXTON
- BAKEWELL
- Chatsworth
- BOLSOVER
- WORKSOP
- RETFORD
- GAINSBOROUGH
- MABLETHORPE
- Harrington Hall
- Clumber Park
- Thoresby Hall
- SHERWOOD FOREST
- CHESTERFIELD
- LINCOLN
- SPILSBY
- Gunby Hall
- SKEGNESS
- Haddon Hall
- Hardwick Hall
- Rufford
- Doddington Hall
- WOODHALL SPA
- MATLOCK BATH
- Newstead Abbey
- NEWARK
- Crowder's Nurseries and Garden Centre
- Lea Gardens
- ALFRETON
- A15
- A153
- Kedleston Hall
- HECKINGTON
- BOSTON
- ASHBOURNE
- ILKESTON
- Wollaton Hall
- NOTTINGHAM
- Ednaston Manor
- DERBY
- DERBYSHIRE
- NOTTINGHAMSHIRE
- LINCOLNSHIRE
- Belton House
- Sudbury Hall
- Holme Pierrepont Hall
- GRANTHAM
- LONG EATON
- Belvoir Castle
- Elvaston Castle Country Park
- Melbourne Hall and Gardens
- LOUGHBOROUGH
- SPALDING
- Ayscoughee Gardens
- SWADLINCOTE
- MELTON MOWBRAY
- ASHBY-DE-LA-ZOUCH
- COALVILLE
- Whatton Gardens
- OAKHAM
- Springfields
- LEICESTER
- Belgrave Hall
- STAMFORD
- Abbey Park and Grounds
- WIGSTON MAGNA
- LEICESTERSHIRE
- HINCKLEY
- University of Leicester Botanic Garden
- Rockingham Castle
- Deene Park
- MARKET HARBOROUGH
- CORBY
- Boughton House
- KETTERING
- Coton Manor Gardens
- Holdenby House Gardens
- Lamport Hall
- Abington Park
- NORTHAMPTON
- Delapre Abbey Gardens
- Castle Ashby Gardens
- NORTHAMPTONSHIRE

□ Tourist Information Centres open all year
○ Tourist Information Centres open summer only

EAST MIDLANDS

Abbey Park and Grounds
Leicester, Leicestershire
Formal 'Victorian' park with boating lake, waterfowl lake and pavilion. Reconstructed site of Leicester Abbey and memorial stone marking approximate site of Cardinal Wolsey's grave. Spring and summer floral displays.
Open all year, daily, 7.30am–dusk. Admission free.
☎ *(0533) 20290.* &

Abington Park
Northampton, Northamptonshire
Large town park with lakes, bowling greens, pitch & putt; well planted with trees; noted for autumn colour. Aviary; garden for the blind.
Open all year, daily, dawn to dusk. Admission free. &

Ayscoughfee Gardens
Spalding, Lincolnshire
Yew hedges in gardens planted in the 15th century.
Open all year, daily exc 25 Dec, Mon to Sat 8am–sunset, Sun 10am–sunset. Admission free.
☎ *(0775) 5468.* &

Belgrave Hall
Belgrave, Leicestershire
Small Queen Anne home built 1709-13, with period and botanic gardens, rock and water gardens.
Open all year exc 25 & 26 Dec, Mon to Thur & Sat 10am–5.30pm, Sun 2pm–5pm. Admission free. No dogs.
☎ *Leicester (0533) 669413.* &

Belton House
nr Grantham, Lincolnshire
17th-century house in 600-acre parkland; formal gardens with Orangery; lakeland and woodland; adventure playground.
Open 29 Mar to end Oct, Wed to Sun, Bank Hol Mon, Park 12 noon–5.30pm, House 1pm–5.30pm. Admission £2.20 adults, £1.10 children.
☎ *(0476) 66116. NT* ✤

Belvoir Castle
nr Grantham, Leicestershire
Historic castle overlooking beautiful Vale of Belvoir. Lovely garden, rare 300-year-old statuary by Cibber.
Open 22 Mar to 4 Oct, Tue, Wed, Thur, Sat, Sun, 12 noon–6pm. Admission Castle & Gardens £2.20 adults, £1.20 children; parties £1.60 adults, £1.20 OAPs. No dogs.
☎ *(0476) 870262.* &

Boughton House
Kettering, Northamptonshire
15th-century monastic building later enlarged around seven courtyards. Delightful gardens and grounds including walled garden, 16th-century fishpond, Victorian rose beds, herbaceous borders; adventure woodland play area and nature trail.
Open 2 to 31 Aug, daily; Grounds 12.30pm–5pm, House 2pm–5pm. Admission £1 adults, 50p OAPs/students; House extra. No dogs (exc Park).
☎ *(0536) 82248.* &

Castle Ashby Gardens
nr Northampton, Northamptonshire
Elizabethan house set in fine 'Capability' Brown landscape, including lakes, follies and temple. Victorian terrace gardens and Italian garden with large conservatory. Arboretum and nature trail in Woodland Park.
Gardens open all year, daily, 10am–6pm or dusk. Admission 50p adults, 25p children. House not open to public.
☎ *Yardley Hastings (0601 29) 234.* &

Chatsworth
Bakewell, Derbyshire
Extensive garden with elaborate cascade and fountains contrasting with a landscaped park and working farmyard.
Open 23 Mar to 26 Oct, daily, 11.30am–5pm. Admission £1.50 adults, 75p children; House extra; parties by arrangement.
☎ *Baslow (024 688) 2204.* &

Clumber Park
Worksop, Nottinghamshire
Notable example of 18th-century landscape design; 3,800 acres with extensive woodland, 80-acre lake, famous 2-mile avenue of limes, lawned lakeside terraces.
Open all year, daily. Admission £1.40 per car; coaches £2.40 weekdays, £5.50 weekends/Bank Hols.
☎ *(0909) 476592. NT* ✤ &

Coton Manor Gardens
Coton, nr Northampton, Northamptonshire
Outstanding old-English garden of exceptional charm; flamingos; wildfowl and tropical birds. Roam at large in the water gardens. Unusual plants for sale.
Open 1 Apr to 31 Oct, Thur, Sun, Bank Hol Mon & Tue; also Wed in July & Aug,
2pm–6pm. Admission £1.50 adults, 50p children; parties of 30+ £1.30.
☎ *(0604) 740219.* &

Crowder's Nurseries and Garden Centre
Horncastle, Lincolnshire
1½ acres of landscaped show-gardens adjoining purpose-built garden centre.
Open all year, daily exc 25 & 26 Dec, 1 Jan, 8.30am–5.30pm. Admission free.
☎ *(065 82) 7686.* &

Deene Park
nr Corby, Northamptonshire
Mainly 16th-century house with large lake and park and extensive gardens with old-fashioned roses, rare trees and shrubs.
Open 30 Mar to 31 Aug, Sun & Bank Hol Mon, Park 1pm–5pm, House & Gardens 2pm–5pm. Admission (1985 prices) £2 adults, £1 children. No dogs.
☎ *Bulwick (078 085) 278/223.* &

Delapre Abbey Gardens
Northampton, Northamptonshire
Walled garden dating back to 15th century; garden and walls laid out as Victorian garden; herbs and herbaceous borders; shrubs; arboretum.
Garden open Mar to Oct, daily, dawn to dusk. Arboretum all year, daily, dawn to dusk. Admission free. &

Doddington Hall
Lincoln, Lincolnshire
Five acres of romantic gardens with fine displays of roses, spring bulbs, flowering shrubs and mature trees: the setting for a magnificent Elizabethan house. Licensed garden restaurant open from 12 noon.
Open 31 Mar & May to Sept, Wed, Sun & Bank Hol Mon, 2pm–6pm. Admission: House & Garden £1.90 adults, 95p children; Garden half price; parties 10% reduction.
☎ *(0522) 694308.* &

Ednaston Manor
Brailsford, Derbyshire
On A52. Lutyens house with garden of botanical interest. Large collection shrubs, shrub roses, clematis and unusual plants. Plants for sale.
Open 30 Mar to Sept, Mon to Fri 1pm–4.30pm, Sun 2pm–5.30pm. Admission free (House not open to the public). No dogs.
☎ *Ashbourne (0335) 60325.* &

CASTLE ASHBY, the seat of the 7th Marquess of Northampton, is a fascinating combination of 18th and 19th century gardening styles; formal gardens overlooking a 'Capability' Brown landscape and mature trees sheltering an Italian Garden.
The Nature Trail, laid out along one of Brown's carriageways, reveals the best of both styles.
CASTLE ASHBY HOUSE, CASTLE ASHBY, NORTHAMPTON. Tel. Yardley Hastings (060 129) 234 M1 Exit 14 or 15. Open all year.

A Guide to English Gardens

41

EAST MIDLANDS

A GUIDE TO ENGLISH GARDENS

Elvaston Castle Country Park
nr Derby, Derbyshire
Country estate with formal gardens (recently restored), and landscaped parkland. Walled Old English Garden featured in BBC TV series 'Gardeners' World'; extensive topiary garden. Unique working estate museum. Tearoom; caravan & camp site.
Park open all year, daily, 9am–dusk (6pm Old English Garden); Museum Easter to Oct, Wed to Sat 1pm–5pm, Sun & Bank Hols 10am–6pm. Admission free to Park; Museum 50p adults, 25p children; car park charge weekends & Bank Hols.
☎ *(0332) 71342.* ♿

Gunby Hall
Gunby, nr Spilsby, Lincolnshire
Seven acres of formal and walled gardens, old roses, herbaceous borders, herb garden, kitchen garden with fruit trees and vegetables. Tennyson's "Haunt of Ancient Peace".
Open Apr to end Sept, Thur, 2pm–6pm; Tue, Wed, Fri by written appointment. Admission House & Gardens £1.10 adults, 55p children; Gardens only 80p & 45p.
NT ✠

Haddon Hall
Bakewell, Derbyshire
Fine example of medieval manorial home; 17th-century terraced gardens, wall and bed roses, clematis.
Open 25 Mar to 30 Sept, Tue to Sun exc Suns in July & Aug, 11am–6pm. Admission £2.20 adults, £1.60 OAPs, £1.10 children; parties £1.60. No dogs.
☎ *(062 981) 2855.*

Hardwick Hall
nr Chesterfield, Derbyshire
Interesting herb garden particularly suitable for visually or physically handicapped to enjoy; delightful orchards and a collection of old-fashioned roses.
Open 29 Mar to end Oct, daily, 12 noon–5.30pm or dusk. Admission £1.20 adults, 60p children.
☎ *(0246) 850430. NT* ✠ ♿

Harrington Hall
Spilsby, Lincolnshire
Climbing roses, flowering shrubs, yew hedges, herbaceous borders; terrace is 'high hall gardens' of Tennyson's poem, 'Maud'.
Open 2 Apr to 30 Oct, Wed & Thur, 12 noon–8pm or dusk; also 30 & 31 Mar, 4, 11, 25 May, 1, 15 June, 6, 20 July. Admission to Gardens free; charge for House and conducted tours.
☎ *(0790) 52281.* ♿

High Peak Garden Centre
Bamford, Derbyshire
Exhibition garden in Peak National Park; tree and shrub borders; rock, rose and heather gardens; craft and walking equipment shop. Café.
Open all year, daily, 10am–6pm. Admission free.
☎ *Hope Valley (0433) 51484.* ♿

Holdenby House Gardens
Holdenby, nr Northampton, Northamptonshire
Beautiful gardens surrounding house once the largest in England. Elizabethan garden with terraces,
ponds, fragrant and silver borders. Rare farm animals; museum; shop; donkey and train rides; play area; pets corner; teas served in Victorian kitchen.
Open Apr to Sept, Sun & Bank Hol Mons; also Thur in July & Aug; 2pm–6pm. Admission (1985 prices) £1.20 adults, £1 OAPs, 60p children.
☎ *(0604) 770786/770241.* ♿

Holme Pierrepont Hall
Nottingham, Nottinghamshire
Early-Tudor brick crenellated manor, boasting a 19th-century courtyard garden with box parterre; also an informal garden.
Open June to Aug, Tue, Thur, Fri, Sun; also Easter & Spring Bank Hols, Sun to Tue; 2pm–6pm. Admission £1.50 adults, 75p children. No dogs.
☎ *Radcliffe-on-Trent (060 73) 2371.* ♿

Kedleston Hall
nr Derby, Derbyshire
The finest Robert Adam house in England, with spacious park and gardens.
Open 30 Mar to 31 Aug, Sun; also Bank Hol Mon & Tue exc 6 May, 12 noon–6pm. Admission: Hall, Park, Gardens, Museum & Church £2.20 adults, £1.10 children; Gardens & Park £1.10.
☎ *(0332) 842191.*

Lamport Hall
Lamport, Northamptonshire
17th/18th-century house set in attractive wooded gardens and park, with the first Alpine Garden in England. Picnic area; nature trail.
Open 30 Mar to 28 Sept, Sun, Bank Hol Mon; also Thur in July & Aug, 2.15pm–5.15pm. Admission £1.50 adults, £1.20 OAPs/students, 75p children; parties £1.20 by arrangement.
☎ *Maidwell (060 128) 272.* ♿

Lea Gardens
Lea, Matlock, Derbyshire
3½ acres of hybrid and species rhododendrons and azaleas; rock garden; refreshments; plant sales.
Open 20 Mar to 31 July, daily, 10am–7pm. Admission 50p adults (£1 May to 20 June), 25p children.
☎ *Dethick (062 984) 380.* ♿ *(check).*

Melbourne Hall and Gardens
Melbourne, nr Derby, Derbyshire
House with historic associations and important collection paintings and furniture. World-famous gardens; waterside walks. 17th-century Tearoom.

Chatsworth, Derbyshire

CHATSWORTH

EXTENSIVE GARDEN
World famous for its waterworks.
Open every day 11.30am to 5.30pm, 23rd March to 26th October
House open every day 11.30am to 4.30pm
Farmyard and Adventure Playground open every day
10.30am to 4.30pm
Home-made refreshments, Shops, Baby Room
For further details please telephone: Baslow (024688) 2204

42

EAST MIDLANDS

Open 1 Apr to 30 Sept, Wed, Sat, Sun &
Bank Hol Mon, 2pm–6pm. Admission £1.
No dogs.
☎ (033 16) 3347/2502. &

Newstead Abbey
Linby, Nottinghamshire
Country mansion where Byron lived;
Japanese garden, fern garden, iris
garden; beautiful parkland.
*Gardens open all year, daily exc 30 Nov,
10am–dusk; House 20 Apr to 30 Sept,
daily, 1.45pm–6pm (last entry 5pm).
Admission: Gardens 70p adults, 20p
children; House 80p adults, 20p children;
parties by arrangement.*
☎ Mansfield (0623) 792822 (grounds),
793557 (house). &

Pavilion Gardens
Buxton, Derbyshire
23 acres of well-laid-out gardens; duck
pond, children's play area, miniature
railway, crazy golf.
Open permanently. Admission free.
☎ (0298) 3114. &

Rockingham Castle
Corby, Northamptonshire
Ancient home set in wild and formal
gardens; rose garden and famous
'elephant' hedge.
*Open 30 Mar to 30 Sept, Sun, Thur, Bank
Hol Mon & Tue; also Tue in Aug;
2pm–6pm. Admission House & Gardens
£1.80 adults, £1.50 OAPs/students/
parties, £1 children; Gardens only £1.*
☎ Rockingham (0536) 770240. &

Rufford
nr Ollerton, Nottinghamshire
152-acre Country Park with 20-acre
lake. Recently-developed garden area
includes a formal garden laid out in
'rooms', an informal garden including
the Reg Hookway Memorial
Arboretum and semi-natural area
developed predominantly for the
benefit of wildlife.
*Open all year, daily, dawn to dusk.
Admission free.*
☎ Mansfield (0623) 824153. &

Springfields
nr Spalding, Lincolnshire
Impressive show garden; dazzling
displays of tulips and daffodils; also
bedding plants, 10,000 rose bushes
(new varieties), dahlias, flowering
trees and shrubs.
*Open 28 Mar to 30 Sept, daily, 10am–6pm.
Admission £1.20 adults (£1.50 special
events), children free; parties 15% discount.
No dogs.*
☎ (0775) 4843/4844. &

Rockingham Castle, Northamptonshire

Sudbury Hall
Sudbury, Derbyshire
Hall lies in landscaped grounds, with
lawns sweeping to the lakeside.
Particularly notable is the Quincunx –
a rare, classic formation of lime trees.
*Open Apr to end Oct, Wed to Sun; also
Bank Hol Mon; 1pm–5.30pm (last
admission 5pm). Admission: Gardens free;
Hall £2 adults, £1 children; parties of 20+
£1.40; Museum extra.*
☎ (028 378) 305. NT &

Thoresby Hall
nr Newark, Nottinghamshire
A Victorian Italianate garden with
grand terraces, shrubberies and open
views of Repton's 18th-century
parkland. Bedding most colourful
July/August. Many beautiful mature
trees.
*Open May to Aug, Sun; also 30 & 31 Mar
& Bank Hol Mons; 11am–6.30pm (House
1pm–5.30pm). Admission House & Garden
£1.70 adults, 80p children, OAPs in parties
£1.10; Gardens only 50p adults, 20p
children.*
☎ Mansfield (0623) 822301.

University of Leicester Botanic Garden
*Beaumont Hall, Oadby, Leicester,
Leicestershire*
Heather, herb, knot and rock gardens;
formal pool; glasshouses; beds
illustrating history of roses.
*Open all year, Mon to Fri, 10am–5pm or
dusk. Admission free. No dogs.*
☎ (0533) 717725. &

Whatton Gardens
*Long Whatton, nr Loughborough,
Leicestershire*
25-acre grounds containing both
formal gardens and wilderness areas.
Rock pools with fish, unusual plants,
roses, lilacs, azaleas, rhododendrons
and fine selection of mature trees.
*Open 30 Mar to end Sept, Sun & Bank
Hols, 2pm–6pm. Admission 70p adults, 40p
OAPs, 30p children; parties on application.*
☎ (0509) 842268. &

Wollaton Hall
Nottingham, Nottinghamshire
16th-century hall housing City of
Nottingham Natural History
Museum; formal gardens, with deer
park and lake. Nature trail.
*Park open all year, daily, dawn to dusk.
Hall open, Mon to Sat summer,
10am–7pm, autumn/winter 10am–dusk;
Sun summer 2pm–5pm, autumn/winter
1.30pm–4.30pm. Admission Park free exc
for special events; Hall on Sun & Bank
Hols 20p adults, 10p children.*
☎ (0602) 282146. &

LOSEHILL HALL
Losehill Hall is a comfortable, modernised and extended Victorian Mansion
set in 25 acres of garden, parkland and woodland.
A wide range of special interest holidays and courses are offered, including
GREAT HOUSES AND GARDENS, and CHRIS BAINES' WILDLIFE
GARDENING WEEKEND.
Full details (SAE please) from: Peter Townsend, Principal, Peak National
Park Centre, Losehill Hall, Castleton, Derbyshire S30 2WB.
Telephone: Hope Valley (0433) 20373.

A Guide to English Gardens

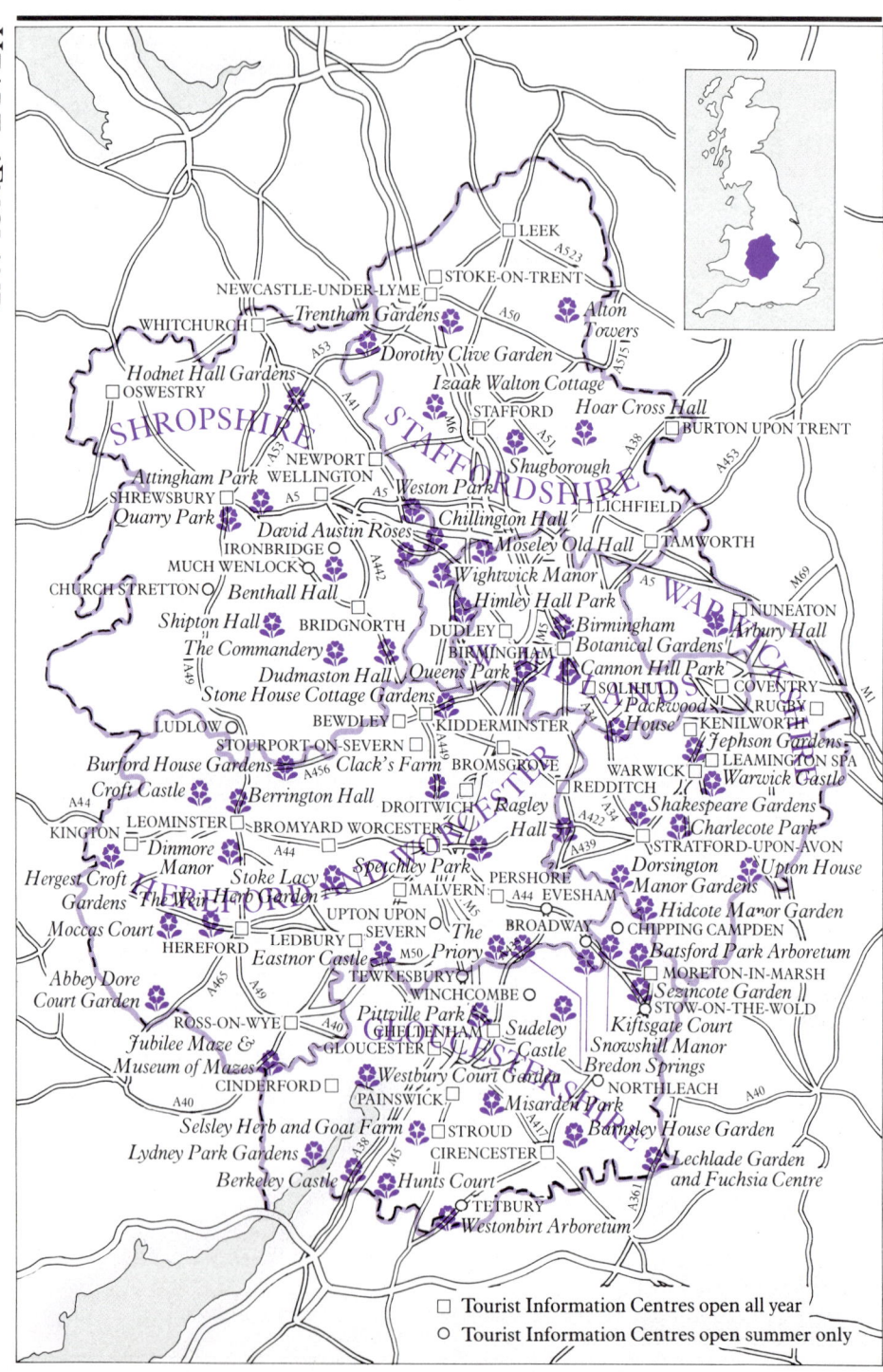

Heart of England

Shropshire
- Whitchurch
- Hodnet Hall Gardens
- Oswestry
- Attingham Park
- Shrewsbury
- Quarry Park
- Newport
- Wellington
- Ironbridge
- David Austin Roses
- Much Wenlock
- Church Stretton
- Benthall Hall
- Shipton Hall
- Bridgnorth
- The Commandery
- Ludlow

Staffordshire
- Leek
- Stoke-on-Trent
- Newcastle-under-Lyme
- Trentham Gardens
- Alton Towers
- Dorothy Clive Garden
- Izaak Walton Cottage
- Stafford
- Hoar Cross Hall
- Burton upon Trent
- Shugborough
- Weston Park
- Chillington Hall
- Lichfield
- Moseley Old Hall
- Tamworth
- Wightwick Manor
- Himley Hall Park
- Dudley
- Birmingham
- Birmingham Botanical Gardens
- Nuneaton
- Arbury Hall

Warwickshire
- Queens Park
- Cannon Hill Park
- Solihull
- Packwood House
- Coventry
- Kenilworth
- Rugby
- Jephson Gardens
- Leamington Spa
- Warwick
- Warwick Castle
- Shakespeare Gardens
- Charlecote Park
- Stratford-upon-Avon
- Upton House
- Hidcote Manor Garden
- Chipping Campden
- Batsford Park Arboretum
- Moreton-in-Marsh
- Sezincote Garden
- Stow-on-the-Wold
- Kiftsgate Court
- Snowshill Manor
- Bredon Springs
- Northleach
- Barnsley House Garden
- Lechlade Garden and Fuchsia Centre

Hereford & Worcester
- Dudmaston Hall
- Stone House Cottage Gardens
- Bewdley
- Kidderminster
- Stourport-on-Severn
- Clack's Farm
- Bromsgrove
- Burford House Gardens
- Croft Castle
- Berrington Hall
- Kington
- Leominster
- Droitwich
- Redditch
- Ragley Hall
- Bromyard
- Worcester
- Dorsington Manor Gardens
- Dinmore Manor
- Stoke Lacy Herb Garden
- The Weir
- Speltchley Park
- Pershore
- Evesham
- Broadway
- Hergest Croft Gardens
- Moccas Court
- Hereford
- Upton upon Severn
- Ledbury
- Eastnor Castle
- The Priory
- Malvern

Gloucestershire
- Abbey Dore Court Garden
- Ross-on-Wye
- Tewkesbury
- Winchcombe
- Pittville Park
- Cheltenham
- Sudeley Castle
- Gloucester
- Jubilee Maze & Museum of Mazes
- Cinderford
- Westbury Court Garden
- Painswick
- Misarden Park
- Selsley Herb and Goat Farm
- Stroud
- Lydney Park Gardens
- Cirencester
- Hunts Court
- Berkeley Castle
- Tetbury
- Westonbirt Arboretum

□ Tourist Information Centres open all year
○ Tourist Information Centres open summer only

HEART of ENGLAND

*T*he Heart of England lives up to the romance of its name: 'black and white' buildings, Cotswold cottages, orchard vales and floral towns provide an irresistible setting for mellow cathedral cities and their modern counterparts. This note of nostalgia is echoed throughout the region in a wealth of houses and gardens which represents the fairest and finest of Old England. There is plenty to remind us that this was Shakespeare country: Elizabethan Berkeley Castle, Sudeley Castle or Charlecote Park, Moseley Old Hall and Shipton Hall all with their period grounds and, of course, the Shakespeare Gardens at Stratford-upon-Avon. Amongst the stately courts and manors, there are show places of every period and of every size, from Izaak Walton's cottage garden to the medieval magnificence of Warwick Castle in its Capability Brown parkland. He also landscaped the grounds of Berrington Hall, Chillington Hall, Himley Hall Park, Moccas Court, Trentham Gardens and Weston Park, and Humphry Repton followed on with Attingham Park and the water gardens at Sezincote. Whilst many gardens in the Heart of England have developed new attractions ranging from picnic sites to adventure playgrounds, the old favourites which they have so carefully preserved number amongst them a carriage collection, a brewhouse, a Roman temple, a maze museum, a medieval dovecote and Europe's largest private toy collection at Sudeley Castle. Natural collections are just as far-ranging, covering things like the Domestic Fowl Trust at Dorsington Manor, the famous deer at Charlecote and Spetchley Park, an indoor display of fuchsias at Lechlade and an outstanding variety of trees at the great arboreta established last century at Westonbirt and Batsford Park. At Hidcote Manor, in the heart of the Cotswolds, you'll find one of the finest and most influential of English 20th-century gardens. Designed by its American owner as a series of more than 20 outdoor rooms, it entrances amateurs and serious gardeners alike. ❦

APRIL

April celebrates the arrival of spring with a season of bulbs: daffodils, narcissi, tulips and less common varieties such as the trout lily or the spring starflower. Hardy perennials compete with colourful shows of their own – the purple of primulas and aubrietia, orange and saffron wallflowers or warm yellow allysum. Two particularly lovely trees are in flower this month; the ornamental cherry seems almost to disappear beneath a sea of frivolous pink blossom, and the magnolia's pure white flowers, so delicately tinted with rose at the base, give the garden an exotic air. April also sees a mass of rhododendrons come into flower in the start of one of the most spectacular displays of the gardening year.

Magnolia soulangeana

HERBS

'There's rosemary, that's for remembrance; there's rue for you – we may call it herb of grace'. Shakespeare was obviously well aware of the symbolism of herbs, a lighter side of the sweet-smelling and aromatic plants whose most serious use at that time was the provision of medicinal cures. But Shakespeare would have met them too in a variety of other practical guises – fashioned into nosegays to ward off unpleasant smells, strewn on the floor to discourage vermin, scattered in chests to perfume clothes, or added to food to bring out the flavour. In the grandest homes they were grown in elaborate knot gardens; today the more modest herb farms and gardens of the Bard's own region are helping us to re-discover the charm of these old-world plants.

Rosemary

For more information contact the
Heart of England Tourist Board,
2-4 Trinity Street, Worcester,
Worcestershire WR1 2PW
☎ (0905) 613132 (written and telephone enquiries only).

HEART of ENGLAND

A GUIDE TO ENGLISH GARDENS

Abbey Dore Court Garden
Abbey Dore, nr Hereford, Herefordshire
Riverside garden of approx. 4 acres, including walled garden and large rock garden with pool. Unusual plants, many propagated for sale. Small Nursery.
Open 15 Mar to 31 Oct, daily, 10.30am–6.30pm. Admission 75p adults, 25p children. No dogs.
☎ *Golden Valley (0981) 240419.* &

Alton Towers
nr Alton, Staffordshire
Britain's only world-rated leisure park, with magnificent gardens created by the 15th Earl of Shrewsbury. Delightful follies include Chinese Temple, Pagoda Fountain, Stonehenge, Corkscrew fountain and beautifully restored conservatories. One of the great gardens of England. 5 restaurants.
Open 2 Mar to 2 Nov, daily, 9am–7pm or dusk. Admission £5.99 adults, £1.99 OAPs, children under 4 free; parties of 12+ £4.99 (price includes admission to over 80 attractions).
☎ *Oakamoor (0538) 702200.* &

Arbury Hall
Astley, nr Nuneaton, Warwickshire
18th-century Gothic mansion with park and landscape gardens including bog garden, roses, herbaceous borders; trees include limes, pines and copper beeches.
Open 30 Mar to 30 Sept, Sun, Bank Hol Mons, also Tue & Wed in July & Aug, 1pm–6pm. Admission: Gardens & Park 80p adults, 40p children; House extra. Parties by arrangement.
☎ *Nuneaton (0203) 382804.* &

Attingham Park
Shrewsbury, Shropshire
House designed in 1785 standing in over 1,000 acres of parkland landscaped in 1797 by Humphry Repton. Grounds open all year, daily exc 25 Dec, dawn–dusk; House 29 Mar to 30 Sept, daily, also Oct, Sat & Sun, 2pm–5.30pm. Admission: House & Grounds £1.80 adults, 90p children; Grounds only 50p.
☎ *Upton Magna (074 377) 203.* NT ⚘ &

David Austin Roses
Albrighton, nr Wolverhampton, West Midlands
Large nursery display garden featuring 700 different old roses, climbers, bush roses. Hardy plants, including large collection of paeonies and irises.

Barnsley House Garden
Barnsley, Cirencester, Gloucestershire
On A433. Established garden with 18th-century summerhouses, redesigned with rare shrubs, trees and herbaceous plants; laburnum walk; knot and herb gardens; kitchen garden laid out as decorative potager. Large selection of plants for sale.
Open all year, Wed, every weekday May to Sept, 1st Sun in May, June, July, 10am–6pm. Admission £1 adults, 70p OAPs/students, children free, parties by arrangement.
☎ *Bibury (028 574) 281.* &

Batsford Park Arboretum
Moreton-in-Marsh, Gloucestershire
Over 1,200 species of trees in 50 acres of delightful Cotswold countryside overlooking the Vale of Evenlode.
Open Apr to early Nov, daily, 10am–5pm. Admission (1985 prices) £1 adults, 50p children/OAPs/parties.
☎ *Blockley (0386) 700409.*

Benthall Hall
Broseley, Shropshire
16th-century house with interesting small garden containing shrubs and plants; topiary.
Open 29 Mar to end Sept, Tue, Wed, Sat, Bank Hol Mon, 2pm–6pm. No dogs. Admission £1.50 adults, 75p children; Garden only, 60p.
☎ *Upton Magna (074 377) 649.* NT ⚘ &

Alton Towers, Staffordshire
Open May to Sept, daily, 9am–5pm (viewing only, Sat & Sun); plant centre open all year, daily. Admission free.
☎ *(090 722) 3931.*

Berkeley Castle
Berkeley, Gloucestershire
Elizabethan terraced gardens including lily pond, grass bowling alley, choice shrubs and climbers against the walls. Butterfly house.
Open 28 Mar to 30 Sept, daily exc Mon, Oct Sun only, Sun 2pm–5pm, Apr and Sept 2pm–5pm, May to Aug 11am–5pm. Admission £2 adults, £1.80 OAPs, £1 children; parties £1.80, £1.60 & 90p. No dogs.
☎ *Dursley (0453) 810322.*

Berrington Hall
nr Leominster, Herefordshire
18th-century house set in beautiful parkland landscaped by 'Capability' Brown.
Open May to Sept, Wed to Sun & Bank Hol Mon, 2pm–6pm; Mar 29, 30, 31, Apr & Oct, Sat & Sun, 2pm–5pm. Admission £1.50 adults, 75p children, £1 parties; joint ticket with Croft Castle £2.50. No dogs.
☎ *(0568) 5721.* NT ⚘ &

Birmingham Botanical Gardens
Edgbaston, Birmingham, West Midlands
Landscaped in 1830 with shrubs, rock garden, herbaceous border; indoor collection includes orchids, cacti, tropical and warm temperate flora.
Open all year, daily exc 25 Dec, 9am–8pm or dusk. Admission £1.25 adults, 60p children/OAPs; parties £1.15 & 50p. No dogs.
☎ *021-454 1860.* &

BATSFORD ARBORETUM & GARDEN CENTRE
1½m NW Moreton-in-Marsh off A44

Delightful scenic walks in 50 acres of glorious wooded countryside. Over 1000 different species of trees, exotic shrubs and bronze statues from the Orient. Picnic and play areas. Shop and tea-room at the Garden Centre.

Entrance £1.00 Adults; Children, O.A.P.s and parties 50p (Coach parties by arrangement. Tel: Blockley (0386) 700409.

HEART of ENGLAND

Bredon Springs
*Paris, Ashton-under-Hill,
nr Evesham, Worcestershire*
Large plant collection in 1½-acre natural setting. Plants for sale.
Open 5 Apr to 30 Oct, Wed, Thur, Sat, Sun, Bank Hol Mon & Tue 10am–dusk. Admission 50p adults, 25p OAPs, children and students free; parties by arrangement.
☎ *Evesham (0386) 881328.*

Burford House Gardens
Tenbury Wells, Shropshire
Gardens containing many interesting trees, shrubs, clematis and plants; ornamental pools and streams in beautiful setting by River Teme.
Open 29 Mar to 26 Oct, Mon to Sat 11am–5pm, Sun 2pm–5pm. Admission £1.50 adults, 50p children; parties by arrangement. No dogs.
☎ *(0584) 810777. & (in dry weather).*

Cannon Hill Park
*Moseley, Birmingham,
West Midlands*
80 acres of urban park particularly noted for its collection of tropical and sub-tropical plants, large-scale bedding and many unusual trees. Bowls, boating, fishing, tennis, putting.
Open all year, daily, dawn to dusk (closes 12 noon Christmas Day). Admission free.
☎ *021-449 0238. &*

Charlecote Park
Warwick, Warwickshire
Parkland containing famous 'Shakespeare' deer and Jacob sheep; restored Elizabethan house contains carriage collection, kitchen and brewhouse, shop and tearoom.
Open Apr & Oct, Sat, Sun 11am–5pm, 1 May to 30 Sept daily exc Mon & Thur 11am–6pm (open Bank Hol Mon). Admission £2.20 adults, £1.10 children; parties by arrangement. No dogs.
☎ *Stratford upon Avon (0789) 840277. NT ⚭ &*

Chillington Hall
Codsall Wood, Wolverhampton, Staffordshire
18th-century house, with landscaped park mainly by 'Capability' Brown featuring 1-mile oak avenue, extensive woodlands and 85-acre lake with temples and bridges.
Open 1 May to 11 Sept, Thur, 2.30pm–5.30pm; also Suns prior to Bank Hols & Suns in Aug. Admission £1.20 adults, 60p children; Grounds only 60p & 30p.
☎ *Brewood (0902) 850236. &*

Clack's Farm
Boreley, Ombersley, Worcestershire
Home of Arthur Billitt of Central TV. Informal garden with ornamental borders, shrubs and trees. Vegetable and fruit plots plus amateur greenhouses. Gardening advice given by experts.
Open Sat & Sun 10/11 May, 7/8 June, 12/13 July, 9/10 Aug, 13/14 Sept, 10am–5pm. Admission 50p adults, 25p children; coach parties by appt. only.
☎ *Worcester (0905) 620250. &*

Dorothy Clive Garden
Willoughbridge, Staffordshire
On A51 near Woore (Salop). Rock and scree gardens, rare trees, rhododendrons, azaleas, alpines and shrub roses.
Open 1 Mar to 30 Nov, daily, 11am–7.30pm or dusk; other times for coach parties by appointment. Admission 75p adults, 20p children; 60p parties of 20+.
☎ *Whitmore (0782) 680322.*

The Commandery
Sidbury, Worcester, Worcestershire
Late-15th-century timber-framed monastic hospital, now English Civil War Centre. Canalside terrace, plus walled gardens including a herb garden with raised beds for the disabled and thermoformed labels for the poor-sighted. Sealed Knot Society regularly stage 17th-century 'living history' camps in the grounds.
Gardens open all year, daily, 8.15am–5.15pm. Centre open all year, Mon to Sat, 10.30am–5pm; Sun, 2pm–5pm. Admission £1 adults, 50p OAPs/children; Gardens free.
☎ *(0905) 355071. &*

Croft Castle
Croft, nr Leominster, Herefordshire
Medieval castle with fine chestnut, beech and oak avenues, many planted in the 17th century. Late-18th-century Fishpool Valley and collection of old-fashioned plants.
Open 29, 30, 31 Mar, Apr & Oct, Sat, Sun, 2pm–5pm; May to end Sept, Wed to Sun, Bank Hol Mon, 2pm–6pm. Admission £1.50 adults, 75p children, £1 parties of 15+; joint ticket with Berrington Hall £2.50 adults, £1.25 children.
☎ *Yarpole (056 885) 246. NT ⚭ &*

Dinmore Manor
Wellington, Herefordshire
Attractive gardens, the setting for cloister, music room and chapel dating from 12th century.

Open all year, daily exc 25 Dec, 10am–6pm. Admission 50p adults, 25p children/OAPs; 40p parties. No dogs.
☎ *Hereford (0432) 71322. &*

Dorsington Manor Gardens
nr Stratford-upon-Avon, Warwickshire
2mSW Bidford-on-Avon, off Bidford-Broadway road. 27 acres of grounds including traditional English garden; home of Domestic Fowl Trust, a unique collection of domestic birds. Nature trail, picnic area, plant centre, adventure playground, pets corner; shops, restaurant, accommodation.
Open 28 Mar to 30 Sept, daily, 11.30am–6pm. Admission £1.50 adults, £1.30 OAPs, 75p children; parties £1.30, £1.20 & 70p.
☎ *(0789) 772442. &*

Dudmaston Hall
Quatt, nr Bridgnorth, Shropshire
Late seventeenth-century house with an extensive lakeside garden, American garden and dingle.
Open 30 Mar to end Sept, Wed, Sun, 2.30pm–6pm. Admission £1.80 adults, 90p children; Gardens only 80p & 40p; reductions for pre-booked parties.
☎ *(0746) 780866. &*

Eastnor Castle
nr Ledbury, Herefordshire
Early-19th-century castle, in medieval style, whose grounds contain one of the great 19th-century arboreta with many fine specimen trees.
Open mid May to end Sept, Sun, Bank Hol Mon; also Wed, Thur in July & Aug, 2.15pm–5.30pm. Admission £1.20 adults, 60p OAPs/children; parties £1 & 60p; Grounds only 50p.
☎ *(0531) 2304. &*

Hergest Croft Gardens
Kington, Herefordshire
An outstanding collection of trees and shrubs, together with spring bulbs, summer borders and an old-fashioned vegetable garden.
Open 27 Apr to 14 Sept, daily; Suns in Oct; 1.30pm–6.30pm. Admission £1.20 adults, 60p children; 90p parties of 20+ by arrangement.
☎ *(0544) 230160. &*

BEFORE SETTING OUT it's always best to 'phone and check garden details. Opening times and prices may be subject to change at short notice!

DORMY HOUSE HOTEL, Willersey Hill, Broadway
Worcestershire WR12 7LF England.
Telephone Broadway (0386) 852711. Telex 338275 DORMY G.

A unique 17th century Cotswold country house hotel combining all the comforts of the 20th century.

Traditional charm, a chef with a touch of genuis and fifty individually appointed bedrooms.

Overlooking Broadway and the Vale of Evesham, the ideal location to visit some of the most beautiful gardens and villages in England.

47

Hidcote Manor Garden
Mickleton, Gloucestershire
17th-century Cotswold house with one of the most beautiful English gardens; different types of plot within various species of hedges.
Open 29 Mar to end Oct, daily exc Tue & Fri, 11am–8pm (last entry 7pm). Admission £2.40 adults, £1.20 children. No dogs.
☎ (038 677) 333. NT ♿ & (part).

Himley Hall Park
nr Dudley, West Midlands
200 acres of parkland with Great Pool and other pools, landscaped by 'Capability' Brown c.1779.
Open all year, daily, 8am–8pm or dusk. Admission free. Car park 30p.
☎ Wombourne (0902) 895223. &

Hoar Cross Hall
Hoar Cross, Burton-on-Trent, Staffordshire
Mansion set in 20 acres of woodland and gardens. Grounds under restoration. Enclosed gardens, yew walks, lime alleys. Variety of fine, rare and majestic trees.
Open Spring Bank Hol to mid-Sept, most weekdays, Sat, Sun & Bank Hols, 2pm–6pm. Admission £1.40 adults, 70p children.
☎ (0283 75) 224. &

Hodnet Hall Gardens
nr Market Drayton, Shropshire
Acres of superb landscaped gardens with fascinating ornamental lakes. Kitchen garden; tearooms; gift shop.
Open Apr to Sept, daily, Mon to Sat 2pm–5pm, Sun, Bank Hols & Tue following, 12 noon–6pm. Admission £1 adults, 60p children; parties 80p & 40p.
☎ (063 084) 202. &

Hunts Court
North Nibley, nr Dursley, Gloucestershire
Two-acre garden with shrubs, lawns and about 200 old roses; herbaceous and heather beds. Nursery plants for sale.

Open 7 May to 24 Sept, Wed, 2pm–6pm; also daily exc Mon, 10 Jun to 13 July. Admission 50p adults, 25p OAPs/children. No dogs.
☎ (0453) 47440. &

Jephson Gardens
Leamington Spa, Warwickshire
Beautifully laid-out lawns, flower-beds and walks; tropical birds, rare trees, shrubs, fountains.
Open all year, daily, dawn to dusk. Admission free.
☎ (0926) 27072, ext 199.

Jubilee Maze and Museum of Mazes
Symonds Yat West, Herefordshire
Delightful garden featuring a traditional hedge maze with unique centrepiece. Maze Museum.
Open 28 Mar to end Oct, daily, 11am–5.30pm; Maze illuminated 12 July to end Aug, each evening exc Sun, 8pm–10.30pm. Admission 80p. No dogs.
☎ (0600) 890360. &

Kiftsgate Court
nr Chipping Campden, Gloucestershire
Magnificently situated house and garden with fine views and trees; unusual shrubs and plants; plants for sale on open days.
Open 30 Mar to 30 Sept, Wed, Thur, Sun, 2pm–6pm. Admission £1.50 adults, 50p children. No dogs.

Lechlade Garden and Fuchsia Centre
Lechlade, Gloucestershire
Landscaped indoor fuchsia garden featuring over 800 varieties.
Open all year, daily, Mon to Sat 9am–5.30pm, Sun, Bank Hols 10am–5pm. Admission free.
☎ Faringdon (0367) 52372.

Lydney Park Gardens
Lydney, Gloucestershire
Extensive woodland garden. Superb trees and shrubs; rhododendrons and azaleas. Roman temple and museum. Picnics in deer park. Teas in house. Dogs on leads.

Open 27 Apr to 15 June, Wed, Sun, Bank Hols, 11am–6pm. Admission £1 adults, children free; parties 90p.
☎ Dean (0594) 42844.

Misarden Park
nr Stroud, Gloucestershire
Spring flowers, shrubs, roses and herbaceous borders; old Tudor manor house standing high overlooking Golden Valley. Plants and shrubs for sale at garden nurseries.
Open 2 Apr to 25 Sept, Wed & Thur, 10am–4.30pm. Admission 70p adults, 30p children, 60p parties.
☎ Miserden (028 582) 303. &

Moccas Court
nr Hereford, Herefordshire
Seven-acre gardens and parkland designed by 'Capability' Brown, overlooking the River Wye.
Open Apr to end Sept, Thur, 2pm–6pm. Admission £1 adults, 50p children, 80p parties.
☎ (098 17) 381. &

Moseley Old Hall
Fordhouses, Wolverhampton, Staffordshire
Elizabethan manor house with small garden reconstructed in 17th-century style with box knot and plants of the period. Small orchard.
Open Mar to Nov, Sun, also Wed & Sat in Apr to Oct, 2pm–6pm. Admission £1.80 adults, 90p children; parties £1.50 & 75p. No dogs.
☎ (0902) 782808. NT ♿ &

Packwood House
Hockley Heath, Warwickshire
Outstanding topiary yew garden and colourful flower garden in grounds of Tudor home.
Open 29 Mar to Sept, Wed to Sun, Bank Hol Mon, 2pm–6pm; Oct, Sat & Sun, 2pm–5pm. Admission: House & Gardens £1.50 adults, 75p children, £1.10 parties; Gardens only £1. No dogs.
☎ Lapworth (056 43) 2024.NT♿ & (part).

Hodnet Hall Gardens
Shropshire

It is a joy to relax in the peace and quiet of these lovely gardens with their superb trees and lawns, tranquil trout lakes and ancient buildings. From April daffodils to September hydrangeas the variety of the flowers delights the eye. Open 1 April to 30 September. Weekdays 2pm to 5pm, Sundays, Bank Holiday Mondays and the Tuesdays following 12 noon to 6 p.m.
Free car park, pleasant tea rooms (Open daily–May to August) – gift shop and plants for sale. Leave M6 at junction 15 and follow the signs for Shrewsbury, Hodnet Hall is situated 12 miles N.E. of the town. Organised parties catered for. Further information may be obtained by telephoning Mrs. A. Hensby on 063 084 202.

PAINSWICK HOUSE GARDENS
Painswick, Gloucestershire

Unique Rococo six-acre garden in the process of restoration to the original Thomas Robins portrayal of 1748. Contemporary garden buildings with vistas and woodland paths. Open mid-April to end of September every Wednesday. First Sundays, May to September. Spring and Summer Bank Holiday Mondays. 12noon–5pm. Parties by Arrangement.
Admission: £1.00 Adults, 70p O.A.Ps, 30p Children. No Dogs. Telephone: Painswick (0452) 813204.

Pittville Park
Cheltenham, Gloucestershire
34-acre park with herbaceous borders, rock gardens, shrubberies and formal bedding. Extensive seasonal bedding displays, mainly April to Autumn. Ornamental lake, pets corner. Regency Pump Room.
Open all year, daily, dawn to dusk. Admission free.
☎ *(0242) 584757.* ♿

The Priory
Kemerton, Tewkesbury, Gloucestershire
Four-acre garden with long herbaceous borders planted in colour groups, using many unusual plants and shrubs. Small nursery.
Open May to end Sept, Thur & Suns 25 May, 22 June, 13 July, 3 Aug, 24 Sept, 2pm–7pm. Admission 50p adults, 20p children.
☎ *Overbury (038 689) 258.*

Quarry Park
Shrewsbury, Shropshire
Formal park with avenues of lime trees, on banks of River Severn. Centrepiece is the Dingle, with woodland garden, annual beddings and water feature.
Open all year, daily, 10am–dusk. Admission free.
☎ *(0743) 61411.* ♿

Queens Park
Harborne, Birmingham, West Midlands
15 acres of well-used urban park with flower-beds and children's playground; bowls, tennis, putting.
Open all year, daily, dawn to dusk. (Closes 12 noon 25 Dec.) Admission free.
☎ *021-427 3334.* ♿

Ragley Hall
Alcester, Warwickshire
Magnificent Palladian country house with gardens, park and lake. Adventure wood, country trail and picnic areas.
Open 29 Mar to 28 Sept, Tue, Wed, Thur, Sat, Sun, Bank Hols; House & Garden 1.30pm–5.30pm, (12 noon–5pm June to Aug); Park 11am–6pm (Park also open Mon & Fri in July & Aug). Admission: Park with Adventure Wood & Country Trail £1 adults, 50p children; House, Garden & Park £2 adults, £1.50 OAPs/children; £1.50 parties.
☎ *(0789) 762090.* ♿

Selsley Herb and Goat Farm
Selsley, nr Stroud, Gloucestershire
Herb farm with formal herb garden, demonstration beds; nursery with container-grown herbs for sale. Barn shop selling herb products.
Open Apr to Sept, Tue to Sun, Bank Hol Mons, 2pm–5.30pm. Admission free.
☎ *Stroud (045 36) 6682.* ♿

Sezincote Garden
Sezincote; Moreton-in-Marsh, Gloucestershire
Oriental water garden by Repton and Daniell surrounding house in Indian style: inspiration for the Brighton Pavilion.
Open all year exc Dec, Thur, Fri, Bank Hol Mon, 2pm–6pm. Admission (1985 prices) £1.50 adults, 50p children. No dogs.

Shakespeare Gardens
Stratford-upon-Avon, Warwickshire
New Place gardens and ancient mulberry tree (Chapel Lane). Entrance to adjoining Elizabethan knot garden through Nash's House, Chapel Street (open Mon to Sat, till 6pm summer, 4pm winter).
Open daily 9am–dusk. Closed 24–26 Dec, 1 Jan. Admission free. No dogs.
☎ *(0789) 204016.* ♿

Shipton Hall
Shipton, Much Wenlock, Shropshire
Elizabethan manor in picturesque setting with attractive stone-walled garden and medieval dovecote.
Open May to Sept, Thur; also Sun, July & Aug, and Bank Hol Sun & Mon; 2.30pm–5.30pm. Admission £1 adults, 50p children; 90p parties of 20+.
☎ *Brockton (074 636) 225.*

Shugborough
Great Haywood, Staffordshire
Notable landscape includes Chinese garden house, classical temple, riverside gardens, beautiful trees and shrubs; county museum.
Open 15 Mar to 26 Oct, Tue to Fri, 10.30am–5.30pm, Sat, Sun 2pm–5.30pm; Oct to Mar, Tue to Fri, 10.30am–4.30pm. Admission: Car park £1 per vehicle (incl. access to gardens & picnic area); House £1 adults, 50p children/OAPs; Museum, Farm extra (all-in ticket £2.50 adults, £1.25 children/OAPs).
☎ *Little Haywood (0889) 881388.*
NT ♿

Warwick Castle, Warwickshire

HEART of ENGLAND

CHELTENHAM SPA

Chosen as Britain's floral city for 1985 in the "Beautiful Britain in Bloom" competition, Cheltenham Spa is a centre of elegance. In the Spring and Summer the Parks and Gardens are ablaze with colour and buildings are decorated with hanging baskets. Pittville Park of approximately 40 hectares is mainly informal in design and possesses a fine Regency Pump Room, with a Gallery of Fashion, two large ornamental lakes, an 18-hole Pitch and Putt Course and an Arboretum with numerous trees of beauty and interest.

The Town Centre is particularly attractive with the Promenade Long Gardens and its fine display of ornamental flower beds, and Imperial Gardens where the visitor can see the most outstanding floral display anywhere in England.

Snowshill Manor
Broadway, Worcestershire
Interesting Tudor house set in small, formal, terraced garden.
Open Mar 29, 30, 31, Apr & Oct, Sat & Sun, 11am–1pm, 2pm–5pm; May to Sept, daily exc Mon & Tue (open Bank Hol Mon), 11am–1pm, 2pm–6pm. Admission £2.30 adults, £1.15 children. No dogs.
☎ *(038 685) 2410. NT* ✻ & *(ground floor only).*

Spetchley Park
Spetchley, Worcestershire
Attractive garden containing rare trees and shrubs; red and fallow deer; garden centre.
Open 28 Mar to 30 Sept, daily exc Sat; Mon to Fri 11am–5pm, Sun 2pm–5.30pm; Bank Hol Mon 11am–5.30pm. Admission £1.20 adults, 60p children; parties of 25+ £1 & 50p. No dogs.
☎ *(090 565) 213/224.* &

Stoke Lacy Herb Garden
nr Bromyard, Herefordshire
Small herb garden and nursery on private-garden scale, with interesting plants, shrubs and small trees.
Open mid-May to mid-Sept, Thur & Sat 2pm–5pm. Admission free; donations to charity.
☎ *Burley Gate (043 278) 232.*

Stone House Cottage Gardens
Stone, nr Kidderminster, Worcestershire
On A448. Sheltered walled garden with rare wall shrubs and climbers, and interesting herbaceous plants. Adjacent nursery with many plants for sale.
Open Mar to Nov, Wed to Sat, 10am–6pm. Admission 50p adults, children free. No dogs.
☎ *(0562) 69902.* &

Sudeley Castle and Gardens
Winchcombe, nr Cheltenham Spa, Gloucestershire
Formal Elizabethan-style herb garden and shrub borders. Yew hedges and rolling lawns with carpets of spring bulbs. Fountains; waterfowl collection. Europe's largest private Toy Collection.
Open 28 Mar to end Oct, daily, 11am–5.30pm (Castle 12 noon–5pm). Admission £2.95 adults, £2.40 OAPs, £1.60 children; parties £2.40, £2 & £1.40. No dogs.
☎ *(0242) 602308.*

Trentham Gardens
Trentham, nr Stoke-on-Trent, Staffordshire
Delightful mature garden by 'Capability' Brown; idyllic parkland setting and formal Italian layout; high-quality restaurant facilities; exhibition/special event/conference centre; adventure playground.
Open Mar to Sept, daily, 10am–4pm. Admission £1 (1985).
☎ *(0782) 657341.* &

Upton House
Edge Hill, Warwickshire
Late 17th-century house containing connoisseur's collections. Extensive lawns and terraced gardens lead down to pool and woodland garden in deep valley.
Open Apr to Sept, Mon to Thur, 2pm–6pm (last entry to House 5.30pm); also weekends 10/11, 17/18 May, 26/27 July, 2/3, 8/10, 16/17 Aug. Admission £1.90 adults, 95p children; parties of 15+ (exc Bank Hols) £1.30.
☎ *Edge Hill (029 587) 266. NT* ✻ &

Izaak Walton Cottage
Shallowford, Stone, Staffordshire
The famous 17th-century angler's restored cottage with period garden being established with plants known in cultivation in England during Walton's lifetime. Angling museum. Picnic area. Plants for sale.
Open mid-Mar to late Oct, daily exc Wed & Thur, 12.30pm–5.30pm; winter, Sat & Sun, 12.30pm–4.30pm. Admission 20p adults, 10p children.
☎ *Stafford (0785) 760278.* &

Warwick Castle
Warwick, Warwickshire
Medieval castle surrounded by 'Capability' Brown-designed parkland on the banks of the Avon; formal garden, conservatory, magnificent trees and shrubs including cedars of Lebanon. River island. Victorian Rose Garden of 1868 faithfully reconstructed from original plans (opens in late July 1986).
Open daily exc 25 Dec, Mar to Oct 10am–5.30pm, Nov to Feb 10am–4.30pm. Admission £3.50 adults, £2.75 OAPs, £2.25 children; parties of 20+ £3.15, £2.50 & £1.95. No dogs.
☎ *(0926) 495421.* &

The Weir
Swainshill, Herefordshire
Spring garden with fine views of River Wye from cliff-garden walks.
Open 30 Mar to 10 May, daily exc Sat; 11 May to end Oct, Wed & Bank Hol Mons; 2pm–6pm. Admission 50p adults, 25p children; no coaches. No dogs. NT ✻

Westonbirt Arboretum, Gloucestershire

Westbury Court Garden
Westbury-on-Severn, Gloucestershire
Formal Dutch water garden dating from 1696–1705 with canals and yew hedges. Planted with 100 species of plants grown in England before 1700.
Open 29 Mar to end Oct, Wed to Sun, Bank Hol Mon, 11am–6pm. Admission £1 adults, 50p children; parties of 15+ 70p. No dogs.
☎ *(045 276) 461. NT* ✻ &

Westonbirt Arboretum
nr Tetbury, Gloucestershire
One of the finest collections of trees and shrubs in the world, magnificent in autumn with fiery maples.
Open all year, daily, 10am–8pm or dusk. Admission £1 adults, 50p OAPs/children. Educational parties only by appointment.
☎ *(066 688) 220.* &

Weston Park
nr Shifnal, Shropshire
Fine trees and shrubs including magnificent azaleas and rhododendrons, set in 'Capability' Brown parkland; nature trails, picnic areas, woodland adventure playground. House, aquarium, museum, butterfly farm, miniature railway, pottery; licensed cafeteria.
Open 29 Mar to 28 Sept; Apr, May & Sept Sat, Sun & Bank Hols; June, July daily exc Mon & Fri; Grounds 11am–5pm, House 1pm–5pm. Admission £1.70 adults, £1.20 OAPs/children.
☎ *Weston-under-Lizard (095 276) 207.* &

Wightwick Manor
Wightwick Bank, Wolverhampton, Staffordshire
William Morris period house having gardens with formal yew and golden holly walks, terraces and topiary; two pools.
Open all year (exc Feb), Thur, Sat, Bank Hols, 2.30pm–5.30pm. Closed Good Fri, Christmas & New Year. Also open for pre-booked school & student tours Wed & Thur am & pm. Admission 80p adults, 40p children.
☎ *(0902) 761108. NT* ✻

LONDON

*I*t's hard to imagine the London of old, completely surrounded by untamed countryside, when Regent's Park and Hyde Park were part of the royal forest where Henry VIII hunted wild boars, or Smithfield was a smooth field used for jousting, when Covent Garden actually did sell fruit and vegetables from a convent garden and highwaymen held sway on Hampstead Heath. But despite the march of time, precious pockets of greenery remain in no less than 80 parks, gardens and open heathlands within 7 miles of Piccadilly. Our ten Royal Parks were once the private grounds of royal palaces; they include Kensington Gardens featuring the Round Pond, Sunken Garden, Flower Walk and Queen Anne's Orangery, St. James's Park with its ornamental Chinese-style lake, Holland Park with, appropriately, a Dutch Garden and Regent's Park, setting for the lovely Queen Mary's Rose Garden and, of course, London Zoo. Some great houses remain in splendid settings. Henry VIII's palace of Hampton Court has a Tudor knot garden, a fountain court and a grape vine planted in the 18th century as well as formal gardens redesigned in the French manner under William and Mary; the grounds of Chiswick House and Ham House have been well restored, and Syon Park Garden which was begun, effectively, by Capability Brown gained a splendid conservatory in the 19th century. The place for glasshouses is, of course, Kew. Originally two gardens, they were amalgamated by George III and given to the nation as the Royal Botanic Gardens in 1840, to become one of the most highly-esteemed collections in the world. In recent years the public has gained better access to another of England's most fascinating gardens in the Chelsea Physic Garden, which has been an important centre of horticultural study since its foundation in 1673. But famous or informal, the majority of London's parks and gardens are there for the same purpose – to provide pleasure and relaxation for the thousands of people who come regularly to listen to the band, feed the ducks or simply to admire the flowers.

MAY
Shrubs have their triumph in May, when azaleas and rhododendrons join forces to transform whole landscapes with their delicate spectrum of colour.

Lilac Other shrubs lend their strong support in the form of the glowing pieris, pink weigela, laburnum or heavily-scented lilacs, while clematis montana gets a firm grip on fences and walls and the taller varieties of broom become engulfed in dense yellow flower. Hawthorn and crab apple trees also flower now, while peonies, columbine, forget-me-not, poppies and lily-of-the-valley make a welcome return to borders and rock gardens.

THE LONDON PLANE
Prized for the beauty of its dappled bark and autumn colours, the London Plane accounts for over 60% of all the trees which grace the capital's streets, parks, squares and gardens. It is perfectly adapted to city life, resisting the harmful effects of air pollution in an intriguing way: as the outer bark of the tree becomes darkened and clogged by dust and soot, it peals off to reveal pale patches of new growth, through which the Plane is able to breathe more freely. Thus it grows vigorously to a height of up to 35 metres, surviving the rigorous pruning necessary to trees in towns. *The Plane* Most planes have been planted this century, but some, like those around Berkeley Square, are about 200 years old. The tree produces pinkish-brown timber, sought after for use by manufacturers of keyboard instruments, and cabinet makers.

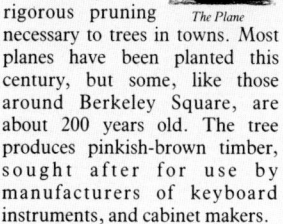

For more information contact the
**London Visitor
and Convention Bureau,**
26 Grosvenor Gardens,
London SW1W 0DU ☎ 01-730 3488
(written and telephone enquiries only).

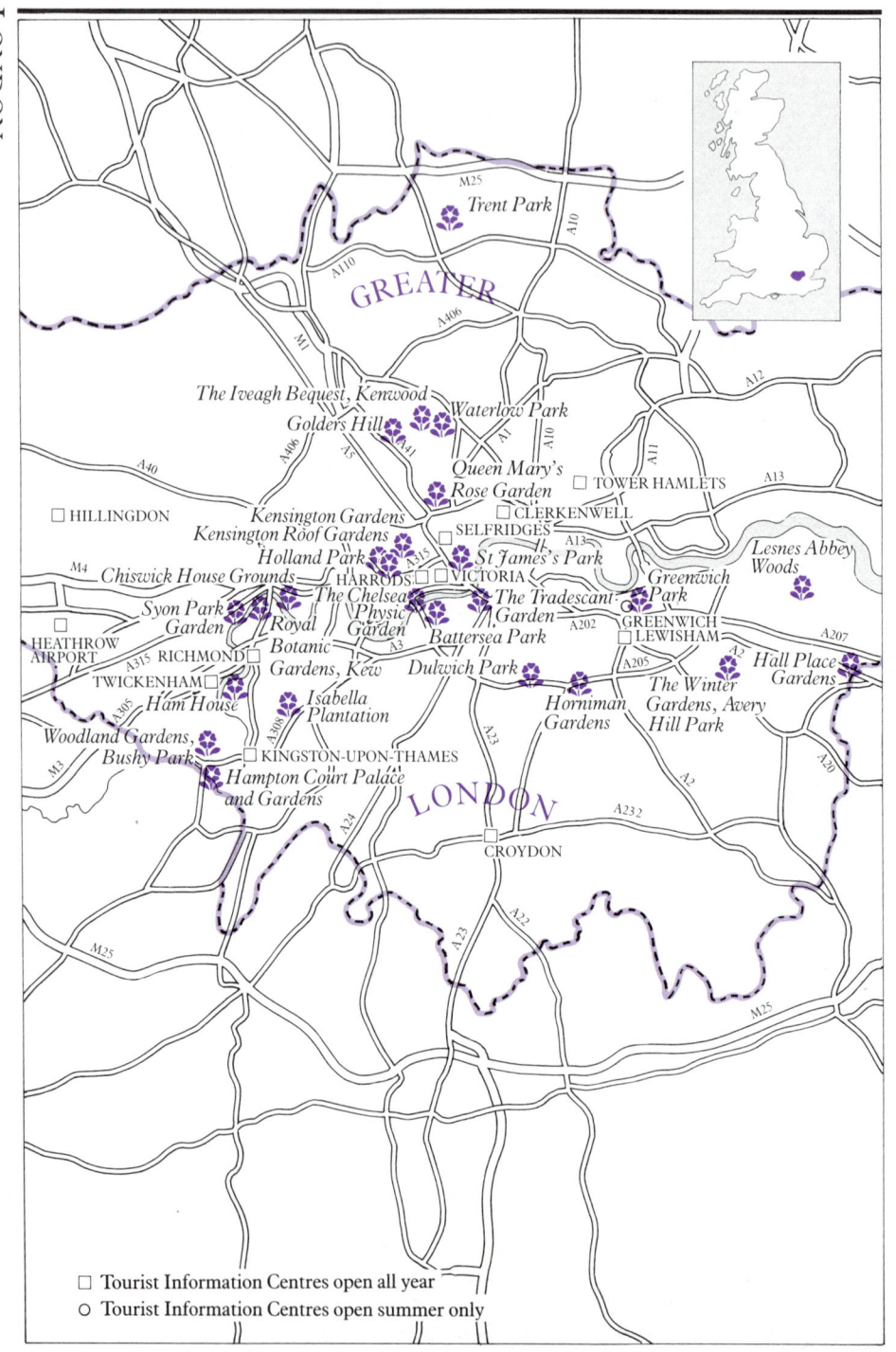

A Guide to English Gardens

LONDON

GREATER LONDON

- Trent Park
- The Iveagh Bequest, Kenwood
- Waterlow Park
- Golders Hill
- Queen Mary's Rose Garden
- TOWER HAMLETS
- HILLINGDON
- Kensington Gardens
- Kensington Roof Gardens
- CLERKENWELL
- SELFRIDGES
- Holland Park
- Lesnes Abbey Woods
- Chiswick House Grounds
- HARRODS
- St James's Park
- VICTORIA
- The Tradescant Garden
- Greenwich Park
- Syon Park Garden
- The Chelsea Physic Garden
- Royal Botanic Gardens, Kew
- Battersea Park
- GREENWICH
- LEWISHAM
- HEATHROW AIRPORT
- RICHMOND
- TWICKENHAM
- Ham House
- Dulwich Park
- Hall Place Gardens
- Isabella Plantation
- Horniman Gardens
- The Winter Gardens, Avery Hill Park
- Woodland Gardens, Bushy Park
- KINGSTON-UPON-THAMES
- Hampton Court Palace and Gardens
- CROYDON

□ Tourist Information Centres open all year
○ Tourist Information Centres open summer only

Greenwich Park, London

Battersea Park
Albert Bridge Road, London SW11
200-acre riverside park between Albert and Chelsea Bridges. Laid out by Sir George Pennythorn in 1852. Much of the original Victorian landscape remains, including 13½-acre lake. Garden for the disabled; old-English garden; heather garden; herb garden; alpine and show glasshouse; Japanese Peace Pagoda. Recreational facilities.
Open all year, daily, 7.30am–dusk. Admission free.
☎ 01-228 2798. &

The Chelsea Physic Garden
Chelsea, London SW3
An important centre for the study of horticulture since its foundation in 1673; whilst preserving its history and identity, the Garden aims to educate in the knowledge and love of horticulture and botany.
Open 13 Apr to 19 Oct, Wed, Sun, Bank Hol Mon, 2pm–5pm. Also open Chelsea Flower Show week, 20–23 May, 12noon–5pm. Groups at other times by appt. Admission £1.50 adults, £1 children/students. No dogs.
☎ 01-352 5646. &

Chiswick House Grounds
Chiswick, London W4
17th-century Italian-style garden, serpentine lake, yew hedges, famous collection of camellias in conservatory.
Open all year, daily, dawn to dusk. Admission free.
☎ 01-994 2861. &

Dulwich Park
College Road, London SE21
72-acre park featuring many sporting facilities, and including a notable collection of rhododendrons and azaleas, at their best in mid-May. Lake; aviary; Tree Trail; disabled garden (opens late 1986).
Open all year, daily, 7.30am–dusk. Admission free.
☎ 01-693 5737. &

Golders Hill
Hampstead, London NW3
39-acre park with flamingos, sea fowl and animal enclosure with goats and fallow deer. Includes the Hill, a tranquil garden alongside Inverforth House and West Heath, with many fine plants and a pergola walk with uncommon plants. Café.
Open all year, daily, 7.30am–dusk. Admission free.
☎ 01-455 5183.

Greenwich Park
Greenwich, London SE10
Lovely, spacious park with views over the Thames. Flower garden; water garden with shrubs and spring flowers; small wilderness with deer. Setting for the Old Royal Observatory and the Greenwich Meridian.
Open all year, daily, 5am–dusk. Admission free.
☎ 01-858 2608. &

Hall Place Gardens
Bexley, Kent
Medieval/Jacobean mansion; spring and summer bedding displays; extensive gardens; herb and peat gardens; topiary 'Queen's Beasts'; conservatory.
Open all year, daily, 9am–sunset. Admission free. No dogs.
☎ 01-303 7777. &

Ham House
Richmond, Surrey
17th-century house with extensive gardens, authentically restored between 1976 and 1979. Parterre with box-edged beds filled with lavender. Orangery.
Grounds open all year, daily, 8am–5pm; House open all year, daily exc Mon, 11am–5pm (last entry 4.30pm); also open Bank Hol Mon (exc 5 May); closed 24–26 Dec, 1 Jan, 28 Mar. Admission: Garden free; House £1.60 adults, 80p children. No dogs.
☎ 01-940 1950. NT ✠ &

Hampton Court Palace and Gardens
East Molesey, Surrey
Henry VIII's famous gardens and parkland; Tudor knot garden, maze and grape vine.
Gardens open all year, daily, dawn to dusk. Palace all year, daily exc 24–26 Dec, 1 Jan; 1 Apr to 30 Sept, Mon to Sat 9.30am–6pm, Sun 11am–6pm; Oct to Mar, Mon to Sat 9.30am–5pm, Sun 2pm–5pm. Admission (1985 prices) £2 adults, £1 OAPs/children; parties of 12+ 10% reduction. Gardens free.
☎ 01-977 8441 (Palace). &

Holland Park
Kensington, London W8
55-acre park, with lawns and gardens. Dutch garden dating from 1812 with tulip displays; iris garden, yucca lawn, bedding and shrubberies; Orangery. 28 acres of natural woodland with exotic trees and plants, and many interesting bird species. Open-air theatre in summer.
Open all year, daily, 8am–dusk. Admission free.
☎ 01-602 2226/6016. &

Horniman Gardens
Forest Hill, London SE23
26-acre park, set on side of hill with views over central London. Colourful sunken, rose and water gardens. Lectures during summer; exhibitions; museum. Animal and bird enclosure; American Indian totem pole.
Open all year, daily, 7.30am–dusk. Admission free. Museum open all year, daily exc 24,25,26 Dec, Mon to Sat 10.30am–6pm, Sun 2pm–6pm.
☎ 01-699 8924. &

THE SOURCE OF IMAGINATIVE PLANTS AND GARDENS

The Chelsea Gardener is the expert for help, advice and service. Imaginative ideas using new colours, new shapes, new scents and new shades offer inspiration and a source with which to transform gardens, terraces or even window boxes.

We advise and provide; new gardens can also be designed, created and even maintained.

The Chelsea Gardener, 125 Sydney Street, King's Road, London S.W.3.
Telephone: 01-352 5656. Open 7 days a week.

LONDON

Royal Botanic Gardens, Kew

Isabella Plantation
Richmond Park, Surrey
Beautiful plantation in Richmond Park, full of heather, magnolias, camellias, rhododendrons and azaleas.
Open all year, daily, 7am–9.15 pm. Admission free.
☎ 01-948 3209. ♿

The Iveagh Bequest, Kenwood
Hampstead Lane, London NW3
18th-century Adam mansion whose 200-acre grounds include gardens with a lime avenue, rhododendrons and herbaceous border; lakes; woodlands of special scientific interest.
Open all year, daily, dawn–dusk. Admission free.
☎ 01-348 1286. ♿

Kensington Gardens
Kensington, London W8
Attractive grounds surrounding palace; famous Orangery, Elfin Oak, Serpentine lake and Peter Pan statue.
Open all year, daily, 5am–dusk. Admission free.
☎ 01-937 4848. ♿

Kensington Roof Gardens
99 Kensington High Street, London W8
1½ acres of roof garden established in 1938, with many exotic plants. Also flamingos and numerous specialised breeds of pheasants and ducks, Chinese Bantam Hens.
Open all year daily, 10am–6pm. Admission free. No dogs.
☎ 01-937 7994.

Lesnes Abbey Woods
Abbey Wood, London SE2
Area of 215 acres, with the ruins of a 12th-century Abbey, extensive woodlands of considerable ecological importance and native daffodils in spring.
Open all year, daily, 7.30am–dusk. Admission free.
☎ 01-311 1674. ♿

Queen Mary's Rose Garden
Regents Park, London NW1
Magnificent collection of roses set in inner circle of park; open-air theatre. Cafeteria.
Open all year, daily, 7am–dusk. Admission free.
☎ 01-486 7905. ♿

Royal Botanic Gardens, Kew
Kew, Richmond, Surrey
Magnificent collection of plants and trees; glasshouses, lakes and beautiful walks.
Open all year, daily exc 25 Dec & 1 Jan, from 10am (closing time varies from 4pm to 8pm according to season). Admission 25p adults, children under 10 free. No dogs.
☎ 01-940 1171. ♿

St James's Park
London SW1
Lawns, colourful plants and flowers in beds and borders; Queen Mother's Rose Walk; large ornamental lake with exotic waterfowl collection.
Open all year, daily, 5am–12midnight. Admission free.
☎ 01-930 1793. ♿

Syon Park Garden
Brentford, Middlesex
Extensive gardens, lake, Garden Centre; Syon House and Conservatory; London Butterfly House and Heritage Motor Museum.
Gardens open all year, daily exc 25 & 26 Dec, 10am–6pm, or dusk (last ticket 1 hr

THE TRADESCANT TRUST

The Tradescant Trust, Museum of Garden History.
St Mary-at-Lambeth (next Lambeth Palace) SE1.

Historic Building and newly-made period garden containing 17th-century plants and in which stand the tomb of the John Tradescants – royal gardeners to Charles 1 – and that of Captain Bligh of the *Bounty*. Gift shop, Tea & Coffee available.

Open Mon–Fri 11am–3pm, Sunday 10.30am–5pm. Closed on Saturday.

before). House open Easter to end Sept, Sun to Thur, 12noon–4.15pm. Admission: Gardens £1 adults, 80p children/OAPs; House & Garden £1.50 & £1. No dogs.
☎ 01-560 0881/2/3. &

The Tradescant Garden
next Lambeth Palace, London SE1
17th-century garden featuring only period plants, and some of the introductions made by the John Tradescants, father and son.
Open 2 Mar to 14 Dec, daily exc Sat, Mon to Fri 11am–3pm, Sun 10.30am–5pm. Admission free; donations welcome.
☎ 01-261 1891. &

Trent Park
Cockfosters, Hertfordshire
A country park of 413 acres, including 150 acres of oak woodland, with wild flowers in a meadow setting and a great variety of wild bird life; water garden; nature & farm trails; fishing lakes. Two special woodland trails for the blind.
Open all year, daily, 7.30am–dusk. Admission free.
☎ 01-449 8706. &

Waterlow Park
Highgate, London N6
27-acre park with colour all year round. Over 20,000 bedding plants; herbaceous borders. Three ponds with wildlife; aviary. Recreational facilities.
Open all year, daily, 7.30am to ½ hour before dusk. Admission free.
☎ 01-435 7171 (Parks Dept). &

The Iveagh Bequest, Kenwood

The Winter Gardens, Avery Hill Park
Eltham, London SE9
Gardens within 210-acre park, with many species of tropical and temperate plants in cold, temperate and tropical houses. Second only as a collection to the Royal Botanic Gardens at Kew.
Park open all year, daily, dawn to dusk. Winter Gardens open all year, Mon to Fri 1pm–4pm, Sat, Sun, Bank Hols 11am–4pm (6pm in summer). Closed 1st Mon each month and Christmas Day. Admission free. No dogs.
☎ 01-850 2666. &

Woodland Gardens – Bushy Park
Teddington, Middlesex
A woodland and water garden developed around the Longford River, which supplies water to Hampton Court Gardens and fountains. Nearly 100 acres, with emphasis on rhododendrons, azaleas, camellias, ericas and water plants.
Open all year, daily, 9am to 1 hr before dusk. Admission free.
☎ Park Superintendent 01-977 1328. &

LONDON

SYON PARK
Brentford, Middlesex 01-560 0881

Syon House open Easter to September
Gardens open all year

Syon Park Art Centre

OTHER ATTRACTIONS AT SYON

The Heritage Motor Museum—01-560 1378
The London Butterfly House—01-560 7272
Syon Park Garden Centre—01-568 0134

A GUIDE TO ENGLISH GARDENS

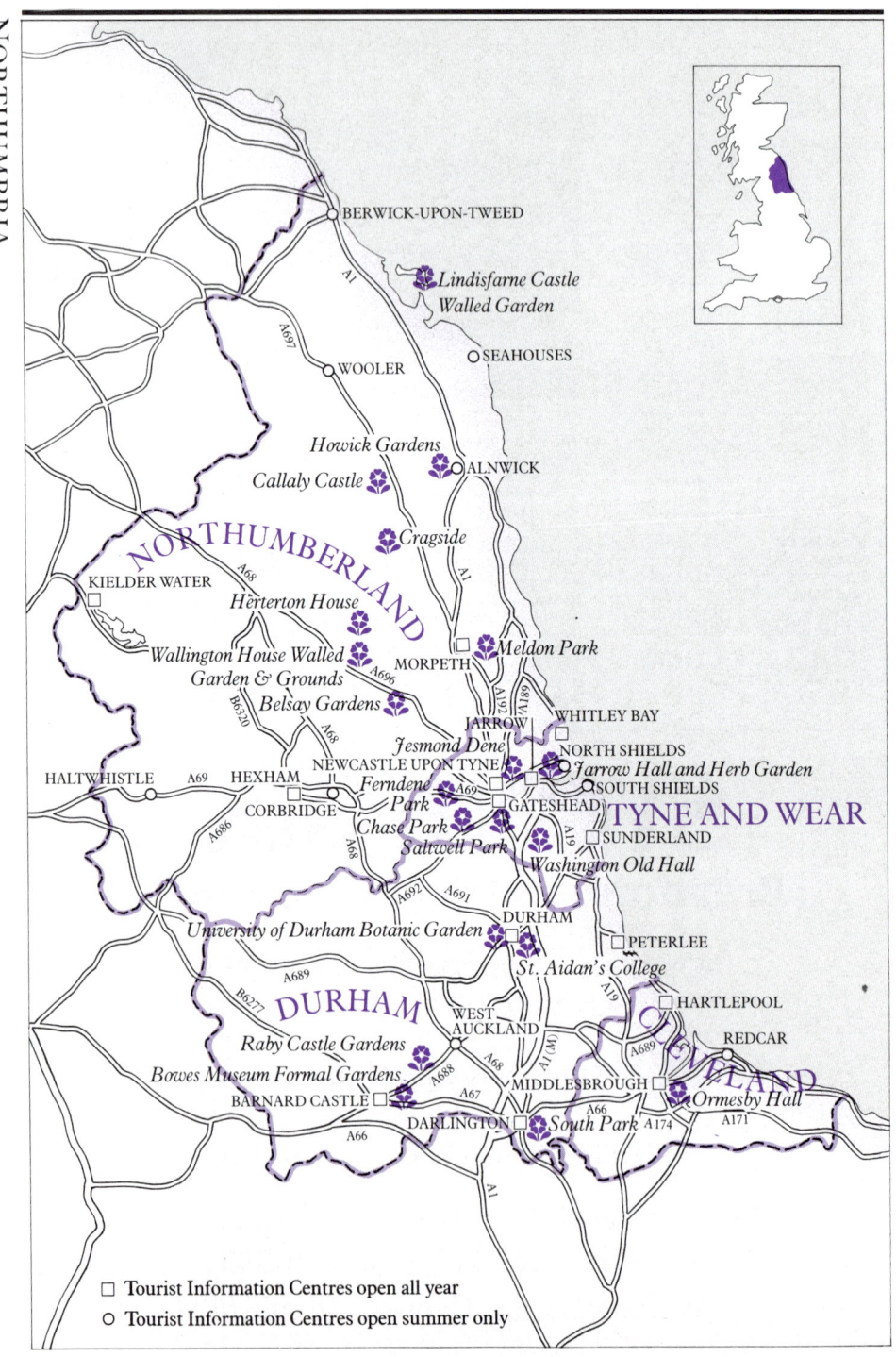

NORTHUMBRIA

Northumberland

- Berwick-upon-Tweed
- Lindisfarne Castle Walled Garden
- Seahouses
- Wooler
- Howick Gardens
- Callaly Castle
- Alnwick
- Cragside
- Kielder Water
- Herterton House
- Wallington House Walled Garden & Grounds
- Meldon Park
- Morpeth
- Belsay Gardens
- Jarrow
- Whitley Bay
- Jesmond Dene
- North Shields
- Newcastle Upon Tyne
- Jarrow Hall and Herb Garden
- Haltwhistle
- Ferndene Park
- South Shields
- Hexham
- Corbridge
- Chase Park
- Gateshead
- Saltwell Park
- Sunderland

Tyne and Wear

- Washington Old Hall

Durham

- University of Durham Botanic Garden
- Durham
- Peterlee
- St. Aidan's College
- Hartlepool
- Raby Castle Gardens
- West Auckland
- Redcar
- Bowes Museum Formal Gardens
- Barnard Castle
- Middlesbrough
- Darlington
- South Park
- Ormesby Hall

Cleveland

□ Tourist Information Centres open all year
○ Tourist Information Centres open summer only

NORTHUMBRIA

*N*ature gave the lands north of the Humber a bold landscape of empty hills, green dales and sweeping moorlands which meet the North Sea in a majestic coastline of rocky cliffs and soft, pale sand. Centuries of 'debate' over ownership of these lands left their mark in the form of magnificent monuments such as Hadrian's Wall, or the great castles of Bamburgh, Alnwick, Dunstanburgh and Warkworth. But one of them, Lindisfarne, shows within its sturdy walls, evidence of a gentler form of conquest where the famous Gertrude Jekyll, 'Artist, Gardener and Craftswoman', established one of Northumbria's loveliest gardens on the steep slopes of St. Cuthbert's Holy Island. The theme of Christian Heritage which began here, leads to two more pleasant gardens – one at Jarrow Hall, built near the site of Bede's monastery, the other in the grounds of St. Aidan's College with its views of Durham cathedral, the finest Romanesque building in the country. History is still the theme at Washington Old Hall, ancestral home of George Washington's family, and again at Barnard Castle where the French chateau-styled Bowes Museum enjoys a formal setting to match. With gardens as your guide, you will come across some of Northumbria's most delightful spots. Picturesque stone villages like Staindrop or Cambo, where Capability Brown attended the village school, and market towns like Alnwick, are a speciality of the region and gardens such as Cragside or Meldon Park are set at the gateway to superb hill and moorland country. But don't go away with the idea that gardens belong only in the countryside as settings for stately homes: Northumbrian towns and cities have a wide variety of parks and open spaces that make them such pleasant places to be: the railway town of Darlington has 100 acres of greenery in South Park; Gateshead's Saltwell Park provides the town with a central recreation ground, Victorian-style gardens and boating lake, and perhaps best known of all, there is Jesmond Dene, a natural oasis and unspoilt haven for wildlife right in the centre of bustling Newcastle upon Tyne.

JUNE

Roses tend rather to steal the limelight in June. Rambling, weeping or climbing, as floribundas or tea roses, shrubs or miniatures, there is hardly a spot in the garden in which one will not grow, or a colour in the plant world which they cannot reproduce. But many other June flowers can equal the traditional appeal of the rose – cornflowers, larkspur, foxgloves, lupins, Canterbury bells – 'Old England' is in their very names. This is a good month too for those firm favourites which every garden visitor is able to identify: asters, begonias, geraniums, pot marigolds, aubrietia, pinks and sweet-smelling stocks. More well-known shrubs like buddleia, berberis and viburnum are coming into flower now, and in the water gardens irises and primulas show their familiar faces.

Rose

MEADOW CRANESBILL

This striking sky-blue flower is to be found along the roadsides and in the hay meadows of Teesdale and Weardale between the months of June and September. A conspicuous plant, it grows to about knee-height, and after flowering produces attractive seed heads which act like a catapult to hurl out the dry seeds. Meadow cranesbill can also be grown in gardens as a hardy perennial, along with many other varieties of the geranium family of which it is a member. The smallest varieties make long-lived and reliable rock plants, whilst the taller ones, which can vary enormously both in the shape of the plant and its flowers, bring a bright touch to the border.

Crane's-bill Geranium

For more information contact the
Northumbria Tourist Board,
9 Osborne Terrace, Jesmond,
Newcastle upon Tyne,
Tyne & Wear NE2 1NT
☎ (0632) 817744.

NORTHUMBRIA

Belsay Gardens
Belsay, Northumberland
Formal terraces around house, and informal, sheltered quarry garden with tender plants unusual for the area. Known for its rhododendrons; colour throughout the year.
Open 1 Apr to 30 Sept, daily, 9.30am–6.30pm. Admission (1985 prices) 40p adults, 20p OAPs/students/children; 15% reduction parties 11+.
☎ *(066 181) 636.* ♿

The Bowes Museum Formal Gardens
Barnard Castle, Co. Durham
20 acres of grounds, designed as framework for chateau-style museum. Gardens around house recently re-designed in French style, with parterre of formal beds, ponds and fountains.
Garden open all year, daily. Museum open weekdays 10am–5pm, Sun 2pm–5pm (winter closes 4pm). Admission (1985 prices): Gardens free; Museum £1.20 adults, 35p children, OAPs, unemployed.
☎ *Teesdale (0833) 37139.* ♿ *(check).*

Callaly Castle
Whittingham, Alnwick, Northumberland
Country house set amidst formal gardens; beautiful walks through woodland to lake.
Open 4 May to 15 June, 5 July to 14 Sept, Sat, Sun, Bank Hols, 2.15pm–5.30pm (last tour 5pm). Admission £1.50 adults, 75p children; special party rates.
☎ *(066 574) 633.* ♿

Chase Park
Whickham, Tyne & Wear
25-acre park with extensive ornamental area of rose beds and flower-beds, and wide variety of trees. Something in flower at all times of the year.
Open all year, daily, 7.30am–dusk (winter 9am–dusk). Admission free.
☎ *091-488 7141.* ♿

Cragside
Rothbury, Northumberland
Extensive grounds on the edge of Alnwick Moor; famous for magnificent trees, rhododendrons and beautiful lakes.
Open 28 Mar to end Sept, daily, 10.30am–6pm; Oct, daily, 10.30am–5pm; Nov to Mar, Sat & Sun, 10.30am–4pm. Admission £1 adults, 50p children; 70p parties.
☎ *(0669) 20333. NT* ♿

Ferndene Park
Ryton, Tyne & Wear
Four acres with extensive spring and summer bedding plants, and wide variety of shrubs. Heather beds; carpet beds. Dene walk with spring bulbs and rock plants. Open-air swimming pool.
Open all year, daily, 7.30am–9pm (4.30pm in winter). Admission free.
☎ *091-414 2822.* ♿

Herterton House
Hartington, nr Cambo, Northumberland
One-acre country garden laid out in formal 18th-century manner. Flower garden; herb garden; small topiary garden. Nursery with plants for sale.
Open May to end Sept, daily exc Tue & Thur, 10am–5.30pm. Admission free; pre-booked parties £11 inc. guided tour and talk. No dogs.
☎ *Scots Gap (067 074) 278.*

Howick Gardens
Alnwick, Northumberland
Lovely gardens full of flowers, shrubs and beautiful rhododendrons.
Open Apr to Sept, daily, 2pm–7pm. Admission 50p adults, 30p OAPs/students/children, 50p parties.
☎ *Longhoughton (066 577) 285.*

Jarrow Hall and Herb Garden
Jarrow, Tyne & Wear
Small herb garden laid out in traditional English style, with medicinal, culinary and fragrant herbs. Hall houses finds from excavations of monastic site.
Open all year exc. Christmas period, daily exc Mon; summer, Tue to Sat 10am–5.30pm, Sun 2.30pm–5.30pm; winter, Tue to Sat 11am–4.30pm, Sun 2.30pm–5.30pm. Admission (1985 prices) 45p adults, 20p children/OAPs.
☎ *091-489 2106.* ♿

Jesmond Dene
Newcastle upon Tyne, Tyne & Wear
Exotic trees, shrubs and rhododendrons in natural, unspoilt river valley parkland. Pets corner.
Open all year, daily. Admission free.
☎ *(0632) 328520 ext 6212.* ♿

Raby Castle, Co. Durham

Lindisfarne Castle Walled Garden
Holy Island, Northumberland
16th-century fort, restored by Lutyens in 1903, with lovely walled garden designed by Gertrude Jekyll and restored by the National Trust.
Open (tide conditions permitting): 28 Mar to 6 Apr, daily; 7 to 30 Apr, Wed, Sat & Sun; May to end Sept, daily exc. Fri; Oct, Sat & Sun, 11am–5pm. For entry to garden apply to administrator. Admission to Castle & Garden £1.70 adults (£2.20 June, July, Aug), £1.30 parties (£2.20 June, July, Aug); children half-price.
☎ *Berwick-on-Tweed (0289) 89244. NT*

Meldon Park
Morpeth, Northumberland
House, built 1832, set in 10 acres of woodland. Different coloured rhododendrons especially in the wild garden.
Open 24 May to 22 June, daily, 2pm–5pm; also Summer Bank Hol weekend. Admission £1 adults, 50p children. No dogs.
☎ *Hartburn (067 072) 661.*

Ormesby Hall
nr Middlesbrough, Cleveland
Small attractive garden, full of variety; spring garden and holly walk.
Open 29 Mar to end Oct, Wed, Sat, Sun, Bank Hol Mon, 2pm–6pm. Admission £1 adults, 50p children; parties 80p & 40p. No dogs.
☎ *(0642) 324188. NT*

Raby Castle Gardens
Staindrop, nr Darlington, Co. Durham
Castle and formal gardens set in landscaped parkland; roses, shrub and herbaceous borders; collection of carriages.
Open 28 Mar to 30 Sept; Easter to June & Sept, Wed, Sun, 1pm–5.30pm; July & Aug, daily exc Sat, 1pm–5.30pm. Admission £1.80 adults, £1 children/OAPs; Gardens only 80p & 50p; parties on application.
☎ *(0833) 60202.*

St Aidan's College
Durham, Co. Durham
Classic views of Durham Cathedral. Easy care garden reflecting marriage between architecture and landscape; secluded courtyard with pond; laburnum walk.

Cragside, Northumberland

Open all year, daily. Admission free; donations to National Gardens Scheme at porter's lodge.
☎ *(0385) 65011. (Part)*

Saltwell Park
Gateshead, Tyne & Wear
Large, intensively-cultivated Victorian park with extensive flower-beds and borders, 4-acre boating lake, rose garden, heather garden, shrubberies and 3,000 mature trees including 73 distinct species.
Open all year, daily, 7.30am–dusk. Admission free.
☎ *(0632) 786405.*

South Park
Darlington, Co. Durham
100-acre park with formal planting of carpet beds and flower-beds, rose garden, variety of trees and shrubs. Rockery, river, small aviary and animal enclosure, lake, wild fowl, nature trail. Café and recreational facilities.
Open all year, daily, 8am–dusk. Admission free.
☎ *(0325) 465841.*

NOTES ON GARDEN VISITING

These entries have been compiled from information supplied by the gardens and were correct at the time of going to press (November 1985). However, opening times can be subject to sudden change, often because of uncontrollable factors such as the weather. We advise you to telephone the garden to check before setting out – check the admission charges, too. Those given in the entries do not always include admission to the house or other facilities in addition to the garden. Some of the gardens are willing to allow visitors by prior appointment at other times apart from their normal opening days. Where dogs are allowed in a garden, they should always be kept on a lead. NT denotes gardens belonging to the National Trust – see also pages 8–9. The symbol shows which gardens are accessible to physically handicapped visitors – see also page.

University of Durham Botanic Garden
Durham, Co. Durham
Teaching and research garden; specific collections of tropical and arid zone plants; North American arboretum and collections of Himalayan, Scandinavian and other areas of the world's flora.
Open all year, daily, 10am–4pm. No dogs.
☎ *(0385) 64971 ext. 743.*

Wallington House, Walled Garden and Grounds
Cambo, Northumberland
Fine house in 100 acres of lakes, lawns and woodlands; magnificent fuchsias in conservatory in walled garden; terraces, pavilions. 'Capability' Brown was born nearby and his work can be seen at north end of wider estate.
Open: Garden 28 Mar to end Sept, daily, 10am–7pm, Oct, daily, 10am–6pm, Nov to end Mar, daily, 10am–4pm; House 28 Mar to 6 Apr, daily, 2pm–6pm, 7 Apr–end Apr, Wed, Sat, Sun, 2pm–6pm, May to end Sept daily exc Tues, 2pm–6pm, Oct Wed, Sat, Sun 2pm–5pm; Grounds open all year, daily, dawn to dusk. (Guided tours of walled garden by Head Gardener, 17 June, 22 July, 7pm). Admission House & Grounds £2.40 adults, £1.20 children, £2 parties; Grounds only £1 adults, 50p children, 70p parties. Guided tours approx. £2.50.
☎ *Scots Gap (067 074) 673. NT*

Washington Old Hall
Washington, Tyne & Wear
Ancestral home of George Washington; formal garden, restored with donations from America, overlooking Jacobean garden; marvellous roses.
Garden open all year, daily, weather permitting. Admission free to garden; Hall extra.
☎ *Newcastle 091-4166879. NT*

A Guide to English Gardens

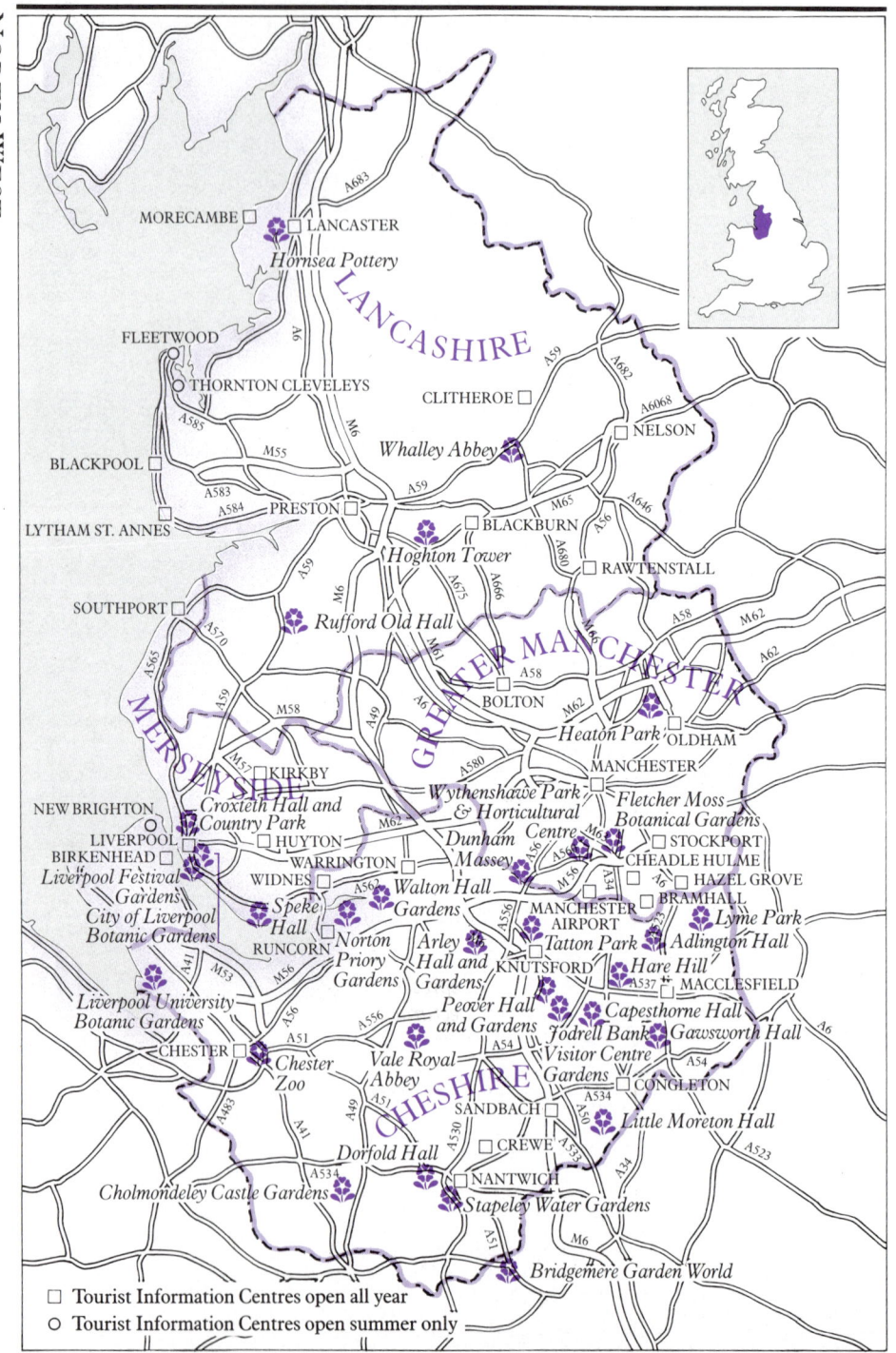

North West

□ Tourist Information Centres open all year
○ Tourist Information Centres open summer only

NORTH WEST

*G*uide books to the North West promise visitors things of beauty, and of interest – the untamed Trough of Bowland, Lancashire's holiday coast, the dramatic scarps of the Peak District National Park towering over Cheshire's fertile plain, and cities such as historic Chester, Manchester or Liverpool, constantly adding to their rich fund of attractions. In the gardens of the North West, interest and beauty combine to make them masters of the unexpected: there are orchids in Liverpool, roses and tigers in Chester, pottery and dahlias in Hornsea and trees and telescopes at Jodrell Bank – and the surprises don't end there. You'll find Europe's largest water-garden centre near Nantwich (Stapeley Water Gardens), medieval fish-ponds and a 16th-century tilting ground at Gawsworth Hall, a shell cottage at Adlington Hall, rare breeds of farm animals browsing peacefully around Cholmondeley Castle and Croxteth Hall and an Elizabethan water mill working in the grounds of Dunham Massey. Hoghton Tower, a fortified hilltop mansion dating from the 16th century, has not one but three walled gardens as well as connections with the Lancashire witches. Period houses like Jacobean Capesthorne Hall, 16th-century Peover Hall and the even earlier Rufford Old Hall are all set in period grounds. Most famous amongst them is exquisite Little Moreton Hall, the moated black-and-white timbered manor house which represents the epitome of Cheshire's traditional architectural style. Other parks and gardens have enormous style of their own: Lyme Park at Disley combines 16 acres of gardens with a magnificent 1320-acre deer park from which there are superb views of the foothills of the Pennines, the Peak District and the Cheshire Plain; Manchester's Heaton Park, a generous 600 acres, was landscaped by a pupil of Capability Brown, while Tatton Park at Knutsford still shows the influence of Humphry Repton whose landscaping work was based on the belief that 'the art could only be perfected by the united powers of the landscape painter and the practical gardener'.

JULY

This magnificent month brings the pages of gardening catalogues to life with an overwhelming abundance of flowers. Nasturtiums and red hot pokers provide a sudden stab of dramatic colour; petunias, clematis and cartwheels lay back their petals to drink in the sun; lilies exude exotic elegance, and anti-rrhinums provide the homely touch. At this time of the year the garden is wonderfully scented with the heady perfume of sweet peas, pinks, tobacco plants and lavender, while from their places at the back of the border, hollyhocks and the superior sunflower look down over it all.

Antirrhinum

THE PRIMULA

The large family of moisture-loving primulas grows well in Cheshire, brightening water gardens and rock gardens with their different coloured flowers from March to June. But one of them, the orange *Primula bulleyana*, has a special significance in this part of the world. It was named in honour of Arthur Gilpin Bulley, one of the most important patrons of 20th-century plant collecting. British gardeners owe many of their favourite plants to the enthusiasm of men like Bulley; from 1904 onwards, he supported and encouraged plant collectors in expeditions to China, the Himalayas, Asia Minor and other far-flung places, as a result of which thousands of new plants were introduced to this country via his gardens at Ness, later to become the University of Liverpool Botanic Gardens. Many of them, like the *Primula bulleyana*, are still grown there today.

Primula vulgaris

For more information contact the
North West Tourist Board,
The Last Drop Village, Bromley Cross,
Bolton, Lancashire BL7 9PZ
☎ (0204) 591511 (written
and telephone enquiries only).

A GUIDE TO ENGLISH GARDENS

NORTH WEST

Adlington Hall
nr Macclesfield, Cheshire
15th-century hall with later additions; gardens include a 'shell cottage', yew walk and lime avenue.
Open 28 Mar to 28 Sept, Sun & Bank Hols, 2pm–5.30pm; also Wed & Sat in Aug. Booked parties on weekdays by arrangement. Admission £1.50 adults, 75p children; £1 for parties 25+.
☎ *Prestbury (0625) 829206.* ♿

Arley Hall and Gardens
Between Northwich and Knutsford, Cheshire
Lovely gardens with great variety of features including very early twin herbaceous borders, shrub roses, azaleas, rhododendrons and an unusual avenue of Ilex trees clipped to the shape of cylinders. Arley Hall and private chapel also open.
Open 28 Mar to 5 Oct, Tue to Sun, Bank Hol Mon, 2pm–6pm. Admission £1.40 adults, 70p children; £1.15 pre-booked parties of 20+.
☎ *(056 585) 353.* ♿

Bridgemere Garden World
Bridgemere, nr Nantwich, Cheshire
Seasonal displays of spring-flowering bulbs and summer bedding; informal heather and rhododendron gardens. Spring, summer, autumn and winter borders.
Open all year, daily exc 25 & 26 Dec, 9am–dusk (8.30pm latest). Admission free. No dogs.
☎ *(093 65) 239/381.* ♿

Capesthorne Hall
Macclesfield, Cheshire
Jacobean house and gardens with spring flowers, shrubs, herbaceous borders overlooking a chain of ornamental pools; best seen in spring and early summer. Woodland walk; touring caravan park.
Open 28 and 30 Mar and Suns in Apr; Wed, Sat, Sun, May to Sept; Tue, Thur, Sun July to Sept; also Bank Hol Mons, Grounds and chapel 12 noon–6pm, Hall 2pm–5pm. Admission Hall & Grounds £1.75 adults, 85p children; Grounds £1 adults, 50p children; special rates for parties. No dogs.
☎ *Chelford (0625) 861221 or 861439.* ♿

Chester Zoo
Chester, Cheshire
110 acres of gardens, with shrubs and flowers imaginatively interspersed amongst the animal enclosures. Magnificent rose garden; Tropical House; rock garden.
Open all year, daily exc 25 Dec, 10am–dusk. Admission £2.70 adults, £1.30 children & OAPs; parties £2.30 adults, £1.10 children. No dogs.
☎ *(0244) 380280.* ♿

Cholmondeley Castle Gardens
Malpas, Cheshire
Ornamental gardens, lakeside picnic area, rare breeds of farm animals, tea room, gift shop, ancient chapel in the park. Plants for sale.
Open 30 Mar to 28 Sept, Sun, Bank Hols, 12 noon–6pm. Admission £1 adults, 50p children; parties 80p.
☎ *(082 922) 383.* ♿

City of Liverpool Botanic Gardens
Calderstones Park, Liverpool 18, Merseyside
125 acres with Japanese, Old English, rose and flower gardens; herbaceous border; fine collections trees and shrubs, including flowering cherry collection. Glasshouses in nearby Sefton Park house continuous exhibitions of seasonal flowers including orchids.
Open all year, daily exc Christmas Day, 8am–dusk; Glasshouses 10am–12 noon, 1pm–4pm. Admission free.
☎ *051-724 2371.* ♿

Croxteth Hall and Country Park
Liverpool, Merseyside
Hall set in 500-acre country park, with splendid walled garden containing 100-year-old trained fruit trees, peach house, herbaceous borders, herb garden and special interpretative panels. Rare breeds farm, miniature railway, café and gift shops.
Open 24 Mar to 29 Sept, daily, 11am–5pm. Admission Hall, farm & garden £1.30 adults, 75p children; discount for parties; Garden only 30p adults, 15p children & OAPs. No dogs.
☎ *051-228 5311.* ♿

Dorfold Hall
Nantwich, Cheshire
18-acre garden under restoration, partially laid out by William Nesfield in 1862. Lawns, rose garden, spring garden, water garden, park and lake.
Open Apr to Oct, Tue; also Bank Hol Mons, 2pm–5pm. Admission £1.50 adults, 75p children.
☎ *(0270) 625245.*

Dunham Massey
Altrincham, Cheshire
Early 18th-century house and park with herd of fallow deer; streams, orangery, woodland garden, spacious lawns and herbaceous and shrub borders. Elizabethan working mill.
Open 29 Mar to 31 Oct; Mon to Thur 12 noon– 5.30pm, Sat, Sun, Bank Hol Mon 11am–5.30pm. Admission £2.50 adults, £1 children, parties on application. No dogs.
☎ *061-941 1025. NT* ♿

Fletcher Moss Botanical Gardens
Didsbury, Manchester
Beautiful gardens, containing rock plants, conifers, rhododendrons and many rare shrubs and plants. Wild garden and museum also open to public. Orchid House.
Open all year, daily, 8am–dusk. Admission free. No dogs.
☎ *061-434 1877.* ♿

Gawsworth Hall
Gawsworth, nr Macclesfield, Cheshire
Manor house in extensive grounds including medieval fish ponds, country house garden and unique tilting ground formed in early 16th century.
Open 26 Mar to 25 Oct, daily, 2pm–6pm. Admission £1.80 adults, 90p children; parties £1.50.
☎ *North Rode (026 03) 456.* ♿

Hare Hill
Over Alderley, nr Macclesfield, Cheshire
Walled garden with pergola, rhododendrons and azaleas; parkland.
Open Apr to Oct, Wed, Thur, Sun, Bank Hols, 2pm–5.30pm. Admission 80p. Parties by written appt with Head Gardener.
☎ *Upton Magna (074 377) 649. NT* ♿

Heaton Park
North Manchester, Greater Manchester
600-acre park landscaped by William Emes, a pupil of 'Capability' Brown, with later improvements by John Webb, a follower of Humphry Repton. The 'Dell' provides a riot of colour in springtime; ornamental areas, rose gardens in front of magnificent Hall with Orangery tea rooms. Natural areas and woodlands.
Open all year, daily, 8am–sunset. Admission free.
☎ *061-773 1085.* ♿

Hoghton Tower
Hoghton, nr Preston, Lancashire
Dramatic 16th-century hilltop mansion, surrounded by three walled gardens.
Open 29 Mar to 26 Oct, Sun, Bank Hols (also Sat in July & Aug), 2pm–5pm. Admission £1.50 adults, 50p children.
☎ *(025 485) 2986.* ♿

Hornsea Pottery
Lancaster, Lancashire
Hornsea Pottery set in 42 acres of landscaped leisure park. Amenities include tea garden, picnic area, rare breeds survival unit, alpine slide, adventure playground, as well as shops and factory tours.
Open all year, daily, 10am–5pm. Admission (1985 prices) 60p adults, 40p children/OAPs.
☎ *(0524) 68444.* ♿

Jodrell Bank Visitor Centre Gardens
nr Holmes Chapel, Cheshire
A comprehensive collection of more than 30,000 trees and shrubs of over 2,000 different types in a 40-acre setting. National collection of Malus. Young trees for sale.
Open 12 Mar to 31 Oct, daily, 10.30am–5.30pm; 1 Nov to 11 Mar, weekends only, 2pm–5pm. Admission £2 adults, £1 children/OAPs; schools at reduced rates in winter. No dogs.
☎ *Lower Withington (0477) 71339.* ♿

Little Moreton Hall
Congleton, Cheshire
Traditional knot and herb gardens surround a perfect example of a moated, timbered manor house.
Open Mar & Oct, Sat, Sun, 2pm–6pm; Apr to Sept, daily exc Tue, 2pm–6pm. Last entry 5.30pm. Admission £1.60 adults (£1.90 weekends & Bank Hols), 80p

62

THE FESTIVAL GARDENS

The magnificent Festival Gardens re-open in Spring '86.

And they're better than ever!

All the family will enjoy over 70 acres of flowers, fun and exciting free entertainments.

All on the superb riverside site of the International Garden Festival – Britain's largest tourist attraction of 1984.

The perfect setting for a great family day out!

Two Summer Spectaculars. Two Minutes Apart.

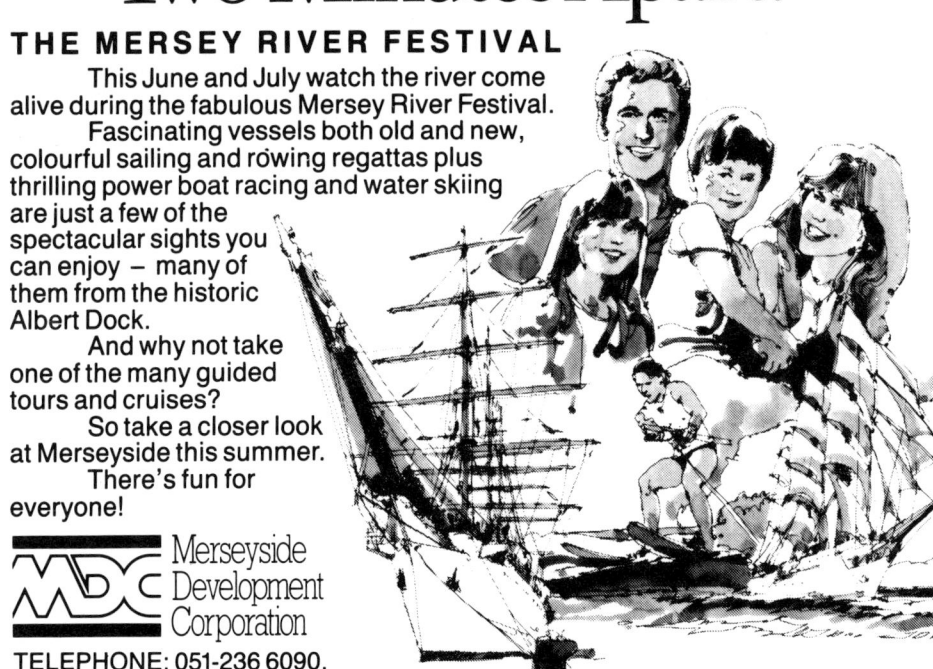

THE MERSEY RIVER FESTIVAL

This June and July watch the river come alive during the fabulous Mersey River Festival.

Fascinating vessels both old and new, colourful sailing and rowing regattas plus thrilling power boat racing and water skiing are just a few of the spectacular sights you can enjoy – many of them from the historic Albert Dock.

And why not take one of the many guided tours and cruises?

So take a closer look at Merseyside this summer.

There's fun for everyone!

Merseyside Development Corporation

TELEPHONE: 051-236 6090.

NORTH WEST

children (90p weekends & Bank Hols), family ticket £5, parties by appt. No dogs.
☎ (0260) 272018. NT ✻ ⚄

Liverpool Festival Gardens
Liverpool, Merseyside
Over 70 acres of flowers, fun and free entertainment, on site of the 1984 International Garden Festival. Contact Merseyside Development Corporation for details of admission times and charges. (See advertisement on page 63).
☎ (051) 236 6090.

Liverpool University Botanic Gardens
Ness, Wirral, Cheshire
Extensive displays of trees and shrubs; rock, terrace, herbaceous and water gardens. One of the best-known heather gardens in the country.
Open all year, daily exc 25 Dec., 9am to dusk (last admission 1hr before). Admission £1.50 adults, 80p children/OAPs; £1.30 parties of 20+.
☎ 051-336 2135. ⚄

Lyme Park
Disley, Cheshire
1,320 acres of moor and parkland with deer and wildfowl; 16th, 18th & 19th-century house with extensive garden; Italian garden; herbaceous borders; children's playground; craft centre; pitch and putt course; cycle hire.
Open: Park & Gardens all year, daily, 8am–dusk; House end-Mar to end-Oct, Tues to Sun 2pm–5pm (last entry 4.30pm or 4pm in Oct). Admission free to Gardens, House 90p adults, 40p children.
☎ (066 32) 2023. NT ✻ ⚄

Norton Priory Gardens
Runcorn, Cheshire
7 acres of attractive woodland gardens, bounded by the historic Bridgewater Canal. Laid out in the late 18th century, the grounds contain a Georgian summerhouse, a Victorian summerhouse and rock garden, a stream glade and a herb garden.
Open all year, daily exc 24–26 Dec, Mar–Oct, Mon–Fri 12noon–5pm, Sat, Sun, Bank Hol Mon 12noon–6pm; Nov–Feb, daily, 12noon–4pm. Admission (1985 prices) 70p adults, 30p children/OAPs; parties by arrangement.
☎ (092 85) 69895. ⚄

Peover Hall and Gardens
Over Peover, Knutsford, Cheshire
Dating from 1585, gardens feature much topiary work, herb garden, lily-pond garden; rose garden, pink and white gardens; Elizabethan summer house and 'theatre' garden; 18th-century landscaped park; 19th-century Rhododendron and Azalea Dell; Rhododendron Walks.
Open May to Sept, exc Bank Hols; Hall, Stables, Gardens, Mon, 2pm–5pm; Stables & Gardens, Thur, 2pm–4.30pm. Gardens only open Oct. Admission: Hall, Stables, Gardens £1.80 adults, 90p children; Stables & Gardens £1 adults, 50p children; parties by arrangement. No dogs.
☎ (056 581) 2135.

Rufford Old Hall
nr Ormskirk, Lancashire
Outstanding 15th-century building with fine collection of oak furniture, arms and armour, set in lovely period garden.
Open 26 Mar to 2 Nov, daily exc Fri, Garden 11am–6pm; Hall 1pm–6pm (last entry 5.30pm). Admission Garden only 60p adult, 30p children; House & Garden £1.40 adult, 70p children; parties by arrangement.
☎ (0704) 821254. NT ✻ ⚄ *(gardens only)*

Speke Hall
Liverpool, Merseyside
Tudor house with grounds laid out in mid 19th-century. Herbaceous borders in moat garden; rose garden, surrounding shrubberies and woodland; raised walk overlooking Mersey.
Open all year, daily, exc 28 Mar, 24–26 Dec, 1 Jan, Apr to Sept, Mon to Sat 10am–5pm, Sun 2pm–7pm (2pm–5pm in winter), last admission 1 hour before closing. Admission to grounds free; extra for Hall, children, unemployed and OAPs half-price. No dogs.
☎ 051-427 7231. ⚄

Stapeley Water Gardens
Stapeley, Nantwich, Cheshire
Europe's largest water-gardening centre, with display gardens, pumps, fountains, waterfalls, plants; musical fountain.
Open all year, daily: Easter to 1 Sept, Mon to Fri 9am–6pm, Sat, Sun, Bank Hols 10am–7pm; winter, Mon to Fri 9am–5pm, Sat, Sun 10am–5pm. Admission free. No dogs.
☎ (0270) 623868. ⚄

Tatton Park
Knutsford, Cheshire
Stately home set in beautiful gardens and park with lakes, nature and village trails, Home Farm, Old Hall, restaurant and shop.
Open all year, daily exc 25 Dec., 1 Apr to 18 May, 2 Sept to 31 Oct 11.30am–5pm (Sun, Bank Hols 10.30am–5.30pm); 19
May to 1 Sept 11am–5.30pm (Sun, Bank Hols 10.30am–6pm). House opens 1½ hours after Gardens. Admission 80p adults, 60p OAPs, 40p children. House & Hall extra. Car parking £1 (inc. access to park).
☎ (0565) 54822. NT ✻ ⚄

Vale Royal Abbey
Whitegate, nr Northwich, Cheshire
Mature grounds and gardens with new plantings, surrounding 16th-century abbey on the site of an abbey dating back to 13th century. Lake, with fountain within walled garden area. Nun's grave, historic monument accessible to east of Abbey.
Open all year, Sat, Sun, Bank Hols, 11am–5pm. Closed Christmas weekend. Admission £1 adults, 50p children/OAPs; parties by arrangement.
☎ Sandiway (0606) 888684. ⚄

Walton Hall Gardens
Higher Walton, Warrington, Cheshire
Formal garden with rose garden and wide variety of bedding plants, set in country park with fine trees and extensive network of footpaths.
House open Thur to Sun, Bank Hol Mon (Sun & Bank Hol Mon only in winter), 1pm–5pm. Admission: Gardens free; House 20p adults, 10p children/OAPs.
☎ Warrington (0925) 601617.

Whalley Abbey
Whalley, Lancashire
Conference centre and ruins of old Cistercian abbey in 15 acres of lawns, roses, heathers, formal bedding plants. Craft centre and gift shop.
Open all year, daily, dawn–dusk; craft centre and gift shop Easter to end Sept. Admission 50p adults, 25p OAPs/children; parties 30p & 15p.
☎ Blackburn (0254) 822268. ⚄

Wythenshawe Park and Horticultural Centre
Northenden, Greater Manchester
Extensive park containing many rare trees and shrubs. Walled garden and rose garden. Elizabethan House recently renovated. Horticultural Centre with glasshouses showing wide variety of 'plant stock' and propagation methods. Charles Darrah Cactus collection and tropical plant house can also be visited.
Open all year, daily; Park 8am–dusk; Horticultural Centre 11am–4pm. Admission free. Guided tours on request. No dogs; children must be accompanied.
☎ 061-945 1768. ⚄

LYME PARK, Disley, Cheshire. The magnificent 1323–acre deer park makes a splendid setting for Lyme Hall, which dates from Elizabethan times, with additions in the 18th and 19th centuries. From the park are breathtaking views of the Peak District, Pennine foothills and the Cheshire Plain.
The wild moorlands are in stark contrast to the 16 acres of gardens surrounding the Hall. The formal East gardens and the sunken Dutch gardens are at their most attractive in spring and late summer. A fine stone bridge arches over a pool and waterfall, from which the stream flows through a steep ravine known as Killtime. Moisture-loving plants and flowering shrubs tumble down from the high banks.
Children's playground, pitch & putt, cycle hire, cafeteria.
1986 EVENTS INCLUDE LYME PARK FESTIVAL SHEEPDOG TRAILS & GUIDED WALKS.
Open park & gardens all year, daily 8pm–dusk, house Apr to Oct, Tues to Sat 2pm–5pm (last entry 4.30pm). Sun, Bank Hols 1pm–6pm (last entry 5.30pm). Tel: Disley 2023
Dates and timings subject to alteration.

SOUTH of ENGLAND

The finest landscapes in the South of England owe very little to man's contrivance: the heaths and woodlands of the New Forest, the old-English countryside of Thomas Hardy's Dorset, Hampshire's rolling farmlands and picturesque river valleys and a sheltered coastline of tucked-away estuaries and inlets have a distinctive charm for all connoisseurs of English scenery at its best. But craftsmen through the ages have embellished corners of this countryside in a variety of ways from cottage gardens to country parks. Lord Palmerston built Broadlands on a wonderful site overlooking the River Test and the Duke of Wellington chose the downlands of the Berkshire/Hampshire border for Stratfield Saye, while Beaulieu and its numerous attractions enjoy a lovely setting on the edge of the New Forest. Like Beaulieu, Mottisfont also boasts an abbey whose riverside grounds are open to the public. After the abbeys come houses and gardens of every period: Southampton's Tudor House with its Elizabethan gardens, Gilbert White's 18th-century garden at Selborne or Barton Manor, where the gardens were laid out by Queen Victoria and Prince Albert and extended by King Edward VII. Many of the smaller gardens are equally delightful – Corfe Castle's model village is also a beautiful old-English garden; Ivy Cottage at Ansty is small but exquisite and Jane Austen's garden at Chawton looks just as it did in the 18th century. You can expect some superb specialist displays in this part of the world, in the spring and autumn colours at the Hillier Arboretum, in the trees, rhododendrons, azaleas and camellias at Exbury or in the wonderful world of Compton Acres, whose series of Japanese, Italian, Roman, English and other gardens is internationally famous. And just across the Solent lies the Holiday Isle itself; blest with more hours of sunshine than any other spot in Britain, the south-facing gardens of the Isle of Wight combine a bright abundance of flowers and shrubs with a host of bright ideas for family entertainments.

AUGUST

A peak holiday period, August lures visitors into the garden in time to catch the final glory of summer flowers before they make way for autumn. There is plenty to enjoy, as many of the plants which began blooming last month are still in flower, and to these August has made some attractive additions – lilies of the African, Peruvian and strongly-scented lilium auratum varieties; dainty pink and white cyclamen, or hibiscus and hardy fuchsias, covered in flower. Borders are bright with the mixed colours of new arrivals with lovely old names: there's henbane or viper's bugloss; love-in-a-mist names two blue varieties after Gertrude Jekyll, while morning glory offers us Heavenly Blue, Flying Saucers and Wedding Bells.

Cyclamen

RHODODENDRONS

The rhododendron gets its name from the Greek 'rhodon' – rose, and 'dendron' – tree. It came here from central Europe in 1656, and its genus was established in 1753 by Linneaus, who mistakenly created a separate genus of azalea. Although the two were later reclassified together, to many gardeners they will always remain two different plants. Rhododendrons are mainly evergreen shrubs, but azaleas, with the main exception of the popular Japanese variety, are deciduous. They vary in size from rock plants to trees and this region, which grows them to great advantage, can produce a succession of specimens in flower for several months at a time.

Azalea

For more information contact the
Southern Tourist Board,
Town Hall Centre, Leigh Road,
Eastleigh, Hampshire SO5 4DE
☎ (0703) 616027 and the
Isle of Wight Tourist Board,
21 High Street, Newport, Isle of Wight
PO30 1JS ☎ (0983) 524343.

A Guide to English Gardens

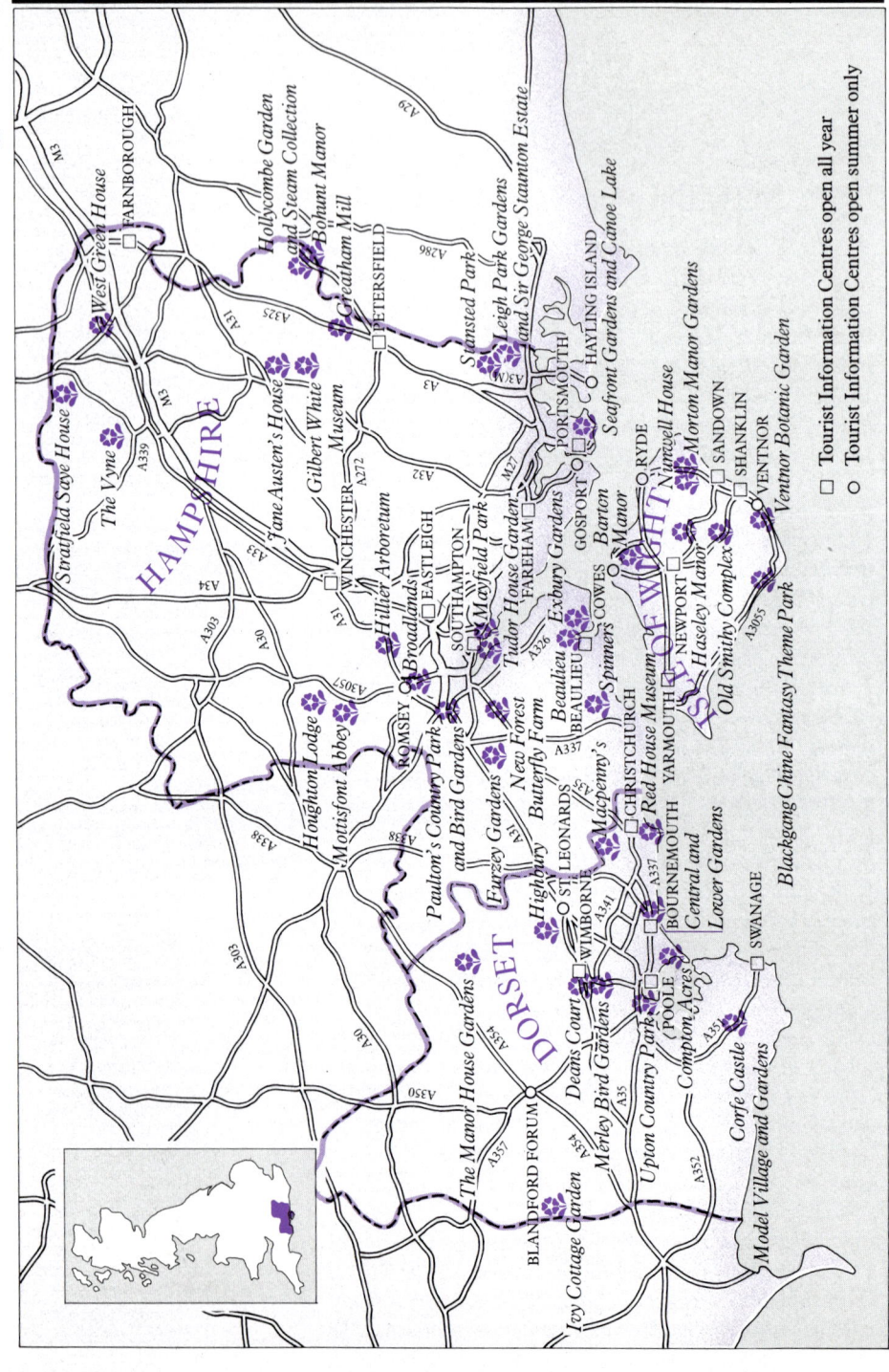

South of England

SOUTH of ENGLAND

Jane Austen's House
Chawton, nr Alton, Hampshire
House and garden containing old-fashioned plants and flowers appropriate to the late 18th century.
Open Apr to Oct daily; Nov, Dec & Mar, Wed to Sun; Jan, Feb, Sat & Sun, 11am-4.30pm. Admission 85p adults, 35p children, 70p parties. No dogs.
☎ (0420) 83262. ⚲

Barton Manor
Whippingham, Cowes, Isle of Wight
20-acre gardens laid out by Queen Victoria and Prince Albert, extended by Edward VII; vineyard, winery and wine bar; wine, vines and produce for sale.
Open May to 12 Oct, daily, 10.30am-5.30pm; also open Sat, Sun in Apr & 28-31 Mar. Admission £1.50 adults, £1.25 OAPs, accompanied children free; parties (by appt.) £1. No dogs.
☎ (0983) 292835. ⚲

Beaulieu
nr Lyndhurst, Hampshire
Beautiful garden with lots to do; National Motor Museum, Palace House; abbey ruins with medieval herb garden.
Open all year, daily exc 25 Dec, May to Sept 10am-6pm, Oct to May 10am-5pm. Admission (inclusive) £3.70 adults, £2.60 OAPs, £2.20 students/children; parties £3, £2.10 & £1.70.
☎ (0590) 612345. ⚲

Blackgang Chine Fantasy Theme Park
nr Chale, Isle of Wight
20-acre scenic gardens opened in 1843. 100 different trees and shrubs, water gardens, and one of England's best mazes laid out in 1964.
Open end Mar to end Oct, daily, Mar, Apr, May, Oct 10am–5pm, June to Sept 10am–10pm. Admission (1985 prices) £1.70 adults, 95p children; parties by arrangement.
☎ (0983) 730330. ⚲

Bohunt Manor
Liphook, Hampshire
Woodland gardens with lakeside walk, water garden, herbaceous borders and flowering shrubs, tulip tree, rare plants. Over 50 species of waterfowl and trees.
Open all year, Mon to Fri, 12 noon–6pm, weekends by arrangement. Admission 50p adults, 10p children. No dogs.
☎ (0428) 722208. ⚲

Compton Acres, Dorset

Broadlands
Romsey, Hampshire
Previously the home of Lord Palmerston, built in classical Palladian style. Lovely landscaped lawns beside the River Test remain a tribute to the genius of 'Capability' Brown.
Open 27 Mar to 30 Sept, Tue to Sun; also Mon in Aug, Sept & Bank Hols; 10am-5pm. Admission £2.70 adults, £1.50 children (under 12 accompanied free), £2 OAPs; parties £2.20 adults, £1.25 children. No dogs.
☎ (0749) 516878. ⚲

Central and Lower Gardens
Bournemouth, Dorset
Civic gardens featuring 'Paradise' area of bulbs and temperate plants; formal bedding displays, aviary.
Open all year, daily. Admission free.
☎ (0202) 22066. ⚲

Compton Acres
Canford Cliffs, Poole, Dorset
Seven different gardens in one with interesting statues, palm court, wishing well; Japanese garden with pagoda and waterfall.
Open Apr to Oct, daily, 10.30am-6.30pm. Admission £1.50 adults, £1 OAPs, 75p children; parties £1.30 & 65p. No dogs.
☎ (0202) 708036. ⚲

Corfe Castle Model Village and Gardens
Corfe Castle, Dorset
Scale model of castle and village before its destruction by Cromwellian forces in 17th century. Set in beautiful old-English gardens.
Open 28 Mar to 30 Sept, daily, 10am-6pm.
Admission 70p adults, 35p OAPs/children; parties 35p adults, 25p children.
☎ (0929) 480091. ⚲

Deans Court
Wimborne Minster, Dorset
13 acres of partly wild garden on the river Allen. Monastery fishpond, specimen trees, woodland park, peacocks, waterfowl and other birds. 18th-century kitchen garden with serpentine wall, herb garden and vegetable sanctuary. Organic produce and plants for sale.
Open Easter Sun & Mon, then 26 May to 28 Sept, Sun & Thur 2pm–6pm, Bank Hol Mons 10am-6pm. Admission 60p adults, 30p children; parties by appt. No dogs. ⚲

Exbury Gardens
Exbury, nr Southampton, Hampshire
200-acre woodland garden of botanical interest, containing the Rothschild collection of rhododendrons, azaleas and camellias. 2-acre rock garden, ponds and rose garden.
Open 8 Mar to 13 July, daily, Mar 1pm-5.30pm, Apr to July 10am-5.30pm. Admission £2 adults, £1.50 OAPs/children (under 12 free); parties £1.50.
☎ Fawley (0703) 891203. ⚲

Furzey Gardens
Minstead, nr Lyndhurst, Hampshire
Lovely gardens full of variety in peaceful setting; ancient cottage and art-and-craft gallery to visit.
Open all year, daily, exc 25 & 26 Dec, 10am–5pm or dusk. Admission £1.25 adults (75p Nov to Feb), 75p children (40p Nov to Feb); reductions for parties. No dogs.
☎ Southampton (0703) 812464. ⚲

EXBURY GARDENS
Welcome Spring in an English Garden

Includes the famous Rothschild Collection of Rhododendrons
Open daily Saturday 8th March to Sunday 14 July inclusive
Prior to Good Friday 1pm-5.30pm
Rest of Season 10am-5.30pm
EXBURY GARDENS LTD.,
EXBURY, Nr. SOUTHAMPTON
(3 miles from Beaulieu)
Tel: Fawley (0703) 891203

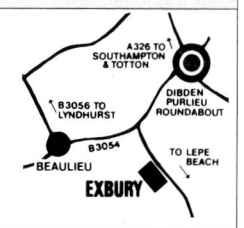

Greatham Mill
Greatham, nr Liss, Hampshire
Interesting garden with large variety of plants surrounding mill house, with mill stream. Plants for sale.
Open 20 Apr to 28 Sept, Sun & Bank Hols 2pm–7pm. Admission 50p adults, children free. No dogs.
☎ *Blackmoor (042 07) 219.*

Haseley Manor
Arreton, nr Newport, Isle of Wight
Herb garden with over eighty varieties of herbs. Water garden with waterfalls running down to a stream and small lake with bog plants. Plants available for sale.
Open all year, daily, 9am–6pm. Admission £1.50 adults, £1 OAPs/children; parties by arrangement.
☎ *(0983) 865420.* &

Highbury
West Moors, nr Wimborne, Dorset
Half-acre garden in mature setting; many rare and unusual plants and shrubs. Specialist collections of botanical and horticultural interest.
Open Apr to Sept, Sun & Bank Hol Mons, 2pm–6pm. Admission 40p adults, 20p children. No dogs.
☎ *Ferndown (0202) 874372.* &

Hillier Arboretum
Ampfield, nr Romsey, Hampshire
The largest collection of trees and shrubs of its kind in the British Isles, planted within an attractive landscape.
Open all year, Mon to Fri 10am–5pm; also Sat, Sun & Bank Hols Mar to 9 Nov, 1pm–6pm. Admission £1 adults, children free; parties of 30+ 80p. No dogs.
☎ *Braishfield (0794) 68787.* &

Hollycombe Garden and Steam Collection
Liphook, Hampshire
Ten-acre woodland garden. Large area rhododendrons and azaleas, including ¼-mile azalea walk. Rare trees and shrubs. Walks with fine views. Steam engine collection.
Open 30 Mar to 28 Sept, Suns & Bank Hols, also 17 to 31 Aug, 12 noon–6pm. Admission £1.80 adults, £1.20 OAPs/children; parties £1.50 & £1. No dogs.
☎ *(0428) 723233.* &

Houghton Lodge
Stockbridge, Hampshire
18th-century 'cottage orne' with fine views over Test Valley. Rare chalk cob walls surround produce garden. Extensive glasshouses and vinery, with fine displays of flowers.

18th-century folly.
Open Mar to end Aug, Wed & Thur 2pm–5pm; also Easter Sun & Mon. Admission £1 adults, 50p children. No dogs.
☎ *Andover (0264) 810502 or 01-352 7478.* &

Ivy Cottage Garden
Ansty, nr Dorchester, Dorset
An informal cottage garden specialising in herbaceous perennials, moisture-loving plants and specimen trees. Plants for sale.
Open Apr to end Sept, Thur, 10am–5pm. Admission 50p adults, 20p children; parties by appt. 40p. No dogs.
☎ *Milton Abbas (0258) 880053.*

Leigh Park Gardens and Sir George Staunton Estate
Havant, Hampshire
Estate garden with lovely walks, rhododendrons, lawns and lake; large cedars and tulip tree. Picnic area; play area and farm animals.
Open 22 Mar to 31 Oct, daily, 10am–6pm. Admission 80p adults, 40p OAPs/children, 30p parties. No dogs.
☎ *Portsmouth (0705) 834148/834770.*

Macpenny's
Bransgore, nr Christchurch, Hampshire
Large woodland garden. Nurseries with many new varieties of plants; camellias, rhododendrons, azaleas, heathers and herbaceous plants.
Open all year, daily, Mon to Fri 8am–5pm, Sat 9am–5pm, Sun 2pm–5pm. Admission free, charity collecting box.
☎ *(0425) 72348.*

The Manor House Gardens
Cranborne, Dorset
Walled gardens, yew hedges and lawns; wild garden with bulbs, herb garden, Jacobean mount garden, knot garden, flowering cherries and old-fashioned and species roses.
Open Apr to Oct, 1st Sat & Sun in month, Bank Hols, Sat & Bank Hol Mon 9am–5pm, Sun 2pm–5pm. Admission £1 adults, 20p children. Garden centre open daily, 9am–5pm, Sun 2pm–5pm. No dogs.
☎ *(072 54) 289.* &

Mayfield Park
Southampton, Hampshire
Recreational park with herbaceous borders and woodland garden of rhododendrons, camellias and other woodland plants.
Open all year, daily, dawn to dusk. Admission free.
☎ *(0703) 832675.* &

Broadlands, Hampshire

Merley Bird Gardens
nr Wimborne Minster, Dorset
Formal gardens, shrubberies and water gardens set in one of the largest and most beautiful historic gardens in the country. Collection of exotic birds.
Open all year, daily, 10am to 6pm. Admission £1.65 adults, £1.30 OAPs, 85p children, £1.30 parties. No dogs.
☎ *(0202) 883790.* &

Morton Manor Gardens
Brading, Isle of Wight
Beautifully terraced landscape gardens with ornamental ponds, historic home and old-world thatched cottage to visit. Vineyard, winery and winemaking museum. Wines and plants for sale.
Open Easter to Oct, daily exc Sat, 10am–5.30pm. Admission (approximate) £1.35 adults, £1.20 OAPs, 60p children, £1 parties.
☎ *(0983) 406168.* &

Mottisfont Abbey
Mottisfont, nr Romsey, Hampshire
Interesting house with lovely grounds bordering river; fine lawns and trees; collection of old-fashioned roses.
Garden open 29 Mar to end Sept, Sun to Thur, House 2pm–6pm Wed & Sun (guided tours only), last entry 5pm. Admission: Grounds £1.30 June & July, £1 Apr, May, Aug, Sept; House 30p extra; children half-price. No dogs.
☎ *Lockerley (0794) 40757.* NT ⚘ &

THE HILLIER ARBORETUM
JERMYNS LANE, AMPFIELD, NR. ROMSEY, HAMPSHIRE
Signposted from A31 Winchester–Romsey. Tel: Braishfield (0794) 68787

The Hillier Arboretum contains the largest collection of trees and shrubs of its kind in the British Isles, all planted within an attractive landscape. Its most colourful seasons are the spring and autumn with the massed flamboyant blooms of the Rhododendrons, Azaleas, Cherries and Magnolias in the spring, followed in the Autumn by the subtle and spectacular tints and hues of the Oaks, Maples and Rowans.

The Arboretum is open weekdays throughout the year from 10am to 5pm, and at weekends and bank holidays from March to second Sunday in November from 1pm to 6pm. Prearranged parties are welcome at anytime.

A GUIDE TO ENGLISH GARDENS

SOUTH of ENGLAND

New Forest Butterfly Farm
Ashurst, nr Lyndhurst, Hampshire
Indoor tropical garden filled with exotic free-flying butterflies from all over the world. Passion flowers and shrubs. English garden with British butterflies. Dragonfly pond. Garden centre.
Open Apr to Oct, daily, 10am–5pm. Admission (1985 prices) £1.80 adults, £1.30 OAPs, £1 children; reductions for parties of 15+. No dogs.
☎ (042 129) 2166. &

Nunwell House
Brading, Isle of Wight
Four acres of garden set in parkland with lovely views of the Solent. Formal garden with fountains, lawns, trees and shrubs.
Open 25 May to 25 Sept, daily exc Fri & Sat, 1.30pm–5.30pm. Admission £1.20 adults, 60p children; 10% discount for parties of 20+.
☎ (0983) 407240.

Old Smithy Complex
Godshill, Isle of Wight
Garden shaped and modelled like the Isle of Wight. Bird garden, grottoes, herb garden.
Open Easter to mid-Oct, daily, 10am–5.30pm; also evenings July & Aug. Admission 50p adults, 30p OAPs, 25p children/parties.
☎ (0983) 840242. &

Paultons Country Park and Bird Gardens
Ower, nr Romsey, Hampshire
Attractive gardens with superb cedars are the setting for aviaries and ponds with many varieties of exotic birds and waterfowl. Ten-acre lake; 19th-century waterwheel; Village Life Museum.
Open all year, daily exc 25 Dec, 10am–7pm (last entry 5pm or 1 hr before dusk). Admission £2 adults, £1.70 OAPs, £1 children; parties by arrangement. No dogs.
☎ Southampton (0703) 814442. &

Red House Museum
Christchurch, Dorset
Museum contained in Georgian house with formal herb garden in courtyard and main garden containing old roses.
Open all year, Tue to Sat 10am–5pm, Sun 2pm–5pm. Admission 40p adults, 10p OAPs/children; school parties free by arrangement.
☎ (0202) 482860. &

Seafront Gardens and Canoe Lake
Southsea, Hampshire
One mile of parks and gardens with floral displays and colour all the year round; Castle Gardens and splendid floral clock. Canoe Lake has 2-acre rose garden with circular pergola; formal floral displays; wide views over Solent.
Open all year, daily, dawn to dusk. Admission free.
☎ Portsmouth (0705) 834148. &

Spinners
Boldre, Lymington, Hampshire
Choice shrubs with primulas, blue poppies and other woodland and ground-cover plants. Rare plants for sale.
Open 21 Apr to 1 Sept, daily exc Mon, 10am–6pm. Nursery open all year. Admission 75p. No dogs.
☎ (0590) 73347.

Stansted Park
Rowland's Castle, nr Havant, Hampshire
Home of the Earl and Countess of Bessborough, Stansted House in its magnificent forest setting, offers the visitor a walled garden, arboretum, chapel and theatre museum.
Open 4 May to 30 Sept, Sun, Mon, Tue, 2pm–6pm, last entry 5.30pm. Admission: Garden £1 adults, 80p children, 50p children; House & Garden £1.60 adults, £1.20 OAPs, 80p children; parties £1.20 & 60p. No dogs.
☎ (070 541) 2265. &

Stratfield Saye House
Between Reading and Basingstoke on Berkshire/Hampshire border
Off A33. Home of the Dukes of Wellington; extensive grounds include American, rose and walled gardens, and wildfowl sanctuary. Exhibition.
Open 1 May to 29 Sept, daily exc Fri, 11.30am–5pm; also 29 to 31 Mar, Sat & Sun in Apr. Admission £2.50 adults, £1.65 OAPs/disabled (Tue only), £1.25 children; parties £2.20 & £1.10.
☎ Wellington Office (0256) 882882. &

Tudor House Garden
Southampton, Hampshire
Half-timbered, 16th-century house now a museum, with gardens formally laid out in Elizabethan style, featuring Tudor knot garden.
Open all year, daily exc Mon; Tue to Fri 10am–5pm, Sat 10am–4pm, Sun 2pm–5pm. Admission free. No dogs.
☎ (0703) 224216. &

Upton Country Park
Poole, Dorset
55 acres of parkland garden and meadow on the northern shore of Poole Harbour. Traditional small country estate. Small collection of farm animals. Heather garden, small lake, herbaceous, camellia and rose borders.
Open all year, daily, 9am–dusk. Admission free.
☎ (0202) 676164 ext. 217. &

Ventnor Botanic Garden
Ventnor, Isle of Wight
Most recently founded botanic gardens with fine range of exotic shrubs; museum of smuggling; adventure playground; gift shop; licensed restaurant; Garden Tavern; car park in grounds.
Open all year, daily, dawn–dusk; Museum open Easter to Sept, 10am–5pm. Admission free.
☎ (0983) 852501. &

The Vyne
Sherborne St John, nr Basingstoke, Hampshire
Extensive lawns, herbaceous borders and spectacular lake; historic mansion originally built by Henry VIII's Lord Chamberlain, William Sandys.
Open 29 Mar to 19 Oct, daily exc Mon & Fri, 2pm–6pm (last entry 5.30pm). Open Bank Hol Mon (but closed Tue following) 11am–6pm. Admission 80p adults, 40p children. No dogs.
☎ (0256) 881337. &

West Green House
Hartley Wintney, Hampshire
Small early 18th-century house of great charm in a delightful garden.
Garden open Apr to end Sept, Wed, Thur, Sun, 2pm–6pm. Admission 80p adults, 40p children. No dogs.
☎ Bookham (0372) 53401. NT

Gilbert White Museum
Selborne, nr Alton, Hampshire
Garden of 18th-century naturalist Gilbert White, including original ha-ha, section of his fruit wall, a wild garden, water garden, old-fashioned rose garden and garden of annuals. New herb garden and new garden guide book. Reconstructed bird hide. Museum. See also advertisement on page 109.
Open 1 Mar to 31 Oct, Tue to Sun, 12 noon–5.30pm (last entry 5pm); also Bank Hol Mon. Admission 90p adults, 70p OAPs, 45p children; party reduction. No dogs exc guide dogs.
☎ (042 050) 275. &

TUDOR HOUSE MUSEUM

Fountain in the Tudor Garden, Southampton. Enclosed within medieval walls the Tudor Garden is laid out with raised beds, a knot bed, herber and heraldic posts. In summer bees from the skep in the adjacent secret garden gather pollen from the assortment of aromatic herbs.
Entrance to the garden is through Tudor House Museum, St Michael's Square, Southampton, telephone 0703 224216.
Opening hours: Tuesday to Friday 10.00am–5.00pm, Saturday 10.00am–4.00pm, Sunday 2.00–5pm. Entrance free.

A Guide to English Gardens

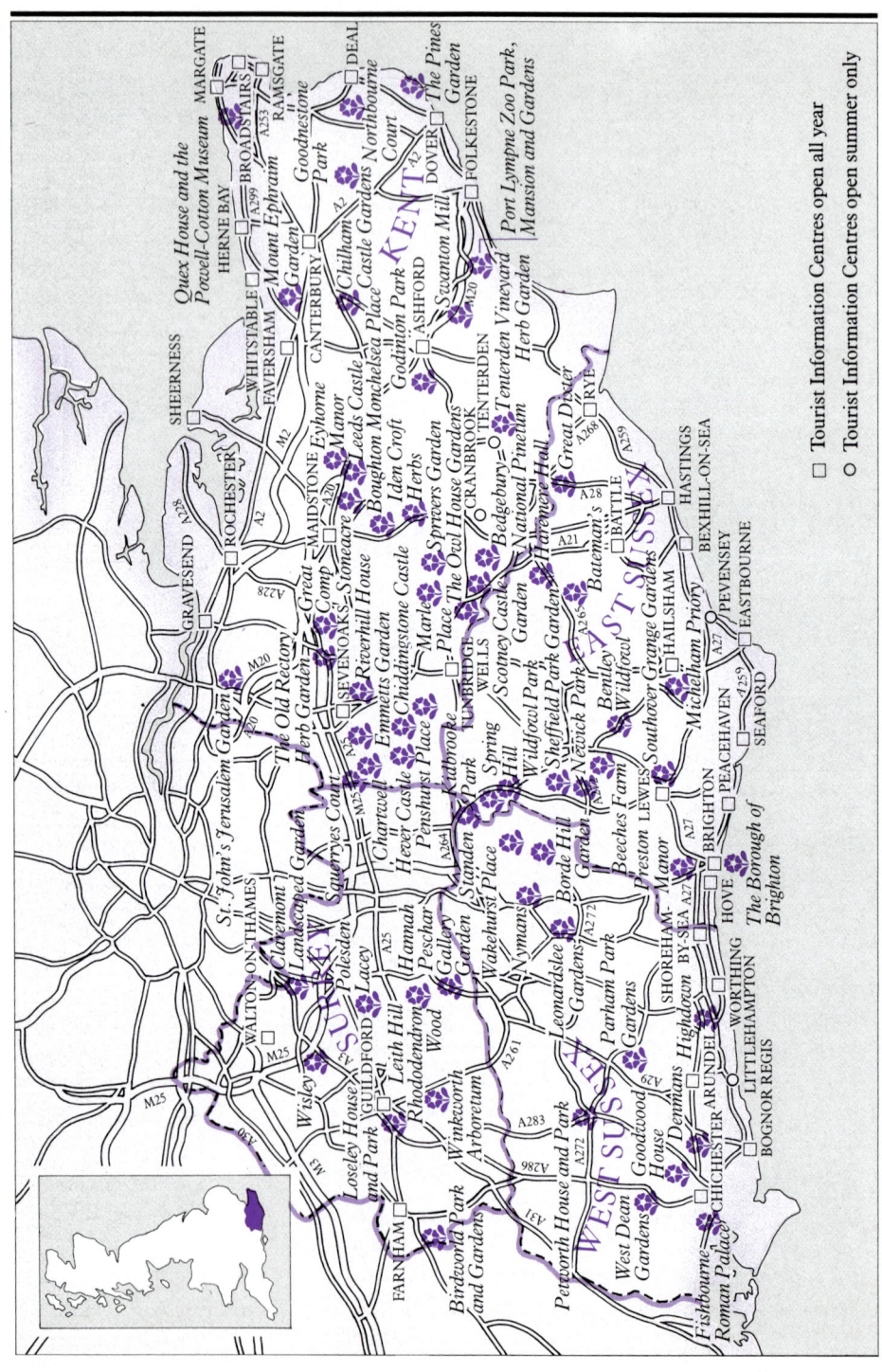

SOUTH EAST

SOUTH EAST

Claremont, Nymans, Sheffield Park, Bedgebury, Wakehurst and Wisley – the names are straight from the parks' and gardens' Roll of Honour. Claremont owes its landscaped gardens to the successive work of Vanbrugh, Kent and Brown; Nymans is a glorious collection of both formal and informal displays from roses to rock gardens; Sheffield Park on London's doorstep represents a marvellous marriage of lakes, trees and shrubs; Bedgebury makes a beautiful site for our National Pinetum, Wakehurst has been described as 'the plantsman's paradise' and the Royal Horticultural Society's gardens at Wisley need no introduction as the place where every aspect of gardening is on show. But don't be dazzled by the big names; dotted around the downs and Weald and holiday coast are others, just as rewarding in a variety of ways. The region which includes the Garden of England itself certainly deserves its title, with gardening grandeur at Parham, Penshurst and Petworth and a host of other places of equal grace and beauty. You can roam the grounds of Churchill's old home at Chartwell, visit Kipling's house at Bateman's or the boyhood home of diarist John Evelyn at Southover Grange. There are lovely, moated gardens in fairy-tale settings like Hever, Scotney and Leeds Castles. You can visit a vineyard near Tenterden, a chalk-pit garden at Highdown, the physic garden of a medieval monastery at Michelham Priory or a smuggler's cottage and garden at picturesque Lamberhurst (Owl House) – and then perhaps you might like to see a mill working in water gardens at Mersham or the reconstruction of a Roman garden at Fishbourne's Roman Palace. The South East rewards its autumn visitors with a brilliant exhibition of woodland colours. Trees are amongst its finest features, on show in particular at Borde Hill, Polesden Lacey, Quex House and others, and at their most stunning on hillside sites like the Winkworth Arboretum which combines a fine collection of deciduous trees with exhilarating views over the downs.

SEPTEMBER

September is a special month in the garden, when for a time summer and autumn go hand in hand. Summer's representatives are still very varied – asters, pelargoniums, gladioli and many more, but the flower that dominates is the dahlia. Pink or purple, dwarf or giant, Blithe Spirit, Fascination, Preference and others offer the rewarding range of shape, size and colour which makes dahlias such firm favourites for decorating houses and gardens alike. But now autumn starts to work its magic on trees and shrubs; purple clematis jackmanii and pale pink 'naked boys' come into flower, while around them leaves begin to 'turn' in earnest. Prunus, whitebeam, mountain ash and rowan join viburnum and the deciduous azalea amongst the leaders in the colourful race for autumn glory.

Dahlia

FRUIT BLOSSOM

Every year, in April and May, the Garden of England stages its spectacular spring show when whole orchards of apple, pear, cherry and plum trees are submerged under a frivolous sea of blossom. Plum trees take the stage first in March, but by April the others too are awash with flowers – white for the pears and cherries, delicate pink for the apples and a splash of darker pink from the ornamental flowering cherries. The blossom means that good things are on their way: cherries from the end of July, apples from the end of August, and pears from the end of September. The AA's special Blossom Route shows off the Kentish orchards at their best, while at Wisley Gardens, 600 different varieties of apple trees put on a rival show of their own.

Apple Tree

For more information contact the
South East England Tourist Board,
1 Warwick Park, Tunbridge Wells,
Kent TN2 5TA ☎ (0892) 40766.

SOUTH EAST

Bateman's
Burwash, East Sussex
Rudyard Kipling's house and garden, built 1634. Attractive garden, yew hedges, lawns, daffodils. Restored water-mill.
Open 28 Mar to 31 Oct, daily exc Thur & Fri (open Good Fri), 11am–6pm (last admission 5.30pm). Admission £2 adults, £1 children; parties £1.50 & £1. No dogs.
☎ (0435) 882302. NT ※ &

Bedgebury National Pinetum
nr Goudhurst, Kent
160 acres of trees, including the most comprehensive collection of conifers in Europe, planted round an old hammer pond.
Open all year, daily, 10am–8pm or dusk. Admission 60p adults, 30p children.
☎ (0850) 211392.

Beeches Farm
Buckham Hill, nr Uckfield, East Sussex
On Isfield road. 16th-century tile-hung farmhouse with lawns, yew trees, borders, sunken garden, roses and fine views.
Open all year, daily, 10am–5pm or dusk. Admission 25p adults, 15p children; House (by appt) 75p extra.
☎ (0825) 2391.

Bentley Wildfowl
Halland, nr Lewes, East Sussex
Tudor house set in extensive grounds with formal gardens, including walled gardens separated by yew hedges; woodland walk. Extensive wildfowl collection; Motor Museum.
Open 24 Apr to end Sept, daily; Apr, May, Sept 11am–4.30pm, June, July, Aug, Sun & Bank Hols 10am–5pm (House opens 1pm); Grounds also open weekends, Oct to Dec, Feb & Mar. Admission £2 adults, £1.40 OAPs, £1 children; discounts for parties. No dogs.
☎ (082 584) 573. &

Birdworld Park and Gardens
Holt Pound, nr Farnham, Surrey
Exotic birds amongst 17 acres of landscaped parkland and gardens. Many beautiful shrubs and trees. New rose garden. Thousands of bulbs in the spring, bedding plants in the summer with many superb hanging baskets.
Open all year, daily exc 25 Dec, 9.30am–6pm or 1hr before dusk. Admission £1.50 adults, £1.30 OAPs (exc Sun & Bank Hols), 95p children; parties of 20+ £1.10 & 80p. No dogs.
☎ Bentley (0420) 22140. &

Hever Castle, Kent

Borde Hill Garden
Haywards Heath, West Sussex
Large garden with woods and parkland containing unique collection of rhododendrons and many rare trees and shrubs of great botanical interest. A garden to visit at all seasons.
Open Mar, Sat, Sun & Good Fri; Apr to Sept, daily exc Fri & Mon (open Bank Hol Mon), Oct, Sat, Sun; 10am–6pm. Admission £1.50 adults, 50p children; £1 parties 20+.
☎ (0444) 450326. &

The Borough of Brighton
Brighton, East Sussex
The Regency town of Brighton has many colourful parks and gardens amid tree-lined streets and squares, including Preston Park, which celebrated its centenary in 1984, and 38-acre Withdean Park, which has the National Collection of Lilacs.
Open all year, daily, dawn to dusk. Admission free.
☎ Parks Dept (0273) 602271. &

Boughton Monchelsea Place
nr Maidstone, Kent
Elizabethan and Regency manor house with gardens planned in 1818; walled gardens, unusual plants; breathtaking views of landscaped deer park and Kentish Weald.
Open 28 Mar to mid-Oct, Sat, Sun, Bank Hol Mon (also Wed in July & Aug), 2.15pm–6pm. Admission: House & Gardens £1.40 adults, 75p children, £1.10 OAPs/parties; Gardens only 70p adults, 45p children.
☎ (0622) 43120. &

Chartwell
nr Westerham, Kent
Famous former home of Sir Winston Churchill with notable garden including lakes, wide variety of trees and flowers, the wall Sir Winston built himself, his garden Studio, and the Golden Rose Walk commemorating the Churchills' Golden Wedding.
Open 29 Mar to 30 Oct, Tue, Wed, Thur, 12 noon–5pm; Sat, Sun & Bank Hol Mon, 11am–5pm. Admission: House & Garden £2.40 adults, £1.20 children; Garden only £1 adults, 50p children.
☎ Edenbridge (0732) 866368. NT ※

Chiddingstone Castle
nr Edenbridge, Kent
17th/18th-century house with 18th-century landscaped grounds being restored; orangery and gazebo; spring daffodils.
Open end Mar to end Sept, Wed to Sat, also Tue mid-June to mid-Sept, 2pm–5.30pm; also Sat, Sun Oct; Sun & Bank Hols 11.30am–5.30pm. Admission £1.50 adults, 85p children; parties of 20+ by arrangement. No dogs.
☎ Penshurst (0892) 870347. &

Chilham Castle Gardens
Chilham, nr Canterbury, Kent
Beautiful grounds with terraced gardens, lake and Petland; falconry displays, Medieval Jousting on Suns and Bank Hol weekends.
Open 16 Mar to 26 Oct, daily, 11am–5pm. Admission (1985 prices) £1.70 adults, 80p children (weekends/Bank Hols extra); parties on application.
☎ (0227) 730319.

SUTTON PLACE
near Guildford, Surrey

Magnificent garden recently landscaped by Sir Geoffrey Jellicoe. Features include Paradise Garden, Secret Garden, Surreal Garden and Ben Nicholson Wall.

Seven Garden Open Days during Spring and Summer, or may be seen on guided tours throughout the year.

For full details and bookings: Tel. Bookings Manager, Guildford (0483) 504455. 10am–4pm, weekdays.

A Guide to English Gardens

SOUTH EAST

Claremont Landscaped Garden
Esher, Surrey
The earliest surviving English landscape garden, recently restored; lake, grotto, viewpoints, avenues and magnificent turf amphitheatre.
Open all year, daily exc 25 Dec & 1 Jan: Easter to end Oct, 9am–7pm or dusk; Nov to end Mar, 9am–4pm; last entry ½ hour before closing. Admission 70p adults, 35p children.
☎ *Bookham (0372) 53401. NT* ※ & *(part).*

Denmans
Fontwell, nr Arundel, West Sussex
Walled gardens extravagantly planted for all-year interest in form, colour and texture. School of Garden Design in adjacent Clock House.
Open 31 Mar to 31 Oct, Wed to Sun; also Bank Hol Mons, 1pm–6pm. Admission £1.50 adults, £1.40 OAPs, 75p children; parties of 30+ £1.40. No dogs.
☎ *Eastergate (024 368) 2808.* &

Emmetts Garden
Ide Hill, Sevenoaks, Kent
Five-acre hillside garden, one of the highest gardens in Kent, noted for its fine collection of rare trees and shrubs. Lovely spring and autumn colours; additional parts of garden now open and restoration work in progress.
Open 28 Mar to 31 Oct, Tue to Fri, Sun, Bank Hol Mon 2pm–6pm (last entry 5pm). Admission £1 adults, 50p children.
☎ *Lamberhurst (0892) 890651. NT* ※ &

Eyhorne Manor
Hollingbourne, Kent
Outstanding early-15th-century manor house with intimate garden specialising in herbs and old-fashioned roses.
Open 3 May to 31 Aug, Sat & Sun; also Tue to Thur in Aug, & Bank Hols; 2pm–6pm. Admission £1.10 adults, 60p children.
☎ *(062 780) 514.*

Fishbourne Roman Palace
Fishbourne, nr Chichester, West Sussex
Roman garden reconstructed as realistically as possible. Courtyard garden, terrace and herb garden.
Open Mar to Nov, daily; Sun only, Dec to Feb; 10am–6pm or dusk. Admission £1.30 adults, £1 OAPs/students, 60p children; parties of 20+ £1. No dogs.
☎ *(0243) 785859.* &

Godinton Park
Ashford, Kent
Jacobean house set in gardens originally laid out in 18th century and improved and extended in 19th century. Topiary work and formal gardens.
Open June to Sept, Sun & Bank Hols; also 31 Mar & 26 May, 2pm–5pm. Admission: House & Garden £1.20 adults, 60p children; parties of 20+ £1; Gardens only 60p.
☎ *(0233) 20773.*

Goodnestone Park
nr Canterbury, Kent
Large garden with fine trees and good views. Old walled rose garden. Connections with Jane Austen, who stayed here.
Open 13 Apr to 10 July, Sun to Thur (closed Suns 4, 11 & 18 May, 10 July); 2pm–6pm. Admission 80p adults, 10p children; parties of 30+ 50p. No dogs.
☎ *Nonington (0304) 840218.* &

Goodwood House
Goodwood, Chichester, West Sussex
House set in beautiful parkland with specimen trees, including Lebanon Cedars and Cork trees.
Park open all year, daily; House open 4 May to 6 Oct, Sun & Mon (exc 9, 22 June, 29 Sept), also 30 & 31 Mar, Tue, Wed, Thur in Aug; closed event days. Admission free.
☎ *(0243) 774107.* &

Great Comp
Borough Green, nr Sevenoaks, Kent
Lovely 7-acre garden designed, constructed and until recently maintained by owners; wide variety of shrubs, trees, heathers and herbaceous plants.
Open 1 Apr to 31 Oct, daily, 11am–6pm. Admission £1.20 adults, 60p children; parties £1.20. No dogs.
☎ *(0732) 882669.* &

Great Dixter
Northiam, East Sussex
Medieval Hall house restored by Lutyens, who designed the gardens. Wide variety of plants; topiary; sunken garden with lily pond and flowering meadows; unusual plants for sale.
Open 1 Apr to 12 Oct, plus 18/19 & 25/26 Oct, Tue to Sun, Bank Hol Mon, 2pm–5pm (last entry). Open 11am 25/26 May, Suns in July & Aug and 25 Aug. Admission £1 adults, 25p children. House extra. No dogs.
☎ *(079 74) 3160.*

Hannah Peschar Gallery Garden
Ockley, Surrey
Natural water garden with a variety of work on display by contemporary British and foreign sculptors against a background of large leaved plants.
Open 1 June to 31 Oct, Fri & Sat 11am–6pm, Sun 2pm–5pm; also Tue & Thur by appt. Admission £1 adults, 50p children.
☎ *Oakwood (030 679) 677.* &

Haremere Hall
Etchingham, East Sussex
Delightful formal and kitchen garden of historic Haremare Hall. Spring bulbs, herb garden and formal rose garden all set in 500 acres of parkland.
Open Easter to 31 Oct, daily exc Mon (open Bank Hol Mons), 10am–5pm. House open Sun & Bank Hol Mon. Admission 70p, House extra. No dogs.
☎ *(0580 81) 245.*

Hever Castle
nr Edenbridge, Kent
13th-century moated castle with Italian-style garden, rose garden, topiary and herb garden, maze and lake set in beautiful grounds.
Open 28 Mar to 2 Nov, daily exc 11 June, 11am–6pm (last entry 5pm). Admission: Castle & Garden £3 adults, £1.50 children; parties £2.50 & £1.25; Gardens only £1.75 adults, 90p children; parties £1.45 & 75p.
☎ *(0732) 865224.* &

Highdown
nr Worthing, West Sussex
Gardens laid out in chalk pit on Highdown Hill, with rock plants, flowering shrubs, daffodils; excellent views.
Open 1 Apr to 30 Sept, Mon to Fri 9am–4.30pm, Sat, Sun 10am–8pm; 1 Oct to 31 Mar, Mon to Fri, 10am–4.30pm. Admission free.
☎ *(0903) 501054.*

Iden Croft Herbs
Staplehurst, Kent
Herb farm specializing in fragrant, culinary, decorative and medicinal herbs. Traditional and modern gardens illustrating a fresh approach to planting for colour and design. Aromatic garden for visually handicapped. National Origanum collection. Pot plants and herb products for sale.
Open all year, Mon to Sat (closed 25, 26 Dec, 1 Jan); 9am–5pm; also open Sun, 31 Mar to 30 Sept, 11am–5pm. Admission free; charity collection box.
☎ *(0580) 891432.* &

Kidbrooke Park
Forest Row, East Sussex
18th-century mansion with attractive water gardens and park landscaped by Humphry Repton.
Open 1 to 31 Aug, daily, 10am–5pm. Admission 30p. Ground floor of House open by appt.
☎ *(034 282) 2275.* &

Leeds Castle
nr Maidstone, Kent
Fairytale medieval castle built in middle of lake in 500 acres of landscaped parkland. Water and woodland gardens. Culpeper Flower Garden; Greenhouses; Vineyard; Maze; Duckery and Aviary.
Open 28 Mar to 31 Oct, daily, 11am–5pm; Nov to Mar, Sat & Sun, 12 noon–4pm. Admission: Castle & Grounds £3.65 adults, £3.15 OAPs/students, £2.65 children; Grounds only £2.65 adults, £2.15 OAPs/students, £1.65 children; parties by arrangement. No dogs.
☎ *(0622) 65400.* &

Leith Hill Rhododendron Wood
Leith Hill, Dorking, Surrey
Wooded gardens, with azaleas and rhododendrons. Best viewed in late spring.
Open all year, daily. Admission by donation.
☎ *Bookham (0372) 53401. NT* ※

73

SOUTH EAST

Leonardslee Gardens
Lower Beeding, Horsham, West Sussex
Renowned valley garden; camellias, magnolias, rhododendrons and azaleas; lakes and streams. Herd of wallabies.
Open 19 May to 15 June, daily, 10am–6pm; 21 June to 28 Sept, Sat & Sun, 2pm–6pm; also Sat & Sun in Oct for Autumn tints; 10am–5pm. Admission £1.50 adults (£2.20 in May), £1 children; parties £1.20 (£1.80 in May). No dogs.
☎ (040 376) 212.

Loseley House and Park
nr Guildford, Surrey
Elizabethan house set in glorious parkland with old mulberry tree and moat walk by Edwin Lutyens and Gertrude Jekyll.
Open 26 May to 27 Sept, Wed, Thur, Fri, Sat, 2pm–5pm; also Summer Bank Hol Mon, 2pm–5pm. Admission £1.60 adults, £1.40 OAPs (Fri only), 90p children; parties of 20+ £1.40. No dogs.
☎ (0483) 571881. &

Marle Place
Brenchley, Kent
Herb garden and nursery featuring Victorian rockery planted with wide range of named herbs. Container-grown herbs and shrubs for sale.
Open 1 Apr–1 Oct, daily exc Sun, 11am–4pm. Admission £1.50 for coach parties; otherwise free. No dogs.
☎ (089 272) 2304.

Michelham Priory
Upper Dicker, Hailsham, East Sussex
Augustinian Priory with extensive grounds; roses, fine specimen trees including English hardwoods, herbaceous border, and 'Physic' garden with plants as used in medieval monastery.
Open 25 Mar to 31 Oct, daily, 11am–5.30pm. Admission £1.50 adults, 70p children; £1.30 parties 20+, by appt. No dogs.
☎ (0323) 844224. &

Mount Ephraim Garden
Hernhill, nr Faversham, Kent
Terraced garden with beautiful views, leading to small lake. Herbaceous border, topiary, Japanese rock garden. Rhododendrons, fine trees and a wide variety of plants and shrubs.

Open 1 May to 14 Sept, Sun & Bank Hols only, 2pm–6pm. Admission £1 adults, 25p children, 80p parties.
☎ Canterbury (0227) 751496.

Newick Park
nr Newick, East Sussex
Wild shrub garden featuring rhododendrons and azaleas, herb and wild flower plant nursery, daffodils, bluebells, primulas; fine trees, snowdrop wood, Farmland walk.
Open Mar–end Oct, Fri, Sat, Sun, Mon, 2pm–5.30pm. Admission £1 adults, 50p children, 75p parties of 4+.
☎ (082 572) 2915. &

Northbourne Court
nr Deal, Kent
Lovely brick terraces of earlier mansion, set with wide range of shrubs and plants on chalk soil; geraniums, fuchsias and grey-leaved plants. Elizabethan Great Barn. Plants for sale when available.
Open June to Aug, Wed, 2pm–5pm; also Suns 25 May, 22 & 29 June, 13 & 20 July, 24 Aug, 14 Sept, 2pm–6pm. Admission £1 adults, 50p OAPs/children; parties 80p & 40p.
☎ (0304) 360813.

Nymans
Handcross, West Sussex
Lovely garden with world-wide collection of trees, shrubs, plants; picturesque ruins overlook lawns, topiary and fine cedars.
Open 29 Mar to end Oct, daily exc Mon & Fri (open Bank Hol Mon), 11am–7pm or sunset. Last entry 1 hr before closing. Admission £1.30 adults, 65p children, 90p parties. No dogs.
☎ (0444) 400321. NT ⚲ &

The Old Rectory Herb Garden
Ightham, Kent
Herb garden and nursery with dried herbs and plants for sale.
Open all year, daily exc Sun & 25/26 Dec, 1 Jan; Mon to Fri 9am–4pm, Sat 9am–12 noon. Admission free. No dogs.
☎ Sevenoaks (0732) 882608. &

The Owl House Gardens
Lamberhurst, Kent
13 acres of romantic walks, spring flowers, rare flowering shrubs and ornamental fruit trees surrounding 16th-century 'Owlers' or Smuggler's cottage. Expansive lawns lead to a woodland of oak, birch and informal sunken water gardens.
Open all year, daily, 11am–6pm. Admission £1 adults, 50p children.
☎ (01) 235 1432. &

Parham Park Gardens
Pulborough, West Sussex
Fine gardens of Elizabethan mansion including 4-acre walled garden with herbaceous borders, re-designed by Peter Caots in the modern manner. Seven-acre 18th-century garden, with fine trees, statuary, lake and Church. Children's play area; tea room.
Open 30 Mar to 5 Oct, Sun, Wed, Thur, Bank Hol Mon, 1pm–6pm (House 2pm–6pm), last entry 5.30pm. Admission: House & Gardens £2.50 adults, £2 OAPs, £1.50 children, £2 parties; Gardens only £1 adults, 75p children.
☎ Storrington (090 66) 2866/2021. &

Penshurst Place
Penshurst, Kent
Magnificent medieval manor house set in a lovely 10-acre walled garden with hedged enclosures (a Tudor legacy); home park with delightful walks.
Open 28 Mar to 5 Oct, daily exc Mon (open Bank Hol Mons), 12.30am–6pm.
Admission (1985 prices) £2.40 adults, £2 OAPs/ parties, £1.10 children; Park & Gardens only £1.65, £1.30 & 80p. No dogs.
☎ (0892) 870307. &

Petworth House and Park
Petworth, West Sussex
Petworth House overlooks 700-acre deer park, landscaped by 'Capability' Brown; pleasure grounds.
Park open all year, daily, 9am–dusk. House & Pleasure Grounds 29 Mar to end Oct, daily exc Mon & Fri, 2pm–6pm (last entry 5.30pm)—open Bank Hol Mon but closed Tue following. Admission £2 adults, £2.50 on Tues; children half-price, parties £1.50 (Wed, Thur, Sat); Park free.
☎ (0798) 42207. NT ⚲ & (part).

The Pines Garden
St Margaret's Bay, nr Dover, Kent
Lovely 6½-acre garden. Specimen shrubs and trees. Lake, waterfall and bog garden. Statue of Sir Winston Churchill and other items of interest.
Open all year, daily; summer 9am–7pm, winter 9am–5pm, weather permitting. Admission 50p adults, 30p children/OAPs; parties by arrangement. &

Polesden Lacey
nr Dorking, Surrey
30 acres of wooded grounds, lawns and informal gardens surrounding a delightful mansion; detailed garden guide identifies species. Views from Sheridan's Walk, designed by Sheridan the playwright, a former owner.

PARHAM PARK, HOUSE & GARDENS,
Pulborough, West Sussex

(A.283 Storrington – Pulborough Road)
Fine Gardens of Elizabethan Mansion
Children's playground, picnic area and tea room.
Open Wednesdays, Thursdays, Sundays and Bank Holidays 1pm–6pm
(House open 2pm) Easter to first Sunday in October.
Telephone Storrington 2021

SOUTH EAST

Garden open all year, daily, 11am–dusk. House 28 Mar to end Oct, Wed to .Sun, 2pm–6pm (open Bank Hol Mon & preceding Sun, 11am–6pm); also open weekends, Mar & Nov, 2pm–5pm). Admission: Garden £1 adults; House £1 extra; children half-price; parties £1.50. No dogs.
☎ *Bookham (0372) 58203/52048.*
NT ※ & *(part).*

Port Lympne Zoo Park, Mansion and Gardens
Lympne, nr Hythe, Kent
Important zoo park; interesting house with 15 acres of spectacular gardens; grand stairway; magnolia walk; 100yd herbaceous border, chessboard and striped gardens; vineyard, fig yard.
Open all year, daily exc 25 Dec, 10am–5pm (or 1 hour before dusk). Admission £3 adults, £2 children/OAPs; parties of 20+ £2.50 & £1.50. No dogs.
☎ *(0303) 64646.*

Preston Manor
Preston Park, Brighton, East Sussex
Georgian house with 1905 additions; garden in late-Victorian/Edwardian layout, 'old-fashioned' walled garden.
Garden open all year, daily; dawn to dusk. Manor open all year exc 28 Mar, 25/26 Dec, Tue to Sun; also Bank Hol Mon, 10am–5pm (closed 1pm–2pm Tue & Sun). Admission: Garden free; House (1985 prices) 85p adults, 70p OAPs, 50p children, 80p parties. No dogs.
☎ *(0273) 603005 ext 59.*

Quex House and The Powell-Cotton Museum
Quex Park, Birchington, Kent
Peaceful gardens in 200 acres of park and woodland with extensive lawns and mature native and exotic trees and shrubs. Ancient wisteria and fruiting figs, roses and carpets of bulbs, sunken lawn and pool.
Open Apr–Sept, Wed, Thur, Sun, Bank Hol Mon; also Fri in Aug; 2.15pm–6pm. Admission 80p adults, 50p children/OAPs; parties by arrangement. No dogs.
☎ *Thanet (0843) 42168.* &

Riverhill House
Sevenoaks, Kent
Small country house and gardens. Fine collection of mature trees. Sheltered terraces with shrubs and roses. Azaleas and rhododendrons. Picnics allowed.
Open 30 Mar to 1 Sept, Mon, also Suns in Apr, May & June, 12 noon–6pm. Admission £1 adults, 30p children; parties on application. No dogs.
☎ *(0732) 452557/458802.*

St John's Jerusalem Garden
Dartford, Kent
Large and beautiful garden moated by the River Darent, with borders bright in spring and summer with bulbs, herbaceous plants, dahlias and buddleias.
Open Apr to Oct, Wed, 2pm–6pm. Admission 40p. No dogs.
☎ *Lamberhurst (0892) 890651.*
NT ※ &

Scotney Castle Garden
Lamberhurst, Tunbridge Wells, Kent
Ruins of a 14th-century moated castle, situated in one of England's most romantic garden landscapes.
Open 29 Mar to 16 Nov, Wed to Fri, 11am–6pm or dusk, Sat, Sun, Bank Hol Mon 2pm–6pm or dusk (last entry ½hr before closing); Old Castle open 1 May–26 Aug. Admission £1.80 adults, 90p children, parties £1.40 & 90p. No dogs.
☎ *(0892) 890615.* NT ※

Sheffield Park Garden
Uckfield, East Sussex
100-acre garden and five lakes laid out in 18th century by 'Capability' Brown; mature trees, rare shrubs and water lilies, beautiful at all times of the year; splendid autumn colours.
Open 29 Mar–9 Nov, Tue to Sat, 11am–6pm or dusk, Sun & Bank Hol Mon 2pm–6pm (last entry 1hr before closing), 1pm–dusk in Oct & Nov. Admission £1.90 adults (£2.50 May, Oct, Nov), £1 children (£1.30 May, Oct, Nov), £1.40 parties (£1.90 May, Oct, Nov). No dogs.
☎ *Danehill (0825) 790655.* NT ※ &

> BEFORE SETTING OUT it's always best to 'phone and check garden details. Opening times and prices may be subject to change at short notice!

JOHN ASPINALL INVITES YOU TO VISIT

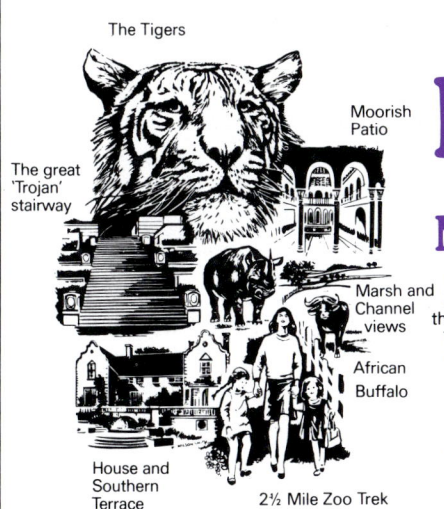

PORT LYMPNE
Zoo Park Mansion & Gardens

The Tigers
Moorish Patio
The great 'Trojan' stairway
Marsh and Channel views
African Buffalo
House and Southern Terrace
2½ Mile Zoo Trek

Roam free in 270 magnificent acres. Take the 2½ mile Zoo Trek through the lovely fields and woodlands. Visit the historic house with its Moorish Patio, the Rex Whistler Tent Room, the Octagonal Library, Wildlife Art Gallery & Museum. Marvel at the exquisite gardens and the great 'Trojan' stairway. Picnic, enjoy the glorious views, see the rare and beautiful animals. Safari Trailer.
Open every day except Christmas Day. Free car parking

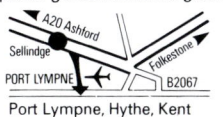

A20 Ashford — Sellindge — PORT LYMPNE — Folkestone — B2067

Port Lympne, Hythe, Kent
Tel: Hythe (0303) 64646

SOUTH EAST

Southover Grange Gardens
Lewes, East Sussex
Old-world Sussex gardens of 16th-century house, boyhood home of diarist John Evelyn. Magnificent old trees; colourful bedding displays.
Open all year, daily exc 25 Dec, 8am–dusk. Admission free. No dogs.
☎ (0273) 471600 ext 246. ⚙

Spring Hill Wildfowl Park
Forest Row, East Sussex
Fourteen acres in beautiful Ashdown Forest setting—ponds, shrubs and terraces. One of the largest and finest collections of wildfowl in the country. Picnic area.
Open all year, daily, 10am–6pm. Admission £1.60 adults, £1 OAPs, 80p children; parties of 12+ 10% reduction. No dogs.
☎ (034 282) 2783. ⚙

Sprivers Garden
Horsmonden, Kent
Garden with flowering and foliage shrubs, herbaceous borders, old walls, spring and summer bedding.
Open 7 May to 24 Sept, Wed, 2pm–5pm. Admission 70p adults, 35p children. No dogs.
☎ Brenchley (089 272) 3553/3008. NT ⚙

Squerryes Court
Westerham, Kent
William and Mary manor house with attractive landscaped gardens and lake. Fine display of spring bulbs, rhododendrons and azaleas. Home-made teas weekends.
Open Mar, Sun only; Apr to Sept, Wed, Sat, Sun, Bank Hol Mon, 2pm–6pm. Admission: House & Grounds £1.40 adults, 70p children; Grounds only 70p & 35p. Parties of 20+ (exc on Suns) by arrangement.
☎ (0959) 62345/63118. ⚙

Standen
East Grinstead, West Sussex
1890s house with 10½-acre hillside garden maintained in style of that period. Fine views across Medway Valley.
Open Apr to end Oct, Wed, Thur, Sat, Sun, 2pm–6pm (last entry 5.30pm). Closed Bank Hols. Admission: House & Garden £1.70 adults, £1.20 parties of 15+; Garden only 80p; children half-price.
☎ (0342) 23029. NT ⚙

Stoneacre
Otham, nr Maidstone, Kent
Mainly 15th-century manor house, with enclosed herb and Shakespeare garden, hosta/hellebore borders, white garden, terrace.
Open Apr to end Sept, Wed & Sat, 2pm–6pm. Admission £1.10 adults, 55p children. No dogs.
☎ (0622) 861861. NT ⚙

Swanton Mill
Mersham, Ashford, Kent
Working water-mill with 3-acre garden, including water, rose, herb and iris gardens.
Open Apr to end Oct, Sat & Sun, 3pm–6pm. Admission £1 adults, 50p children. No dogs.
☎ Aldington (0233) 223. ⚙

Tenterden Vineyard Herb Garden
Spots Farm, Smallhythe, nr Tenterden, Kent
Vineyard winery farm walk and large formal herb garden. Collection of over 400 different types of herbs. Very wide range of herb and wild flower plants for sale.
Open 3 May to 26 Oct, 10am–6pm. Admission £1 adults, children free; Guided tour for parties by arrangement.
☎ (058 06) 3033. ⚙

Wakehurst Place
Ardingly, West Sussex
Interesting large garden full of unusual plants and trees; run by Royal Botanic Gardens, Kew.
Open all year, daily exc 25 Dec & 1 Jan; Jan, Nov, Dec 10am–4pm; Feb, Oct 10am–5pm; Mar 10am–6pm; Apr to Sept 10am–7pm (last entry ½ hour before closing). Admission £1.50 adults, 60p children; parties £1 & 40p. No dogs.
☎ (0444) 892701. NT ⚙

West Dean Gardens
nr Chichester, West Sussex
35 acres of semi-formal gardens, with fine specimen trees; walled garden undergoing restoration. Teas available; garden shop.
Open 28 Mar to 30 Sept, daily, 11am–6pm. Admission £1 adults, 90p OAPs/students, 50p children; parties 75p. No dogs.
☎ Singleton (024 363) 301. ⚙

Winkworth Arboretum
Hascombe, nr Godalming, Surrey
Hillside woodland garden with many rare trees and shrubs; lovely walks by the lakes with superb views of the countryside.
Open all year, daily, dawn to dusk. Admission £1 adults, 40p children.
☎ (048 632) 379. NT ⚙

Wisley
nr Ripley, Surrey
World-famous Royal Horticultural Society's garden showing every aspect of gardening including garden for the disabled and small model gardens. Advisory service. Licensed restaurant/cafeteria, book/gift shop, plant centre. Large free car park, picnic area.
Open all year, daily exc 25 Dec, Mon to Sat 10am–7pm or dusk, Sun 2pm–7pm or dusk. Admission £1.80 adults, 90p children; parties £1.60 by arrangement. No dogs.
☎ Guildford (0483) 224163. ⚙

Kew in the country
The world famous gardens of
WAKEHURST PLACE, Ardingly
Enter via B2028, 1 mile north of village
Open all year
except New Year's Day & Christmas Day
Display of antique furniture in the Lady Price Room
Ardingly 892701

Have a lovely day out at – WISLEY GARDEN 'A garden for all seasons'
Open to the public Monday to Saturday from 10am and Sundays after 2pm. Every day of the year except Christmas Day.
Admission. Adults £1.80, Children 90p (Children under 6 years of age free)
Cost of parties of 20 or more paying in advance £1.60
Licensed Restaurant and Cafeteria, Plant Centre & Shop.
Large Free Car Park (Special concessions for coach drivers)
For full details write to The Director:
**THE ROYAL HORTICULTURAL SOCIETY'S GARDEN,
WISLEY, WOKING, SURREY GU23 6QB.** (on A3 London-Guildford).

THAMES & CHILTERNS

Splendid scenery in the Thames and Chilterns offers landscape gardeners nothing but the best to work with: a network of attractive rivers like the Thames, Evenlode, Cherwell, Windrush or the Great Ouse, broad fertile vales, the limestone Cotswolds or the chalky ridges of the Berkshire Downs and the beech-clad Chilterns. The years have produced houses and gardens worthy of their settings: Cliveden and Dorney Court on the Thames, Rousham on the Cherwell, and great estates like Blenheim, Stowe and Luton Hoo, fashioned from the spreading acres of the vales by the genius of masters like Capability Brown. The work has been going on for centuries – Stonor House dates from the 12th century, Broughton Castle from the 14th and ruined Minster Lovell Hall from the 15th, whilst in Hatfield House, Knebworth House and others we have some of the finest Tudor houses and gardens in the country. Everywhere work continues to restore some gardens to their rightful period – from medieval Chenies Manor with its physic garden and labyrinth to the Edwardian kitchen garden and orchard at Cogges Farm Museum – while others look to the future: Shinfield Grange and Capel Manor are just two of the region's centres of research, while the farm and gardens at Arkley Manor pre-empted the fashion for organic cultivation by 20 years! A wide variety of gardens boasts a wide variety of attractions: the romance of the Swiss Garden; the sheer splendour of the displays at the rose gardens in St. Albans and Nuneham Courtenay (John Mattock Rose Nurseries) or the rhododendrons at Ashridge; the spacious setting of the Savill Gardens in Windsor Great Park; the old world charm of Milton's Cottage garden; the all-the-year-round colour in Reading's Forbury Gardens; sculpture and a herd of Japanese Sika deer at Waddesdon Manor or the peace and quiet of Waterperry Gardens bordering the River Thame. Be it the Bekonscot village, the Burford animals or the Stagsden birds, every garden puts on a special show of its own.

OCTOBER

With autumn into its stride, gardens, hedgerows and woodlands erupt in a blaze of colour. Amongst the most exuberant are the maple and the sumach, whose decorative leaves produce a kaleidoscope of orange, red, purple and yellow, said to be at its most brilliant after a hot, dry summer. They have some stunning companions in the deciduous spindle tree, the bright scarlet nyssa, the amber and crimson parrotia, and in those trees such as the amelanchier or the maidenhair tree which favour the bronze and yellow tints. Many shrubs put on an equally startling display: the dogwood's foliage turns crimson, cotoneaster adpressa's leaves turn scarlet and whole buildings are aglow with colour when Virginia creepers lose their leaves in a spectacular shower of scarlet and orange.

Dogwood Cornus sanguinea

THE ROCK ROSE

The wild variety of this pretty, low-growing shrub can be found nestling amongst the grazed turf or rocky patches of the Chilterns, the Berkshire Downs and many of England's other chalky areas. Its Latin title is helianthemum, but our English name is misleading for it is not, in fact, related to the rose. Rock rose has no thorns, and it bears its yellow flowers in June and July. Many of its more cultivated relatives make very popular, long-lived garden plants, producing double or single flowers in white, pink, yellow, red and orange varieties. Though most keep close to the ground, some of the bushier sorts will grow up to a foot high.

Helianthemum polifolium

For more information contact the
Thames & Chilterns Tourist Board,
8 The Market Place, Abingdon,
Oxfordshire OX14 3UD
☎ (0235) 22711.

A Guide to English Gardens

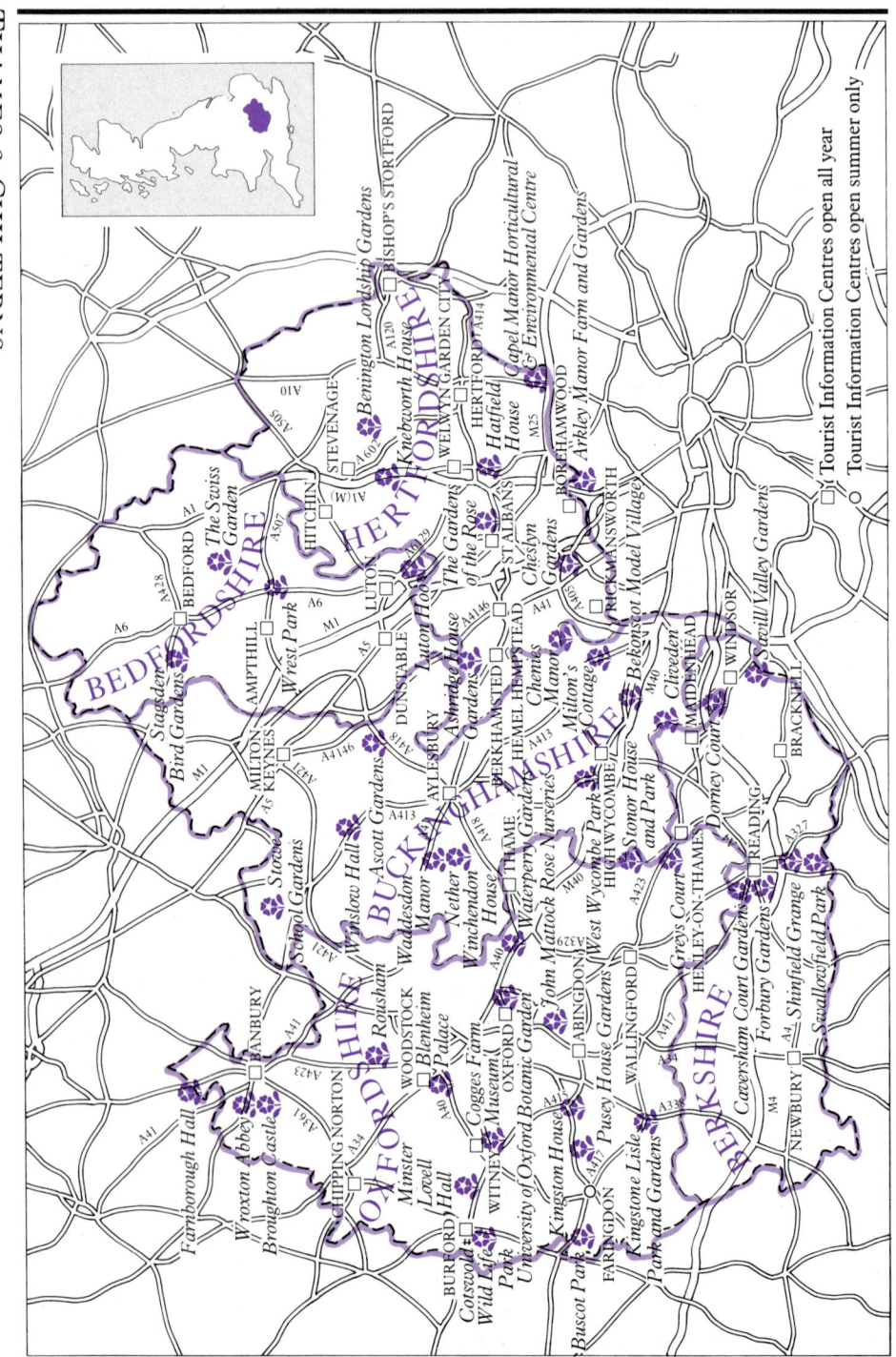

Thames & Chilterns

THAMES & CHILTERNS

Arkley Manor Farm and Gardens
Arkley, Barnet, Hertfordshire
'Organic' for the last 20 years; separate gardens of herbs, roses and ferns; weeping garden.
Open all year, Mon to Fri, 9.30am–5pm. Admission 50p adults, 25p OAPs/students/children; parties by arrangement.
☎ 01-449 7944.

Ascott Gardens
Wing, Buckinghamshire
12 acres of grounds with gardens containing unusual trees, flower borders, topiary sundial, flowering cherry.
House & Gardens open 22 July to 21 Sept, Tue to Sun, also 25 Aug, 2pm–6pm; Gardens also open Apr–28 Sept, Thur & last Sun in month, 2pm–6pm. Admission: House & Gardens £2 adults, £1.40 children; Gardens only £1.20 adults, 60p children. No dogs.
☎ (0296) 688242. NT

Ashridge House Gardens
nr Berkhamsted, Hertfordshire
Garden and house surrounded by woodlands; magnificent collection of rhododendrons; various small gardens; rose gardens.
Open Apr to Oct, Sat & Sun, 2pm–6pm. Admission £1 adults, 50p children; Gardens only 50p & 25p.
☎ Little Gaddesden (044 284) 3491.

Bekonscot Model Village
Beaconsfield, Buckinghamshire
Well laid-out rock gardens and miniature gardens with lakes and waterways, incorporating the oldest model village in the world.
Open 1 Mar to 31 Oct, daily, 10am–5pm. Admission £1 adults, 80p OAPs, students & unemployed, 60p children; parties 80p adults, 40p children.
☎ (049 46) 77486.

Benington Lordship Gardens
nr Stevenage, Hertfordshire
Beautiful mature garden on historic site; double herbaceous borders; rock and rose gardens.
Open 31 Mar; then 4 May to 3 Aug, Wed 11am–5pm, Sun, Bank Hol Mon 2pm–5pm. Admission £1 adults, 50p children. No dogs.
☎ Benington (043 885) 668.

Blenheim Palace
Woodstock, Oxfordshire
Famous house and gardens: water terraces and Italian garden; fine conifers and sweeping lawns; pleasure ground. Tropical butterfly house. Plant centre, garden café.
Open 15 Mar to 31 Oct, daily, 11am–6pm (last entry 5pm). Admission charges on application.
☎ (0993) 811325 or 812678.

Broughton Castle
Banbury, Oxfordshire
Moated Tudor mansion with early-14th-century nucleus; shrubs and herbaceous gardens.
Open 18 May to 14 Sept, Wed & Sun; also Thur, July & Aug, and Bank Hols (Sun &

Hatfield House, Hertfordshire

Mon); 2pm–5pm. Also open any day by appt. Admission £1.70 adults, £1.30 OAPs/students, 90p children; parties £1.30.
☎ (0295) 62624.

Buscot Park
nr Faringdon, Oxfordshire
House built 1780 with landscaped park and lake. Early-20th-century Italianate water gardens by Harold Peto. Attractive garden walks.
Open 1 Apr to 30 Sept, Wed, Thur, Fri; also 2nd & 4th Sat & Sun in each month, 2pm–5.30pm. Admission £1.60 adults, 80p children. No dogs.
☎ (0367) 20786. NT

Capel Manor Horticultural and Environmental Centre
Waltham Cross, Hertfordshire
Large garden in 36-acre estate. Comprehensive collection hardy and glasshouse plants; 17th-century garden, 'old-fashioned' roses, herbs, herbaceous and annual borders. Rock and water gardens. 5-acre 'Gardening from Which?' trials and demonstration garden.
Open all year, Mon to Fri, 10.30am–4.30pm; also Apr to Oct, Sat & Sun, 2pm–5.30pm, and special open weekends May to Oct. Admission (1985 prices) £1 adults (£1.25 special weekends), 50p OAPs/children (60p special weekends); parties by arrangement.
☎ Lea Valley (0992) 763849.

Caversham Court Gardens
Reading, Berkshire
Quiet riverside garden of historical interest, being the garden of the Old Rectory (now demolished), originally a 16th-century monastic priory. Interesting trees, herb garden, island, perennial beds.
Open all year, daily, Apr to Sept 7.30am–8pm; Sept to Mar 7.30am to dusk. Admission free.
☎ (0734) 477917.

Chenies Manor
Chenies, Buckinghamshire
Medieval manor with specially planted physic garden; sunken garden, white garden, 16th-century labyrinth, kitchen garden. Accent on old-world flowers and species roses.
Open 2 Apr to 29 Oct, Wed & Thur, 2pm–5pm; also 26 May & 25 Aug, 2pm–6pm. Admission: House & Gardens £1.50; Gardens only 75p; children half-price. No dogs.
☎ Little Chalfont (024 04) 2888.

Cheslyn Gardens
Watford, Hertfordshire
Two-acre garden consisting of woodland area, landscaped rockeries, waterfall, pond and aviary.
Open all year, daily exc Thur, 25 & 26 Dec, May to Sept 10am–8pm, Oct to Apr 10am–4pm. Admission free.
☎ (0923) 26400 ext 384.

Cliveden
nr Maidenhead, Berkshire
Extensive and historic gardens overlooking Thames; colourful flower borders and water garden.
Open Mar to Dec, daily, 11am–6pm or sunset. House open 3 Apr to end Oct, Thur & Sun, 3pm–6pm (last entry 5.30pm). Admission Grounds only £2 adults (£1.50 Mon exc Bank Hols, Tue, Wed), £1 children; House 60p adults, 30p children; party reduction. No dogs.
☎ Burnham (062 86) 5069. NT

Cogges Farm Museum
Cogges, Witney, Oxfordshire
Medieval farm, with walled kitchen garden and orchard being restored to its Edwardian appearance.
Open 29 Apr to 26 Oct, daily exc Mon (open Bank Hol Mon) 10.30am–5.30pm. Admission £1.50 adults, 80p children, OAPs & students; parties of 10+ £1.20 & 60p.
☎ (0993) 72602.

79

Cotswold Wild Life Park
Burford, Oxfordshire
200-acre, open-plan landscaped zoological park. Beautiful setting of gardens and woodland, centred on old manor house.
Open all year, daily, 10am–6pm or dusk. Admission £2.20 adults, £1.30 OAPs/children; parties of 20+ £1.90 & £1.10.
☎ (099 382) 3006. ♿

Dorney Court
Dorney, nr Windsor, Berkshire
Impressive Tudor manor house with gardens noted for the yew hedges, trees and colourful flowers.
Open 28 to 31 Mar, then June to Sept, Sun, Mon, Tue; also 5 & 12 Oct, 2pm–5.30pm. Admission £2 adults, £1 children; parties by arrangement. No dogs.
☎ Burnham (062 86) 4638.

Farnborough Hall
nr Banbury, Oxfordshire
Interesting house and grass terrace walk with temples and fine views.
Open Apr to Sept, Wed, Sat, also 4 & 5 May, 2pm–6pm. Terrace Walk only, Thur, Fri, Sun, 2pm–6pm. Admission £1.50 adults, £1.20 children. Gardens only 80p & 60p.
☎ (029 589) 202. NT ♿

Forbury Gardens
Reading, Berkshire
19th-century gardens with 50,000 bedding plants giving colour all the year round; cornus tree, snowdrops and crocuses, daffodils and tulips, magnolias, herbaceous plants, roses and dahlias. Heather garden.
Open all year, daily, Apr to Sept 7.30am–8pm, Sept to Mar 7.30am–dusk. Admission free.
☎ (0734) 598263. ♿

The Gardens of the Rose
(Royal National Rose Society) Chiswell Green, St Albans, Hertfordshire
Attractive, landscaped display gardens containing 30,000 roses in over 1,650 varieties; also trials of new varieties.
Open June to Sept, daily, Mon to Sat 9am–5pm, Sun & Bank Hols 10am–6pm. Admission £1.30 adults, children under 16 free; parties £1.
☎ (0727) 50461. ♿

Greys Court
nr Henley-on-Thames, Oxfordshire
Beautiful gardens surrounded by ancient walls, including a white garden, rose garden, wisteria walk, nut avenue and recently-built 'Archbishop's Maze'.
Open 29 Mar to end Sept, Mon to Sat (House Mon, Wed, Fri), 2pm–6pm (last entry 5.30pm). Admission: House & Garden £1.80 adults, 90p children; Garden only £1.30 adults, 65p children. No dogs.
☎ Rotherfield Greys (049 17) 529. NT ♿

Hatfield House
Hatfield, Hertfordshire
Celebrated Jacobean house set in parkland with colour throughout the year. Elizabethan knot garden; wilderness garden; herb & scented garden with sundial. Picnic area.
Open 25 Mar to 12 Oct: Park, daily, 10.30am–8pm; East Gardens, Mon, 2pm–5pm; West Gardens, daily, Mon 2pm–5pm (Bank Hol Mon 11am–5pm), Tue to Sat 12 noon–5pm (closed Good Fri), Sun 2pm–5.30pm. Admission: Exhibition, Park & Gardens £1.40 adults, £1.35 OAPs, £1.10 children; House extra; party reductions.
☎ (07072) 62823. ♿

Kingston House
Kingston Bagpuize, Oxfordshire
Historic house with garden of botanical interest; fine trees; bulbs and flowering shrubs; herbaceous border and hydrangeas.
Open 31 Mar to 30 June, Sat, Sun, Bank Hol Mon, 2.30pm–5.30pm. Admission £1.50 adults, £1 OAPs, students, children; parties by arrangement. No dogs.
☎ Longworth (0865) 820259. ♿

Kingstone Lisle Park and Gardens
Wantage, Oxfordshire
17th- and early-19th-century house in park and gardens featuring rose gardens, herbaceous borders, lawns and shrubs.
Open 1 Apr to 1 Sept, Thur & Bank Hol Sat, Sun, Mon, 2pm–5pm; market garden open daily exc Sun, 9am–5pm. Admission £1.50 adults, 80p children, £1.40 parties.
☎ Uffington (036 782) 223. ♿

Knebworth House
Knebworth, Hertfordshire
Tudor mansion with extensive gardens and 250 acres of beautiful deer park offering something for all the family. Restored herb garden by Gertrude Jekyll.
Open 24 May to 14 Sept, Tue to Sun; also 21 & 28 Sept & Bank Hol Mon, 12 noon–5pm. Admission £2.50 adults, £2 OAPs, students, children; parties £2 & £1.60. No dogs.
☎ Stevenage (0438) 812661. ♿

Luton Hoo
Luton, Bedfordshire
Magnificent house, superb 1,500-acre park, landscaped by 'Capability' Brown; lakes, rose garden.
Open 22 Mar to 12 Oct, Mon, Wed, Thur, Sat, Good Fri 11am–5.45pm, Sun 2pm–5.45pm. Admission £2 adults, £1 children/students; parties £1.70 by appt. Gardens only £1. No dogs.
☎ (0582) 22955. ♿

John Mattock Rose Nurseries
Nuneham Courtenay, Oxfordshire
Internationally-known rose grower's display gardens–over 300,000 roses grown annually from leading rose hybridists.
Open June to Sept, daily, 9am–6pm. Admission free.
☎ (086 738) 265. ♿

Milton's Cottage
Chalfont St Giles, Buckinghamshire
John Milton's cottage; excellently maintained cottage garden; roses,

---

A welcome awaits you at the Gardens of the Rose . . .

OPEN JUNE to OCT
Mon. to Sat. 9am to 5pm.
Sunday 10am to 6pm.
Party rates on application
Car & Coach Park Free
Licensed Cafeteria and Gift Shop
All parts accessible to visitors in wheel chairs. Dogs permitted.

See the most unique collection of roses in the world in a peaceful setting covering 12 acres . . . where the skylarks sing all day.

Roses of every description including miniatures, climbers, shrubs, bushes, species, historical and modern and roses of the future.

■ The Royal National Rose Society, Chiswell Green, St. Albans, Herts. Tel: (0727) 50461

KNEBWORTH HOUSE, GARDENS & PARK

Family home of the Lyttons since 1490 this magnificent Stately Home, standing in 250 acres of rolling parkland, was transformed 150 years ago by spectacular High Gothic decoration. With its splendid Jacobean banqueting hall (where Dickens acted and which Churchill painted; more recently scene of "The Shooting Party") and the beautiful LUTYENS GARDENS, including the JEKYLL HERB GARDEN, Knebworth presents a mirror of English history over the past five Centuries.

British Raj Exhibition, Narrow Gauge Steam Railway and Museum, New Adventure playground, licensed cafeteria in 16th century tithe barn.
**Open Sundays, Bank Holidays, School holidays April – May
Daily 24th May – 14th September except Mondays, plus 21st and 28th September.
Party bookings welcomed April – September (except Mondays)**

**PARK 11am – 5.30pm
HOUSE & GARDENS 12 noon – 5pm.**

For details please telephone Stevenage (0438) 812661
Own direct access from A1(M) at Stevenage South (A602)

flowering shrubs, fruit trees.
Open Feb to 31 Oct, Tue to Sat, Bank Hol Mon 10am–1pm, 2pm–6pm, Sun 2pm–6pm. Admission 60p adults, 20p children; 40p parties 20+. No dogs.
☎ *(024 07) 2313.* ♿

Minster Lovell Hall
nr Burford, Oxfordshire
Ruin of 15th-century manor house, with 15th-century dovecote, in delightfully peaceful riverside setting.
Open all year, daily exc 24–26 Dec & 1 Jan, Mon to Sat 9.30am–1pm, 2pm–6.30pm, Sun 2pm–6.30pm (winter closing 4pm). Admission (1985 prices) 50p adults, 25p children/OAPs; reduction for parties.
☎ *Witney (0993) 75315.*

Nether Winchendon House
nr Aylesbury, Buckinghamshire
Landscape garden, extensively replanted 30 years ago by present owners. Tudor manor house surrounded by wide lawns. Fine trees, of botanic interest; spring bulbs, herbaceous and shrub borders, old roses, autumn colour.
Open May to Aug, Thur, 2.30pm–5.30pm; also May & Aug Bank Hols (Sat, Sun, Mon), and 7/8 June, 9/10 July. Parties at any time by written appt. Admission £1.30 adults, 70p OAPs (Thur only), 70p children. No dogs.
☎ *Haddenham (0844) 290101.* ♿

Pusey House Gardens
nr Faringdon, Oxfordshire
Herbaceous borders, at their best in summer; walled gardens; water garden; large collection of shrubs and roses; many fine trees.
Open 29 Mar to 26 Oct, daily exc Mon & Fri, 2pm–6pm; also Bank Hol Mon 2pm–4pm. Admission £1.30 adults, children under 11 free; parties £1.10.
☎ *Buckland (036 787) 222.* ♿

Rousham
Steeple Aston, Oxfordshire
18th-century William Kent landscape with classic buildings, cascades, statues, vistas, in 30 acres of woodland above River Cherwell.
Open all year, daily, 10am–4.30pm. Admission £1. No dogs or children under 15.
☎ *(0869) 47110.* ♿ *(part).*

Savill/Valley Gardens
Windsor Great Park, Berkshire
400-acre woodland gardens; both interesting all seasons. Valley Garden adjoins Virginia Water.
Open all year, daily, 10am–6pm or dusk. Admission Savill Garden £1.50 adults, £1.30 OAPs, children free; parties £1.30. Valley Gardens free to pedestrians. No dogs in Savill Garden.
☎ *(075 35) 60222.* ♿

Shinfield Grange
University of Reading Horticultural Research Laboratories, Shinfield, Reading, Berkshire
15 acres of teaching garden; old-fashioned roses, herbaceous borders, annuals, shrubs, small trees, water garden, meadow garden of wildflowers etc. Plant sales.

Nether Winchendon, Buckinghamshire

Open Mar to Dec, Wed, 10.30am–4pm; also Mar to Sept, last Sun of each month, 2pm–6pm. Admission 60p adults, 40p OAPs, 20p children. No dogs.
☎ *(0734) 883226.* ♿

Stagsden Bird Gardens
Stagsden, Bedfordshire
Extensive bird-breeding and conservation centre; collection of shrub roses.
Open all year, daily, 11am–6pm or dusk. Admission £1.30 adults, £1 OAPs, 60p children; parties by arrangement. No dogs.
☎ *Oakley (023 02) 2745.* ♿

THE HOME OF GOOD PLANTS AND TRULY A GARDEN FOR ALL SEASONS.

The Savill Garden

IN WINDSOR GREAT PARK

Clearly signposted from Ascot, Egham and Windsor.

Ample Free Car/Coach parking adjoining the garden in Wick Lane, Englefield Green.

The Garden is open daily throughout the year from 10 a.m. to 6 p.m. or sunset if earlier. (Closed December 25-28, 1986.)

Admission: Adults £1.50. Senior Citizens £1.30. Parties of 20 or more £1.30. Half price Nov./Feb.
Accompanied children under the age of 16 free. (Large groups of children by arrangement)

A Licensed Self Service Restaurant is open from March 1st to October 31st. Also our well stocked Plant-Gift-Shop is open throughout the season.

THAMES & CHILTERNS

Stonor House and Park
Henley-on-Thames, Oxfordshire
House dating from 12th century, with beautiful gardens commanding wide views over the park. Terraced rose garden, scenic walk, spring bulbs.
Open 29 Mar to 28 Sept, Wed, Thur, Sun, 2pm–5.30pm (last entry 5pm). Admission (approximate) £1.70 adults, £1.40 OAPs, children free; parties £1.40 & £1.10.
☎ *Turville Heath (049 163) 587.* &

Stowe School Gardens
Stowe, nr Buckingham, Buckinghamshire
Fine landscaped garden, the result of work by many famous designers; Palladian bridge and temples.
Open 28 Mar to 31 Mar, then 13 July to 7 Sept, Fri, Sat, Sun, 11am–6pm. Admission 75p adults, 50p OAPs, students, children; parties of 25+ 10% discount.
☎ *(0280) 813650.* &

Swallowfield Park
Swallowfield, nr Reading, Berkshire
17th-century house with walled garden of about 4 acres containing a variety of flowering shrubs, roses and many interesting trees.
Open May to Sept, Wed & Thur, 2pm–5pm. Admission 50p adults, 25p children.
☎ *(0734) 883815.*

The Swiss Garden
Old Warden, Bedfordshire
Unusual early-19th-century Romantic garden with interesting buildings and features, and rare plants and trees. Lakeside picnic area in adjoining woods.
Open 29 Mar to 31 Oct, Wed, Thur, Sat, Sun (exc last Sun in month), Spring & Summer Bank Hol Mons, 2pm–6pm. Admission (1985 prices) 40p adults, 20p OAPs/children; parties by appt. No dogs.
☎ *Bedford (0234) 228328.*

University of Oxford Botanic Garden
Oxford, Oxfordshire
Famous botanic gardens in the heart of the city, with something of interest all the year round, both outside and in greenhouses.
Open all year, daily exc 25 Dec & 28 Mar, Mon to Sat 8.30am–5pm (4.30pm Oct to Mar), Sun 10am–12 noon, 2pm–6pm (4.30pm Oct to Mar). Greenhouses open daily, 2pm–4pm. Admission free. No dogs.
☎ *(0865) 242737.* & *(check).*

Waddesdon Manor
nr Aylesbury, Buckinghamshire
Extensive grounds, designed 1874–89; 18th-century-style aviary; herd of Japanese Sika deer; sculpture, fountains, fine trees; parkland suitable for picnics; play area for young children.
Open 19 Mar to 19 Oct; House Mar, Apr & Oct, Wed to Fri, 2pm–5pm, Sat & Sun, 2pm–6pm, May to Sept, Wed to Sun, 2pm–6pm; Grounds Wed to Sat, 1pm to 6pm, Sun 11.30am–6pm. House & Grounds also open Good Fri & Bank Hol Mon (closed every Wed following Bank Hols). Admission House & Grounds £2.20 (children under 10 not admitted to House); Grounds only £1 adults, 25p children; reduction for parties of OAPs on Wed, Thur, Sat.
☎ *(0296) 651211/651282. NT* 🍴 &

Waterperry Gardens
Waterperry Horticultural Centre, nr Wheatley, Oxfordshire
Peaceful gardens, grounds and nurseries, bordered by River Thame; garden shop; tea shop.
Open all year, daily exc 25 & 26 Dec, 1 Jan (open only to visitors to Art in Action 17 to 20 July); Apr to Sept 10am–5.30pm (10am–6pm Sat & Sun), Oct to Mar 10am–4pm. Admission 80p adults, 65p OAPs, 40p children (half price in winter); pre-booked parties 60p.
☎ *Ickford (084 47) 254.* &

West Wycombe Park
West Wycombe, Buckinghamshire
18th-century Palladian house and landscape garden with lake and classical temples, including newly reconstructed Temple of Venus.
Grounds open Easter, May Day & Spring Bank Hols Sun & Mon, 2pm–6pm; House & Grounds June, Mon to Fri, July & Aug, daily exc Sat, 2pm–6pm. Admission House & Grounds £2 adults, £1 children; Grounds only £1.20 & 60p. No dogs.
☎ *High Wycombe (0494) 24411.* &

Winslow Hall
Winslow, Buckinghamshire
Country house by Sir Christopher Wren, with 8-acre grounds and gardens laid out in 1695 by celebrated gardeners George London and Henry Wise. Original walls and vegetable garden; rare trees and shrubs.
Open Gardens May & June, Sun, 2pm–5pm; House & Gardens 1 July to 15 Sept, daily exc Mon, also last two weekends in Sept & Bank Hol Mon, 2.30pm–5.30pm. Admission £1.50 adults, children under 12 free; parties £1.25. No dogs.
☎ *(029 671) 3433.* &

Wrest Park
nr Silsoe, Bedfordshire
Garden styles from 17th to mid-19th century, notably semi-formal Great Garden and the Long Water.
Open Apr to Sept, weekends and Bank Hol Mon only, 9.30am–6.30pm. Admission 70p adults, 35p children/OAPs; parties 10% discount.
☎ *Cambridge (0223) 358911 ext 2083.* &

Wroxton Abbey
Wroxton, nr Banbury, Oxfordshire
17th-century manor house surrounded by recently restored 18th-century landscape garden.
Open all year, daily, dawn to dusk. Admission free.
☎ *(029 573) 551.* &

BEFORE SETTING OUT it's always best to 'phone and check garden details. Opening times and prices may be subject to change at short notice!

STOWE SCHOOL, nr. BUCKINGHAM

18th Century House. Former home of the Dukes of Buckingham and Chandos.
Superb landscaped gardens with largest collection of garden buildings in England.
Open: Saturday 12th July to Sunday 7th September, also Good Friday, Saturday, Sunday and Easter Monday.
Adults 75p. Children & OAP's 50p.
Special rates for coaches.
(Tel: 0280 813650).

OPEN DAILY
GARDEN SHOP · TEA SHOP

Near Wheatley · Oxford · Ickford 226
See above

WEST COUNTRY

Warming waters of the Gulf Stream have lent a tender touch to West Country gardens. Though the Isles of Scilly, in the full flow of the Stream, are able to grow plants not found outdoors in any other British garden, from Trengwainton near Penzance to Dorset's sub-tropical gardens at Abbotsbury, palms, magnolias, camellias and a host of other exotic plants thrive on this the mildest part of the English mainland. If the names here have a wonderful, West Country ring – Lanhydrock, Trelissick, Penjerrick or Trewithen – others around the region are equally distinctive: Montacute means superb Elizabethan architecture in a formal setting which includes some planting by Vita Sackville West; Hestercombe House Gardens are the work of Gertrude Jekyll and Edwin Lutyens; Ugbrooke House offers Robert Adam's house in park and grounds by Capability Brown who was responsible too for the grounds at Bowood House, Corsham Court and at Longleat, thought to be his finest achievement. But the world of West Country gardens is full of enjoyable contrasts. The humble gnome rubs shoulders with a host of elegant garden devices; wild beasts roam some estates, in others tropical birds and butterflies lurk amongst the flowers; Thomas Hardy's cottage garden reminds us that both big and small are beautiful and at Babbacombe the model village reduces even its plants to miniature size. Mellow country houses offer the history of gardening through the ages, beginning with Forde Abbey and Gaulden Manor both dating from the 12th century and coming right up to date at the County Demonstration Gardens at Probus which bring the subject to life with a range of modern aids from children's games to videos. But to garden-lovers countrywide, one particular spot in Wiltshire has become a place of pilgrimage. Stourhead was created by its owner Henry Hoare with statues, temples and grottos to emulate an idealised, classical landscape; the result is a 'living painting' which is probably the finest landscape garden in England. ❀

NOVEMBER

November focuses on fruits and berries hanging in rich, glossy clusters that look good enough to eat. Flowering quince fruits now, and malus produces its shiny scarlet and yellow crab apples, while shrubs such as viburnum are weighed down with convincing currant-like berries,

Strawberry Tree Unedo arbutus and the strawberry tree bears the deep orange-red fruits that are so temptingly like its namesake. Others are showier still: berberis and pernettya glow a glorious red; callicarpa's berries are a rich shade of pinky-purple and the ostentatious firethorn has a close relative whose berries bring a blaze of bright yellow to the border.

THE FUCHSIA

The West Country gardener has the mild climate on his side, and with its help he can grow an outstanding variety of the more tender plants. One of the loveliest among them is the fuchsia, a slightly-tender flowering shrub introduced to this country in the late 18th century from South America. Planted in sheltered *Fuchsia* positions, it has since proved itself well able to withstand West Country winters. Fuchsias are remarkable not just for the distinctive shape of their flowers, but also for their colours, presenting a riot of pinks, white, purple, carmine, crimson and violet-blue through the summer and autumn. They vary considerably in size – some like Tom Thumb are suitable for rock gardens, while others such as the popular scarlet and purple *fuchsia magellanica* will develop into wonderful flowering hedges, adding bursts of colour to gardens.

For more information contact the
West Country Tourist Board,
Trinity Court, 37 Southernhay East,
Exeter, Devon EX1 1QS
☎ *(0392) 76351.*

A Guide to English Gardens

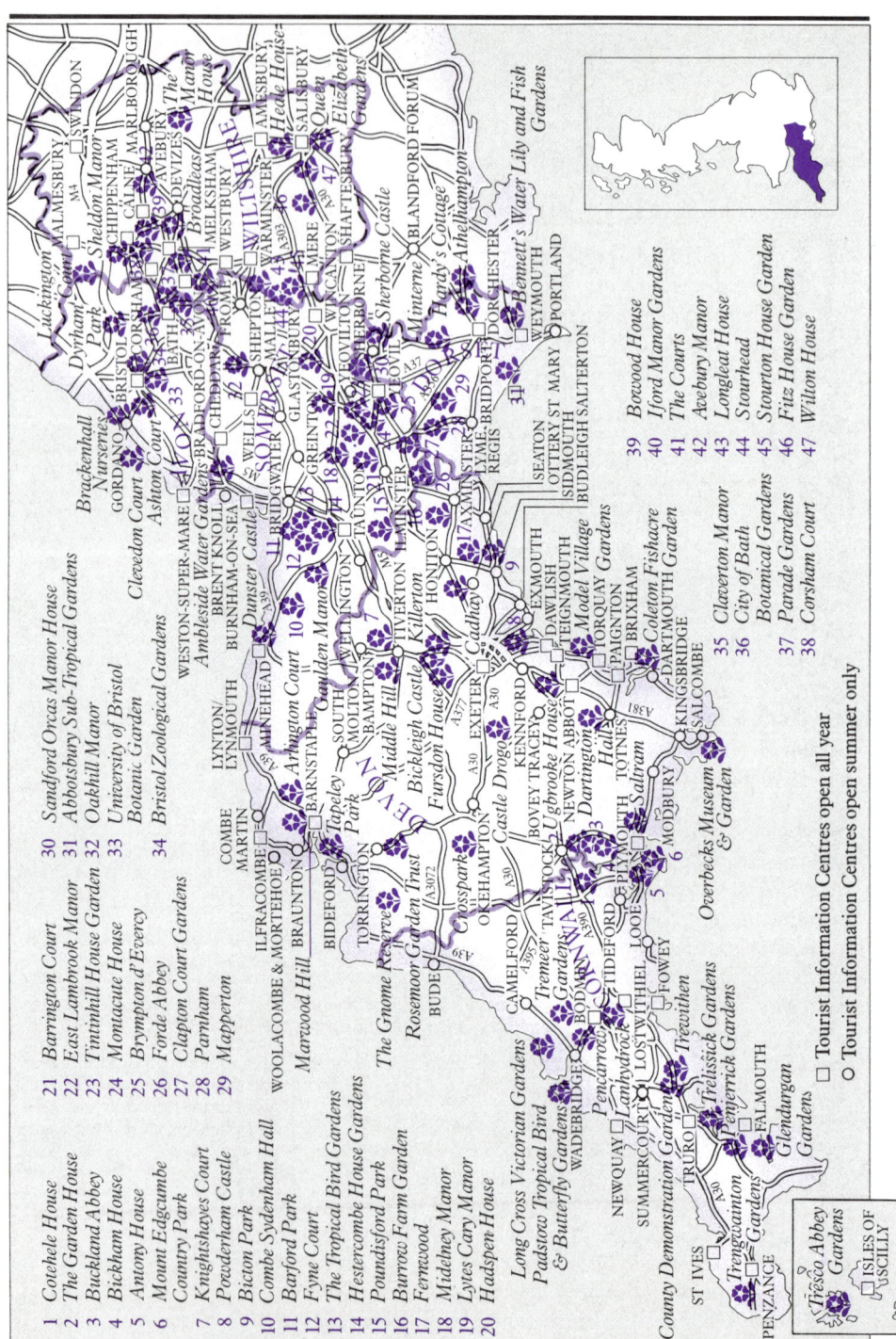

West Country

1. Cotehele House
2. The Garden House
3. Buckland Abbey
4. Bickham House
5. Antony House
6. Mount Edgcumbe Country Park
7. Knightshayes Court
8. Powderham Castle
9. Bicton Park
10. Combe Sydenham Hall
11. Barford Park
12. Fyme Court
13. The Tropical Bird Gardens
14. Hestercombe House Gardens
15. Poundisford Park
16. Burrow Farm Garden
17. Fernwood
18. Midelney Manor
19. Lytes Cary Manor
20. Hadspen House
21. Barrington Court
22. East Lambrook Manor
23. Tintinhull House Garden
24. Montacute House
25. Brympton d'Evercy
26. Forde Abbey
27. Clapton Court Gardens
28. Parnham
29. Mapperton
30. Sandford Orcas Manor House
31. Abbotsbury Sub-Tropical Gardens
32. Oakhill Manor
33. University of Bristol Botanic Garden
34. Bristol Zoological Gardens
35. Claverton Manor
36. City of Bath Botanical Gardens
37. Parade Gardens
38. Corsham Court
39. Bowood House
40. Iford Manor Gardens
41. The Courts
42. Avebury Manor
43. Longleat House
44. Stourhead
45. Stourton House Garden
46. Fitz House Garden
47. Wilton House

□ Tourist Information Centres open all year
○ Tourist Information Centres open summer only

A GUIDE TO ENGLISH GARDENS

WEST COUNTRY

Abbotsbury Sub-Tropical Gardens
Abbotsbury, nr Weymouth, Dorset
Large garden where rhododendrons, palms and camellias of great size grow in extremely mild climate.
Open mid-Mar to mid-Oct, daily, 10am–6pm. Admission £1.50 adults, £1 OAPs, 50p children; parties by arrangement.
☎ (0305) 871387. &

Ambleside Water Gardens and Aviaries
Lower Weare, Axbridge, Somerset
Natural walk-through aviary overlooking lake. Large collection of ornamental waterfowl, also garden with rabbits, guinea pigs and pheasants.
Open 1 Apr to 31 Oct, Tue, Sun, Bank Hol Mon, 10am–5.30pm. Admission 65p adults, 60p OAPs, 45p children. No dogs.
☎ (0934) 732362. &

Antony House
Torpoint, Cornwall
Early-18th-century house, with extensive grounds; much of it is Indianesque, with trees the dominant feature. Unique yew tree-house.
Open 31 Mar to 31 Oct, Tue, Wed, Thur & Bank Hol Mons, 2pm–6pm. Admission £1.90 adults, 95p children. No dogs.
☎ Plymouth (0752) 812191. NT ☘

Arlington Court
nr Barnstaple, Devon
Victorian formal garden set in beautiful wooded parkland; nature trail and walks beside the lake; stables and carriage collection.
Garden open all year, daily, dawn to dusk. House open 28 Mar to 31 Oct, Sun to Fri & Bank Hol Sats, 11am–6pm. Admission: House £2.50 adults, £1.25 children, £2 parties; Grounds £1.50 adults, 75p children.
☎ Shirwell (027 182) 296. NT ☘ &

Ashton Court Mansion and Estate
Bristol, Avon
House (undergoing restoration) set in 825-acre estate, landscaped in early 1800s containing formal gardens, park and woodlands; deer park, nature trail, orienteering course. Pitch and putt, model steam railway, grass ski slope, cafe, and the home of many fine events, including the International Balloon Fiesta in August.
Open all year, daily, dawn to dusk. Admission free, exc model railway, pitch and putt courses and grass ski slope, which have different opening times. House open by appointment.
☎ (0272) 266031 ext 524. &

Forde Abbey, Dorset

Athelhampton
Puddletown, nr Dorchester, Dorset
Six different walled gardens, with pavilions and terraces, pools and fountains, architectural yews, rare plants, dovecote and river gardens.
Open 26 Mar to 12 Oct, Wed, Thur, Sun, Good Fri, Bank Hols; also Mon & Tue in Aug; 2pm–6pm. Admission £2 adults, £1 children; parties of 20+ by arrangement £1.50. Gardens only £1 adults, children free. No dogs.
☎ (030 584) 363. &

Avebury Manor
nr Marlborough, Wiltshire
Elizabethan manor house with extensive traditional English gardens, herb border and old yew and box topiary. Tudor dovecote and wishing well.
Open Apr to end Sept, Mon to Sat 11.30am–6pm, Sun 12.30pm–5.30pm, Oct to Mar, Sat & Sun, 1.30pm–5pm; and by appt. Admission (1985 prices) £2 adults, £1.75 OAPs/parties, £1 children. No dogs.
☎ (067 23) 203.

Barford Park
Spaxton, nr Bridgwater, Somerset
Queen Anne house set in park with fine trees; formal garden, water garden and woodland garden.
House & Garden open May to Sept, Sun, Wed & Thur, 2pm–6pm. Admission £1.40 adults, children free, parties by appt; Gardens only 50p.
☎ (027 867) 269. &

Barrington Court
Ilminster, Somerset
Beautiful Tudor hamstone house and garden surrounded by 'rooms' of gardens inspired by Gertrude Jekyll. Fascinating throughout the year.
Open 30 Mar to 24 Sept: Gardens, Sun, Mon, Tue, Wed, 2pm–5.30pm; House, Wed only, 2pm–5pm (last entry ½hr before closing). Admission £1 adults, 50p children; House £1 extra, parties 70p. No dogs.
☎ (046 05) 2242. NT ☘ &

Bennetts' Water Lily and Fish Gardens
Weymouth, Dorset
Four acres of water with extensive collection of water plants and tropical and hardy water lilies and fish.
Open 1 May to 30 Sept, Mon to Sat, 9am–12.30pm, 2pm–5pm. Admission 50p adults, 20p children.
☎ (0305) 785150.

Bickham House
Barton Roborough, nr Plymouth, Devon
Shrub garden featuring camellias, rhododendrons, magnolias; lovely views and beautiful trees; shrub roses for later openings. Homemade teas.
Open 30 Mar to 25 May, Sun, Bank Hol Mon, also 15 & 29 June, 2pm–6pm. Admission 50p. No dogs.
☎ Yelverton (0822) 852478.

ANTONY WOODLAND GARDENS
Torpoint, Cornwall
(Trustees of the Antony Garden Trust)

A woodland garden bordering the Lynher Estuary containing fine shrubs, Magnolias, Camellias & Rhododendrons set in a Humphry Repton landscape.

Location: 5 miles West of Plymouth via the Torpoint Car Ferry, 2 miles North-West of Torpoint on the northern side of the A.374.

Opening Times: April, May, September & October on Tuesdays, Wednesdays, Thursdays, Sundays & Bank Holiday Mondays (Closed Good Friday) from 2pm to 5.30pm.

Admission £1, Children 50p. No dogs allowed.

WEST COUNTRY

Lytes Cary Manor, Somerset

Bickleigh Castle
Bickleigh, nr Tiverton, Devon
Medieval house with water gardens in castle moat; rare shrubs, rhododendrons, gingko trees. Museum; exhibition: "Mary Rose" and World War II spy and escape gadgets.
Open Easter week, then Wed, Sun & Bank Hol Mon to 26 May; 27 May to 5 Oct, daily exc Sat; 2pm–5pm. Admission £1.80 adults, £1.50 OAPs/students, 90p children; reduced charges for parties of 20+. No dogs.
☎ *(088 45) 363.* &

Bicton Park
East Budleigh, nr Budleigh Salterton, Devon
Over 50 acres of gardens with woodland railway, 18th-century Italian gardens, American garden, pinetum, conservatories, adventure playground/picnic area. New garden layout planned for 1986. Theme halls, countryside collection, teenage assault course, putting and crazy golf. Gift shop, plant centre.
Open 25 Mar to 31 Oct, daily, 10am–6pm (winter opening times on application). Admission £2.50 adults, £2.30 OAPs & first child, others free; parties of 20+ £2 adults, 60p children.
☎ *Colaton Raleigh (0395) 68285.*

Bowood House and Gardens
Calne, Wiltshire
In spring, thousands of daffodils and bluebells; 50 acres rhododendrons and azaleas. Roses in summer. Park by 'Capability' Brown. Terraced gardens, arboretum, lake, grottos and waterfall. Garden centre open all year.
Open 28 Mar to 30 Sept, daily, 11am–6pm (Rhododendron garden open mid-May to mid-June). Admission £2.25 adults, £1.50 OAPs/students, £1.25 children; parties Rhododendron Garden £1 extra; parties 10% discount. No dogs.
☎ *(0249) 812102.* &

Brackenhall Nurseries
Portishead, nr Bristol, Avon
Over 5 acres of mature woodland with magnificent views over the Bristol Channel. Rhododendrons, camellias, azaleas, Japanese maples, rare trees and shrubs; aviaries; ornamental pools. Garden Centre.
Open 28 Mar to mid-Oct, daily, 11am–4.30pm (weather permitting). Garden Centre open all year, daily. Admission 50p adults, 25p children; parties by appointment. No dogs.
☎ *(0272) 843484.*

Bristol Zoological Gardens
Bristol, Avon
Renowned for its brilliant sub-tropical summer bedding and fine trees. Rock garden, herbaceous border and Plant Display House.
Open all year, daily exc 25 Dec, 9am (10am Sun)–6pm (summer), 9am (10am Sun)–5pm (winter). Admission (1985 prices) £2.70 adults, £1.30 OAPs on Mons exc Bank Hols, £1.30 children; parties of 25+ £2.15 and £1.10. No dogs.
☎ *(0272) 738951.* &

Broadleas
Devizes, Wiltshire
Garden with rare and unusual plants and trees. Rhododendrons, magnolias, interesting perennials and ground cover. Plants for sale. Home-made teas by arrangement.
Open 31 Mar to 31 Oct, Sun, Wed, Thur, 2pm–6pm. Admission 80p adults (£1 Sun), children half price.
☎ *(0380) 2035.*

Brympton d'Evercy
nr Yeovil, Somerset
Extensive gardens and vineyard maintained by owners surround this 17th-century mansion; country life museum; teas; exhibitions.
Open 3 May to 30 Sept, Sat to Wed, 2pm–6pm. Admission £2.20 adults, £2 OAPs Tue & Wed only, £1.10 children; parties £1.50. No dogs.
☎ *West Coker (093 586) 2528.* &

Buckland Abbey
Yelverton, Devon
Former 13th-century Cistercian monastery once owned by Drake, with garden featuring flowering shrubs and traditional herbs.
Open 28 Mar to end Sept, Mon to Sat, 11am–6pm, Sun 2pm–6pm; Oct to 26 Mar, Wed, Sat, Sun, 2pm–5pm. Admission (1985 prices) £1.40 adults; special party rates by appt.
☎ *Plymouth (0752) 668000.* NT

Burrow Farm Garden
Dalwood, Axminster, Devon
Extensive bog garden in Roman clay pit featuring rhododendrons, azaleas and mature trees. Rose garden. Plant sales. Cream teas on Suns.
Open 1 Apr to 30 Sept, daily, 2pm–7pm. Admission 70p adults, 10p children, 60p parties. No dogs.
☎ *Wilmington (0297) 285.* &

Cadhay
Ottery St Mary, Devon
16th-century house with gardens featuring herbaceous borders, yew hedges, trees and 16th-century fishponds.
Open 1 July to 28 Aug, Tue, Wed, Thur, 2pm–6pm (last entry 5.30pm). Admission £1.50 adults, 50p children. Reduced rates for parties of 20+ by arrangement.
☎ *(0404 81) 2432.* &

Castle Drogo
Drewsteignton, nr Exeter, Devon
Granite castle built by Sir Edward Lutyens at 900 ft overlooking gorge of River Teign. Garden with herb borders and croquet lawn.
Open 28 Mar to 31 Oct, daily, 11am–6pm. Admission Castle & Grounds £2.30 adults, £1.15 children, £1.60 parties. Grounds only £1.20. No dogs.
☎ *Chagford (064 73) 3306.* NT

City of Bath Botanical Gardens
Bath, Avon
Trees, shrubs and alpines from all parts of the world. Water features, heather garden, spring displays, autumn colour. Part of the 57-acre Royal Victoria Park.
Open all year, daily, Mon to Sat, 8am–dusk, Sun & Bank Hols 10am–dusk. Admission free.
☎ *(0225) 61111 ext 411.* &

Clapton Court Gardens
nr Crewkerne, Somerset
One of Somerset's most beautiful gardens, with fine trees and shrubs of botanical interest in 10 acres of formal and woodland settings. A garden for all seasons. Fuchsias, geraniums; plant centre.
Open all year, Mon to Fri 10.30am–5pm; also Suns, 29 Mar & Sats in May only, 2pm–5pm. Admission £1.20 adults, £1 OAPs, 30p children; parties of 20+ £1. No dogs.
☎ *(0460) 73220.* &

Claverton Manor
nr Bath, Avon
Reproduction of George Washington's garden at Mount Vernon. Colonial herb garden. Arboretum.
Open 28 Mar to 2 Nov, Tue to Sun, 2pm–5pm. Admission charges on application.
☎ *(0225) 60503.* &

Clevedon Court
Clevedon, Avon
14th-century manor house with 18th-century terraced garden with rare shrubs and plants.
Open 30 Mar to end Sept, Wed, Thur, Sun, Bank Hol Mon, 2.30pm–5.30pm. Admission £1.50 adults, 80p children. No dogs.
☎ *(0272) 872257.* NT

Coleton Fishacre Garden
nr Kingswear, Devon
18-acre garden in stream-fed valley; garden created by Lady Dorothy D'Oyly Carte; planted with a wide

86

variety of uncommon trees, rare and exotic shrubs.
Open 28 Mar to 31 Oct, Wed, Fri & Sun, 11am–6pm. Admission £1.20 adults, 60p children, £1 parties.
☎ (080 425) 617. NT ✿

Combe Sydenham Hall
Monksilver, nr Taunton, Somerset
16th-century house under restoration with series of small gardens separated by yew hedges; herb, rose and knot gardens, valley walks; trout farm.
Open 30 Mar to 31 Oct, 11am–5pm (last entry 4.30pm). Admission £1.70 adults, £1.50 OAPs, 80p children; parties by arrangement.
☎ Stogumber (098 46) 284. ⅋

Corsham Court
Corsham, Wiltshire
Elizabethan manor with park and gardens laid out by 'Capability' Brown and Humphry Repton. Fine specimen trees, walled area with herbaceous borders, rose gardens, lily pond, 15th-century gazebo.
Open 14 Jan to 14 Dec, Tue, Wed, Thur, Sat, Sun, 2pm–5.30pm or dusk. Admission House & Garden £2 adults, £1 children; parties of 20+ £1.60. Gardens only £1 adults, 50p children.
☎ (0249) 712214. ⅋

Cotehele House
St Dominick, nr Callington, Cornwall
Victorian terraced garden falling to sheltered valley; ponds, streams and a watermill.
Open 28 Mar to 31 Oct, daily (House closed Fri), 11am–6pm. Admission: House & Gardens £2.60 adults, £1.30 children; Gardens only £1.50 adults, 75p children. Parties by arrangement. No dogs.
☎ Liskeard (0579) 50434. NT ✿

County Demonstration Garden
Probus, nr Truro, Cornwall
Display plots showing every aspect of cultivation; children's gardens; plots for retired or disabled people; frequent demonstrations.
Open all year: May to Sept, Mon to Fri 10am–5pm, Sun 2pm–6pm; Oct to Apr, Mon to Fri only, 10am–4.30pm. Adviser on duty Thurs, 2pm–5pm. Admission charges on application. No dogs.
☎ (0872) 74281. ⅋

The Courts
Holt, Wiltshire
Garden of great charm with interesting topiary, an arboretum and a beautiful lily pond. Conservatory and wildflower reserve.
Open 3 Feb to 28 Nov, Mon to Fri,

2pm–6pm or dusk. Admission £1 adults, children free. No dogs.
☎ North Trowbridge (0225) 782340. NT ✿ ⅋

Crosspark
Northlew, Okehampton, Devon
One-acre garden of interest throughout the year. Rock garden, bog garden, trees, heather, azaleas. White garden. View of Dartmoor.
Open 1 June to 14 Sept, Suns & Bank Hols, 2pm–6pm. Admission 40p adults, 10p children. No dogs.
☎ Beaworthy (040 922) 518.

Dartington Hall and Gardens
nr Totnes, Devon
Interesting terraced garden with superb views of medieval Hall and Tiltyard; woodland trails with fine views of valley and river; craft centre.
Open all year, daily, dawn to dusk. Admission free; guided tours by appt, £1.20 adults, 75p OAPs, 60p children. Parties by appt.
☎ (0803) 862271.

Dunster Castle
Dunster, Somerset
Dating from 13th century with 28-acre park; terraced garden of rare shrubs, fine trees and sub-tropical plants by river; conservatory in Castle.
Open 29 Mar to end Oct, daily; Mar to end Sept 11am–5pm, Oct 12 noon–4pm. Admission £2.20 adults, £1.10 children, £1.60 parties; Gardens only £1, 50p & 70p. No dogs.
☎ (0643) 821314. NT ✿

Dyrham Park
nr Bath, Avon
17th-century house with 250 acres of parkland and garden; Orangery; old hollies; two lakes; fallow deer.
Open 29 Mar to 29 Oct, Apr, May, Oct Sat to Wed, June to Sept daily exc Fri; 2pm–6pm. Admission £2.20 adults, £1.10 children, £1.60 parties. No dogs.
☎ Abson (027 582) 2501. NT ✿

East Lambrook Manor
South Petherton, Somerset
Renowned cottage-style garden with many rare plants. Silver garden, green garden and one of the finest collections of hellebores in the country. Nursery with unusual stock. Memorial to its late owner, Margery Fish.
Open 5 Jan to 19 Dec, daily, 9am–5pm. Admission 50p adults, children under 10 yrs free. No dogs.
☎ (0460) 40328. ⅋

Fernwood
West Hill, Ottery St Mary, Devon
Two-acre woodland garden with flowering shrubs, conifers and bulbs selected to give colour over long periods; species and hybrid rhododendrons and azaleas a special feature in spring.
Open 1 Apr to 30 Sept, daily, all day. Admission 50p adults, accompanied children free. No dogs.
☎ (040 481) 2820.

Fitz House Garden
Teffont Magna, nr Salisbury, Wiltshire
Garden belonging to small historic house, laid out in 1920s. Informal planting in 'rooms' within yew and beech hedges. Bulbs and spring blossom, terraces of scented plants; old orchard and many clematis, old-fashioned roses. Cream teas.
Open 30 Mar to 29 Oct, Wed, Sun, 2pm–6pm. Admission £1 adults, 50p children. No dogs.
☎ (072 276) 257.

Forde Abbey
nr Chard, Dorset
Originally 12th-century Cistercian monastery set in 25 acres of lovely gardens and lakes; water and rock gardens, wooded countryside. Fruit picking in season.
Gardens open 1 Apr to 31 Oct, Mon to Fri, 11am–4pm. Abbey 1 May to 31 Sept, Wed & Sun, also Bank Hol Mon; 2pm–6pm. Admission prices on application.
☎ South Chard (0460) 20231. ⅋

Fursdon House
Cadbury, Devon
Georgian-fronted manor house with walled gardens, set in parkland with superb views.
Open 30 & 31 Mar, 1 May to 30 Sept, Sun, Thur, & Bank Hols, also Wed in July & Aug; 2pm–5.30pm. Admission House & Grounds £1.70 adults, 80p children over 10; parties of 20+ £1.40. Grounds 85p adults, 40p children. No dogs.
☎ Exeter (0392) 860860.

Fyne Court
Broomfield, Bridgwater, Somerset
Original gardens used as nature reserve for associated species of plants and animals; arboretum. Picnic area.
Open all year, daily, 9.30am–5.30pm. Admission free. No dogs.
☎ Kingston St Mary (082 345) 587. ⅋

COUNTY DEMONSTRATION GARDEN

and Centre for Rural Studies at Probus on A390 between St Austell and Truro. A unique garden covering 7 acres designed to illustrate a very wide variety of gardening designs, plant utilisation and collections, the result of modern techniques, garden practices and research. Demonstration Apiary, Nature Trail, Historical Garden etc.
Opening times:
October to April Mondays to Fridays 10am to 4.30pm. Adviser on Duty Thursdays 2.00pm to 5.00pm.
May to September Mondays to Fridays 10.00am to 5.00pm. Adviser on Duty Thursdays 2.00pm to 5.00pm. Sundays 2.00pm to 6.00pm.

WEST COUNTRY

The Garden House
*Buckland Monachorum,
nr Yelverton, Devon*
Eight-acre garden of all-year-round interest, including fine 2-acre walled garden. Good collection of herbaceous and woody plants. Unusual plants for sale.
Open 1 Apr to 30 Sept, daily exc Bank Hols, 2pm–5pm. Admission £1 adults, 20p children; parties of 20+ 75p. No dogs.
☎ (0822) 854769.

Gaulden Manor
Tolland, Lydeard St Lawrence, Somerset
Historic manor dating from 12th century with herb garden and bog garden with primulas and other moisture-loving plants. Plants for sale. Tea room.
Open Easter Sun & Mon; then 4 May to 14 Sept, Thur, Sun, Bank Hol Mon; 2pm–5.30pm; also Wed July to Sept. Admission 70p, House extra. No dogs.
☎ (098 47) 213. & (part).

Glendurgan Gardens
nr Falmouth, Cornwall
A valley garden with fine trees and shrubs running down to the Helford river.
Open 1 Mar to 31 Oct, Mon, Wed, Fri exc 28 May, 10.30am–4.30pm. Admission £1.30 adults, 65p children. No dogs.
☎ Bodmin (0208) 4381. NT

The Gnome Reserve
West Putford, nr Bradworthy, Devon
Bringing an old tradition into the open – gnomes living in a woodland garden setting. Pixie nature trail. Studio making pottery pixies also open to the public.
Open 1 Apr to 31 Oct, daily exc Sat (open Bank Hol Sats), 10am–1pm (last entry 12.30pm), 2pm–6pm, also 7pm–9pm in June, July & Aug. Admission 60p adults, 40p OAPs/students/children.
☎ (040 924) 435.

Hadspen House, Gardens and Nursery
Castle Cary, Somerset
An 8-acre garden on a south-facing slope containing many unusual and interesting plants in an 18th-century setting.
Open all year exc Jan, Tue to Sat, 10am–5pm; also Suns, Apr to Oct & Bank Hols, 2pm–5pm. Admission £1 adults, 50p children; parties of 15+ 80p. No dogs.
☎ (0963) 50200/50427. &

Hardy's Cottage
Higher Bockhampton, nr Dorchester, Dorset
Picturesque birthplace of Thomas Hardy, set in delightful old-fashioned cottage garden designed by the writer.
Open 28 Mar to Oct, daily, 11am–5.30pm (Tue 2pm–5.30pm). Interior by appt only. Admission free, Cottage £1.20. No dogs.
☎ (0305) 62366. NT

Heale House Gardens
Woodford, Salisbury, Wiltshire
Early Carolean house with beautiful river garden; hybrid, musk and other roses; authentic Japanese teahouse.
Open 28 Mar to autumn depending on weather, Mon to Sat, 1st Sun of month & Bank Hols, 10am–5pm. Admission £1 adults, accompanied children under 14 free; parties by arrangement.
☎ Middle Woodford (072 273) 207. &

Hestercombe House Gardens
Cheddon Fitzpaine, Taunton, Somerset
Garden designed by Gertrude Jekyll and Edwin Lutyens. Large parterre surrounded by raised walks. Magnificent stonework. Formal rose garden. Orangery.
Open all year, Tue, Wed, Thur, 12noon–5pm; also last Suns of May, June, July, 2pm–6pm. Admission free but donations of 50p requested towards restoration costs.
☎ (0823) 87222.

Ilford Manor Gardens
Ilford Manor, Bradford-on-Avon, Wiltshire
Romantic Italian-style garden by the Edwardian architect and garden designer Harold Peto, whose home it was. Terraces, cloister, ponds and statues in beautiful riverside setting.
Open early May to end July, Wed, Sun & Bank Hol Mons, 2pm–5pm. Admission £1 adults, 70p OAPs/children, 80p parties.
☎ (022 16) 3146.

Killerton
Broadclyst, nr Exeter, Devon
18th-century house with acres of woodland and forest, contrasting with gardens of sweeping lawns; rare trees and shrubs.
Garden open all year, daily, dawn to dusk; House 28 Mar to 31 Oct, daily, 11am–6pm. Admission £2.30 adults, £1.15 children, £1.60 parties; Grounds only £1.50 adults, 75p children. No dogs.
☎ (0392) 881345. NT &

Knightshayes Court
nr Tiverton, Devon
19th-century house in outstanding gardens; spring bulbs at their best in the 'garden in the wood'; arboretum; huge yew hedges; unique topiary. Plants for sale.
Open 28 Mar to 31 Oct, Garden daily, 11am–6pm, House daily exc Fri, 1.30pm–6pm. Admission House & Garden £2.30 adults, £1.15 children, £1.70 parties; Garden £1.50 adults, 75p children. No dogs.
☎ (0884) 254665. NT &

Lanhydrock
nr Bodmin, Cornwall
Terraced garden full of rhododendrons, azaleas and magnolias; impressive avenue in rolling parkland.
Open all year, daily, 28 Mar to 31 Oct 11am–6pm; Nov to Mar, Garden only, dawn to dusk. Admission House & Garden £2.60 adults, £1.30 children; parties by arrangement. Garden only £1.50 adults, 75p children. No dogs.
☎ (0208) 3320. NT &

Long Cross Victorian Gardens
Trelights, Port Isaac, Cornwall
Late-Victorian gardens set amidst majestic pines with panoramic sea views.
Open Easter to Oct, daily, 11am–dusk. Admission free; charity collecting box.
☎ Bodmin (0208) 880243. &

Longleat House
Warminster, Wiltshire
Superb grounds surround house. Formal gardens, azalea drive. Park landscaped by 'Capability' Brown.
Open all year, daily exc 25 Dec; Easter to end Sept, 10am–6pm, remainder of year 10am–4pm. Admission: House & Grounds £2.30 adults, £1.80 OAPs, £1 children; parties £1.85 adults, £1.45 OAPs, 80p children; Gardens only 50p in summer.
☎ Maiden Bradley (098 53) 551. &

Luckington Court
Luckington, Wiltshire
Small, privately owned, mainly Queen Anne house with beautiful formal garden with fine collection of ornamental trees and shrubs.
Garden open all year, Wed, 2pm–6pm; also Sun 18 May. Admission 50p adults, children free.
☎ (0666) 840205. &

Lytes Cary Manor
nr Ilchester, Somerset
14th- and 15th-century manor house with chapel; formal garden with varied topiary, box hedges, old English garden, lily pool; recorded in Lytes Herballe, 1578.
Open Apr to end Oct, Wed & Sat, 2pm–5.30pm. Admission £1.50 adults, 80p children. No dogs.
☎ Somerton (0458) 223297. NT &

The Manor House
Milton Lilbourne, Pewsey, Wiltshire
Gardens feature lawns, walled vegetable garden, flower borders, roses, azaleas, rhododendrons.
Open May to Oct, Wed, 2pm–6pm. Admission free; donations welcome.
☎ (067 26) 3344. &

Mapperton
Beaminster, Dorset
Terraced and hillside gardens with formal borders, specimen shrubs and trees and orangery; 18th-century stone fishponds and summerhouse.
Open 10 Mar to 10 Oct, Mon to Fri, 2pm–6pm. Admission £1 adults, 60p children over 5. No dogs.
☎ (0308) 862441.

BEFORE SETTING OUT it's always best to 'phone and check garden details. Opening times and prices may be subject to change at short notice!

88

Marwood Hill Gardens
nr Barnstaple, Devon
12-acre garden with three small lakes; bog garden, formal rose garden, collection of Australian plants, rare trees and shrubs. Collections of camellias, clematis and eucalyptus.
Open all year, daily, dawn to dusk. Admission 50p adults, 10p children.
☎ *(0271) 42528. & (part).*

Middle Hill
Washfield, nr Tiverton, Devon
Medium-sized cottage-style garden with a wide variety of plants growing in different situations. Plants for sale.
Open 27 Apr to 14 Sept, Sun, (exc 1 & 15 June, 13 July, 3 & 17 Aug); also Mons 5 & 26 May, 25 Aug. Admission free; collecting box. No dogs.
☎ *Oakford (039 85) 380. & (part).*

Midelney Manor
Drayton, nr Langport, Somerset
Follow signs from Curry Rivel. 16th/18th-century house with period gardens, including heronry and private falcon mews.
Open 31 Mar then 4 June to 17 Sept, Wed & Bank Hols, 2pm–5.30pm. Admission £1.50 adults, 50p children. No dogs.
☎ *(0458) 251229. &*

Minterne
Cerne Abbas, Dorset
Important shrub garden set in beautiful valley, landscaped in 18th century with streams, small lakes and rare trees.

Open 1 Apr to 1 Nov, daily, 10am–7pm. Admission £1 adults, accompanied children free; parties by arrangement.
☎ *(030 03) 370.*

Model Village Gardens
Babbacombe, Torquay, Devon
Set in 4 acres of beautiful, miniature landscaped gardens with a unique collection of miniature trees and conifers.
Open all year, daily exc 25 Dec; Good Fri to mid-Oct 9am–10pm, rest of year 9am–5pm. Admission £1.60 adults, £1.40 OAPs, 90p children; parties £1.40 & 80p.
☎ *(0803) 38669. &*

Montacute House
Yeovil, Somerset
Magnificent Elizabethan house with fine formal gardens. Pavilions and ornaments of local stone; restaurant and tea room.
Open 28 Mar to 31 Oct, daily (House closed Tue), 12 noon–6pm. Admission £2.20 adults, £1.10 children, £1.60 parties; Gardens only 80p & 40p. No dogs.
☎ *Martock (0935) 823289. NT ♣ &*

Mount Edgcumbe Country Park
Cremyll, nr Plymouth, Cornwall
800 acres, 18th-century landscaped park. Formal gardens in French, English and Italian styles.
Open all year, daily, 8am–dusk. Admission free.
☎ *(0752) 822236. &*

Oakhill Manor
Oakhill, nr Shepton Mallet, Somerset
45-acre country estate; Mansion House set in 8 acres of gardens in the Mendip Hills. Transport model collection; miniature railway; picnic area.
Open 27 Mar to 6 Apr, 3 to 5 May, 24 May to 28 Sept, daily; also Sat & Sun to 2 Nov, 11am–5pm. Admission charges on application.
☎ *(0749) 840210.*

Overbecks Museum and Garden
Sharpitor, nr Salcombe, Devon
Small garden with rare plants and shrubs; fine views of estuary; house containing local museum.
Garden open all year, daily; Museum, 28 Mar to 31 Oct, daily 11am–1pm, 2pm–6pm. Admission £1.30 adults, 65p children; Garden only £1.
☎ *(054 884) 2893. NT ♣*

Padstow Tropical Bird and Butterfly Gardens
Padstow, Cornwall
Delightful landscaped garden of approximately 2 acres, with many unusual plants and shrubs. Tropical House with free-flying birds; butterfly display.
Open all year, daily exc 25 Dec, 10.30am–7pm (summer) or 5pm (winter). Admission £1.75 adults, £1.40 OAPs, 80p children; parties of 20+ 20% discount.
☎ *(0841) 532262. & (check).*

WEST COUNTRY

The Imperial

Three more dates for the Gardening Calendar.

The Imperial proudly announces the continuation of our Garden Lovers activity events for 1986.

We are fortunate to have the legendary talents of Percy Thrower hosting our specialised programmes for garden lovers. He will be giving informed talks and demonstrations, illustrated with slides, coupled with his own, inimitable, down-to-earth style, which is ideal for experts and beginners alike. Indoors or out, no aspect of horticulture will go unmentioned, and invariably his talks will end with question sessions. He will also conduct visits to well-known local gardens.

Rosemary Jenkins, well-known writer and lecturer, will also be here to advise and instruct, with her unrivalled knowledge of flower arranging.

This years dates are as follows:
9th-12th May Friday-Monday
4th-7th July Friday-Monday
21st-25th September Monday-Thursday

For further information and reservations:
The Reservations Manager, The Imperial, Torquay, Devon TQ1 2DG, England.

The Imperial, Torquay, England
(0803) 24301
A Trusthouse Forte Exclusive Hotel

WEST COUNTRY

Parade Gardens
Bath, Avon
Centrally situated ornamental gardens; intensive floral displays; three-dimensional carpet bedding; band concerts; fine views of River Avon, Pulteney Bridge and weir.
Open 1 Mar to 30 Sept, daily, 10am–dusk. Admission charges on application.
☎ (0225) 61111. &

Parnham
Beaminster, Dorset
Tudor manor house in 14 acres of varied gardens — courts, terraces, topiary, water-channels and cascades — parkland and woods. John Makepeace Furniture Workshops.
Open 28 Mar to 29 Oct, Sun, Wed & Bank Hols, 10am–5pm. Admission £2 adults, £1 children over 10.
☎ (0308) 862204. & (part).

Pencarrow
Bodmin, Cornwall
Georgian mansion with large formal garden and woodlands; granite rockery; ancient encampment; lake; noted conifer collection.
Open 30 Mar to 30 Sept, Sun to Thur; Apr, May, June, July, Aug & Bank Hols 11am–5pm. Admission (1985 prices) House & Garden £1.75 adults, 90p children, parties of 25+ £1.30; Garden only 50p adults, 25p children.
☎ St Mabyn (020 884) 369. & (part).

Penjerrick Gardens
Budock, Falmouth, Cornwall
Beautiful sub-tropical gardens with famous collection of trees, shrubs and rhododendrons including weeping beech 'Penjerrick' and 'Cornish Cross' hybrids.
Open 1 Mar to 30 Sept, Sun & Wed, 1.30pm–4.30pm. Admission 30p adults (50p Apr & May), 25p children. No dogs.
☎ (0326) 250659.

Poundisford Park
Pitminster, nr Taunton, Somerset
Tudor house in former deer park of Taunton Castle. Gardens (under restoration) with fine brick gazebo and views to Quantock and Blackdown Hills. Many interesting plants.
Open 30 Apr to 18 Sept, Wed & Thur, also Fri in July & Aug; 11am–5pm. Admission £1.50 adults, £1 students, 60p disabled/children over 10, £1 parties. No dogs.
☎ Blagdon Hill (082 342) 244. &

Powderham Castle
Kenton, Exeter, Devon
A small, sheltered rose garden with particular emphasis on the older, highly scented varieties. Magnificent views over the park and River Exe estuary. Medieval castle (restored).
Open 25 May to 11 Sept, daily exc Fri & Sat, 2pm–5pm. Admission £1.75 adults (Thur £2), £1.50 OAPs (Thur £1.75), £1 children (Thur £1.25); parties by arrangement. No dogs.
☎ Starcross (0626) 890243. &

Queen Elizabeth Gardens
Salisbury, Wiltshire
Mature gardens, famous as the foreground of Constable's view of Salisbury Cathedral.
Open all year, daily, dawn to dusk. Admission free.
☎ (0722) 334956. &

Rosemoor Garden Trust
Great Torrington, Devon
Garden with ornamental trees and shrubs; species and old-fashioned roses; dwarf conifers; scree and alpine plants; arboretum. Unusual plants for sale. Teas for groups.
Open 1 Apr to 31 Oct, daily, dawn to dusk. Admission £1 adults, 80p OAPs/students, 50p children; parties 80p.
☎ (0805) 22256. & (part).

Saltram
Plympton, nr Plymouth, Devon
Magnificent George II mansion in landscaped park and garden with orangery.
Garden open all year, daily, 11am–6pm (Nov to Mar daylight hours). House 28 Mar to 31 Oct, Sun to Thur & Bank Hol Sat, 12.30pm–6pm. Admission £2.40 adults, £1.20 children, £1.80 parties; Garden only £1.
☎ (0752) 336546. NT ✤ &

Sandford Orcas Manor House
nr Sherborne, Dorset
Tudor house and gardens with herbaceous borders, yew and box topiary hedges, mature trees, wisteria, climbing roses and ornamental cherries.
Open May to Sept, Sun 2pm–6pm, Mon 10am–6pm. Admission £1.10 adults, 50p children; reduced rates for parties by arrangement.
☎ Corton Denham (096 322) 206.

Sheldon Manor
Chippenham, Wiltshire
Plantagenet manor house with beautiful terraced gardens; daffodils, spring blossom, old-fashioned roses, water garden, ancient yew trees, rare plants.
Open Apr to Oct, Thur, Sun, Bank Hols; 12.30pm–6pm. Admission £1.50 adults, £1.40 OAPs, 75p children; reduced rates for parties by arrangement.
☎ (0249) 653120. &

Sherborne Castle
Sherborne, Dorset
16th-century house, with 20 acres of landscaped lakeside grounds planned by 'Capability' Brown. Many native trees. Tea room and shop.
Open 29 Mar to end Sept, Thur, Sat, Sun, Bank Hol Mon, 2pm–6pm (Grounds open 1.30pm Thur, 12 noon other days). Admission: Castle & Grounds £2.20 adults, £1.70 OAPs/students, £1.10 children, £1.70 parties; Grounds only 80p & 40p.
☎ (0935) 813182.

Stourhead
Stourton, nr Mere, Wiltshire
Celebrated 18th-century landscape gardens with lakes and temples; many rare trees and shrubs.
Open all year, daily, 8am–7pm or dusk if earlier. Admission £1.50 adults, 80p children, £1 parties.
☎ Bourton (0747) 840348. NT ✤ &

Stourton House Garden
nr Mere, Wiltshire
Off A303, next to NT Stourhead. Four acres of charmingly informal, privately-owned gardens. Lovely mature specimen shrubs and a wealth of herbaceous. Much that is unusual. Bouquets of dried garden flowers and unusual plants for sale.
Open 15 Apr to Nov, Sun, Thur & Bank Hol Mon, 11am–6pm. Admission £1 adults, 25p children; parties by arrangement. No dogs.
☎ Bourton (0747) 840417. &

Tapeley Park
Instow, nr Bideford, N.Devon
Superbly situated house (tours as convenient); Italian garden; Chinese Ghost Tree; walled kitchen garden; woodland pond; putting, children's rope course, picnic area; refreshments in Queen Anne Dairy.
Open 28 Mar to Oct, daily exc Mon (open Bank Hol Mon), 10am–6pm. (Gardens open all year.) Admission: House & Gardens £2 adults, £1 children, disabled free; Gardens only £1 & 50p.
☎ (0271) 860528. &

Tintinhill House Garden
Tintinhill, nr Yeovil, Somerset
5 acres of formal garden laid out as 'rooms' in the 1930s. Azalea garden.
Open 31 Mar to 27 Sept, Mon, Wed, Thur, Sat, 2pm–6pm or dusk. Admission £1.50. No dogs.
☎ Martock (0935) 822509. NT ✤ &

Trelissick Gardens
nr Truro, Cornwall
Wooded park with views of River Fal; sub-tropical shrubs, fine camellias and rhododendrons, woodland walk.
Open Mar to Oct, daily, 11am–6pm. Admission £1.50 adults, 75p children.
☎ (0872) 862090. NT ✤ &

Tremeer Gardens
St Tudy, Bodmin, Cornwall
Gardens feature many rare plants and shrubs; walled kitchen garden and lake. Best viewed March to June.
Open 1 Mar to 30 Sept, daily, all day. Admission free; charity collecting box.
☎ (0208) 850313.

Trengwainton Gardens
nr Penzance, Cornwall
Magnificent collection of magnolias and rhododendrons with superb views of St Michael's Mount and bay.
Open Mar to Oct, Wed to Sat, Bank Hols, 11am–6pm. Admission £1.40 adults, 70p children. No dogs.
☎ (0736) 63148. NT ✤

Tresco Abbey Gardens
Tresco, Isles of Scilly
A unique selection of sub-tropical flora; lake garden and island walks leading to beaches.

WEST COUNTRY

Open all year, daily, 10am–4pm. Admission £2 adults, £1 children. ☎ (0720) 22849.

Trewithen
Probus, Cornwall
A privately owned, internationally famous garden with renowned collection of rare camellias, magnolias and rhododendrons in a wooded and beautifully landscaped 18th-century setting. Also includes original rose garden and water gardens.
Open 1 Apr to 30 Sept, Mon to Sat, 2pm–4.30pm. Admission (1985 prices): Apr to June £1 adults, 90p OAPs, July to Sept 90p adults, 70p OAPs; children under 10 free.
☎ St Austell (0726) 882418/882585. &

The Tropical Bird Gardens
Rode, nr Bath, Somerset
Over 1,000 brilliant, exotic birds, many at liberty, in a colourful garden for all seasons. Rare trees (tree trail), shrubs, roses, bulbs, clematis collection.
Open all year, daily exc 25 Dec, 10.30am–7pm (last entry 6pm) or dusk. Admission (1985 prices) £1.85 adults, £1.50 OAPs, 95p children; parties by arrangement. No dogs.
☎ Frome (0373) 830326. &

Ugbrooke House
Chudleigh, Devon
Robert Adams house with park and grounds designed by 'Capability'

Brown including two lakes and magnificent sweeps of unbroken scenery. Adventure playground; pets corner.
Open 19 May to 20 Sept, daily, 12.30pm–5.30pm (House 2pm–5pm). Admission: House and Grounds £1.50 adults, 80p children, parties £1.20 & 60p; Grounds only 50p.
☎ (0626) 852179. &

University of Bristol Botanic Garden
Woodland Road, Bristol, Avon
Mature garden with wide range of plants, featuring special displays, small collections of regional floras and different British ecological situations. Large collection of New Zealand plants.

NOTES ON GARDEN VISITING

These entries have been compiled from information supplied by the gardens and were correct at the time of going to press (November 1985). However, opening times can be subject to sudden change, often because of uncontrollable factors such as the weather. We advise you to telephone the garden to check before setting out – check the admission charges, too. Those given in the entries do not always include admission to the house or other facilities in addition to the garden. Some of the gardens are willing to allow visitors by prior appointment at other times apart from their normal opening days. Where dogs are allowed in a garden, they should always be kept on a lead. NT ⚘ denotes gardens belonging to the National Trust – see also pages 8–9. The & symbol shows which gardens are accessible to physically handicapped visitors – see also page 97.

Open all year, weekdays exc Bank Hols, 9am–5pm. Admission free. No dogs.
☎ (0272) 733682. &

Wilton House
nr Salisbury, Wiltshire
20 acres of lawn with fine cedar trees form parkland setting for this beautiful house (home of the Earl of Pembroke); garden centre for pot plants and shrubs.
Open 25 Mar to 12 Oct, Tue to Sat & Bank Hols 11am–6pm, Sun 1pm–6pm (last entry 5.15pm). Admission: House £2.40 adults, £1.60 OAPs/students, £1.20 children, £1.60 parties; Grounds 90p adults, 60p children/parties. No dogs.
☎ (0722) 743115. &

THE POLURRIAN HOTEL
A treasure chest of holiday pleasures in a secret Cornish cove.

The Lizard peninsula is famous for its wildlife and gardens. Here in 12 acres of superb terraced gardens stands the Polurrian Hotel. Surrounded by National Trust countryside and with panoramic views across Mounts Bay to St. Michael's Mount and distant Lands End the position is ideal for visits to many famous Cornish gardens. Glendurgan, Trelissick, Morrab, Trengwainton and Fox Rose-Hill are just some within easy reach. Family owned and managed, the hotel provides personal friendly service and excellent cuisine which includes choice local produce and a variety of seafood specialities.
Well furnished rooms and family suites are available with bathrooms en suite, colour television with video link, radio, telephone and baby listening. Self catering apartments are also available.

Our new indoor centre has a heated indoor pool, spa bath, sauna, solarium, gymnasium, snooker, squash, games room and lounge bar.

The Polurrian is a convivial hotel for relaxed family holidays or ideal as a centre for touring the whole of Cornwall. Our 1986 programme includes a number of Special Interest breaks – please ask for details.

The Polurrian Hotel AA***RAC, Mullion, Helston, S. Cornwall TR12 7EN. Tel. 0326 240421.

A GUIDE TO ENGLISH GARDENS

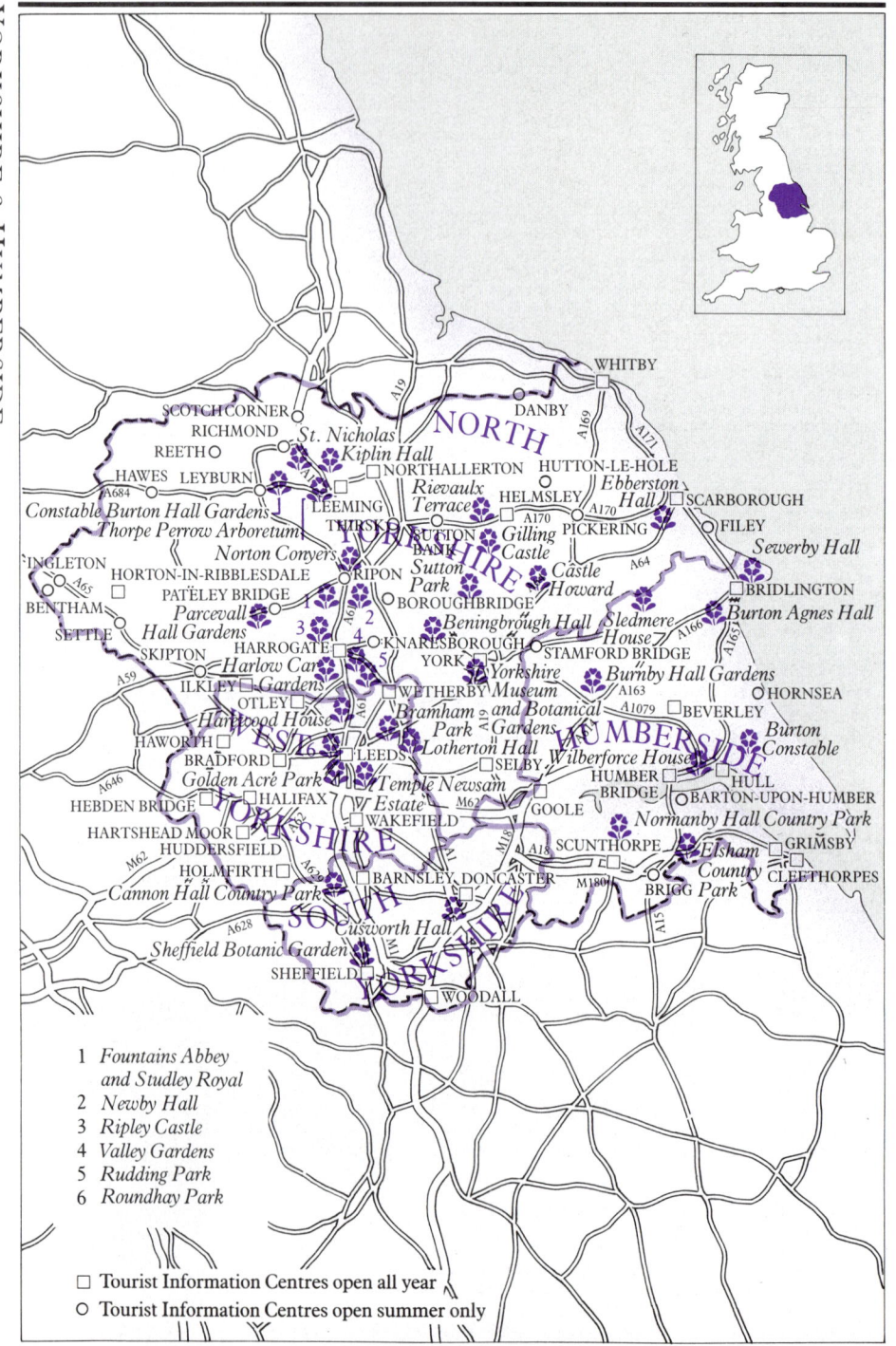

YORKSHIRE & HUMBERSIDE

1 *Fountains Abbey and Studley Royal*
2 *Newby Hall*
3 *Ripley Castle*
4 *Valley Gardens*
5 *Rudding Park*
6 *Roundhay Park*

☐ Tourist Information Centres open all year
○ Tourist Information Centres open summer only

YORKSHIRE & HUMBERSIDE

Yorkshire means space – and plenty of it. The sense of loveliness unlimited which marks the moors and dales and great sweeps of heritage coastline has been carried over into Yorkshire's gardens, creating some splendid examples of gardening very much in the grand manner. Capability Brown was kept busy here; his work includes the woods and terraces of 18th-century Harewood House and the parks and grounds surrounding Sledmere House, whilst he also contributed to the landscaping of Sutton Park, Temple Newsam and the 'pleasure grounds' at Ripley Castle. The genius behind Castle Howard was the owner himself whose grand design combined water, classical buildings and ever-changing panoramic views to create what has been called the masterpiece of the heroic age of English landscape architecture. Though less majestic, other gardens are equally pleasing and wonderfully varied. Burnby Hall Gardens display one of the largest collections of water lilies in the world and Thorpe Perrow Arboretum boasts over 2,000 varieties of trees and shrubs; the gardens at Bramham Park, laid out in the French style of Le Notre who designed Versailles, have remained virtually unchanged over 300 years; in Sheffield you can wander around Victorian rock and heather gardens; at Lotherton Hall you can see over 400 species of exotic birds; Burton Constable has 200 acres of parkland and 25 acres of lakes, and at Norton Conyers you can even pick your own fruit. The map of Yorkshire's gardens also shows some very lovely towns – York, Catterick, Harrogate, Richmond – but Ripon and Helmsley hold the key to two very special places: Studley Royal includes the magnificent ruins of Fountains Abbey, while from Rievaulx Terrace you can look down over Rievaulx Abbey to Ryedale and the Hambleton Hills beyond. Throughout the region views are something of a speciality – and in Herriot Country or the Howardian Hills, from wuthering heights to the gentle Yorkshire Wolds, gardens bring them nicely into focus.

DECEMBER

Gardens are grateful now for the colour supplied by faithful evergreens and winter-flowering shrubs – white Christmas rosés, the delicate yellow of winter jasmine or the pinky-purple of the first winter heathers. Hollies in their different varieties add a festive note. With Christmas approaching, every gardener spares a thought for his greenhouse plants. With their showy red leaves poinsettias are amongst the most popular as presents, but there are many others – delicate, flighty cyclamen, bushy azaleas, warmly-coloured primulas and begonias or the striking aphelandra louisae or 'zebra plant' which are also all at their best to grace the great occasion.

Black Douglas Begonia

HEATHER

The Greek name for heather – 'Calluna', meaning I cleanse – is a reminder of its use in making brooms; in the language of flowers, however, heather means solitude – and it's easy to see why. Common heather, or ling, dominates lonely moorland landscapes such as the North York Moors, turning whole hillsides purple in late summer when it comes into flower. Bees are attracted to its nectar, and beekeepers often move hives out onto the moors to take advantage of this abundant crop. Heather grows well on acid soils, but as it becomes old and woody, it provides less and less food for sheep. For this reason, many heather moors are rejuvenated by burning on a rotation basis, for after burning the heather quickly puts out new and tender shoots.

Erica ciliaris

For more information contact the
Yorkshire & Humberside Tourist Board,
312 Tadcaster Road, York,
North Yorkshire YO2 2HF
☎ (0904) 707961.

Beningbrough Hall
nr York, North Yorkshire
18th-century house standing in wooded park and gardens. Walled garden, adventure playground, picnic area, lime avenue. Victorian laundry with exhibition. Restaurant and shop.
Open 29 Mar to end Oct, daily exc Mon & Fri (open Bank Hol Mon), 12 noon–6pm. Admission: House & Garden £1.90 adults, 80p children; parties £1.50 & 60p. No dogs.
☎ *(0904) 470715/470666. NT* ※ &

Bramham Park
nr Wetherby, West Yorkshire
Unique French-style gardens; ponds, cascades, temples and a 'ha ha'.
Open 9 June to 28 Aug, Sun, Tue, Wed, Thur, 1.15pm–5.30pm; Gardens only also open Easter & Spring Bank Hol. Admission £1.40 adults, 70p children, £1.20 OAPs & parties.
☎ *Boston Spa (0973) 844265.* &

Burnby Hall Gardens
Pocklington, Humberside
Delightful gardens with an outstanding collection of water lilies on two large lakes. Small museum. Scented garden.
Open Easter to 28 Sept, daily, 10am–6pm. Admission 60p adults, 40p OAPs, 20p children over 10.
☎ *(075 92) 2068 or Middleton-on-the-Wolds (037 781) 268.* &

Burton Agnes Hall
Burton Agnes, nr Bridlington, Humberside
Elizabethan house set in woodland gardens; herb and shrub borders, statues.
Open 28 Mar to 31 Oct, daily, 11am–5pm. Admission £1.25 adults, 90p children & OAPs.
☎ *(026 289) 324.* &

Burton Constable
nr Hull, Humberside
Elizabethan house in 200 acres of parkland, with 25 acres of lakes.
Open 30 Mar to 30 Sept, Sun, Mon, also Tue to Thurs in Aug, 1pm–5pm. Open for parties at other times by special appt. Admission £1.20 adults, 70p OAPs, 60p children.
☎ *Skirlaugh (0401) 62400.* &

Cannon Hall Country Park
Cawthorne, nr Barnsley, South Yorkshire
Landscaped by Richard Woods in the early 1760s, with 19th-century rhododendrons and azaleas making this country house museum particularly attractive in early summer.
Open all year, Mon to Sat 10.30am–5pm, Sun 2.30pm–5pm. Closed 25–27 Dec & Good Fri. Admission free.
☎ *(0226) 790270.* &

Castle Howard
nr York, North Yorkshire
Superb house with costume galleries, gardens and parkland; lakes, fountains and beautiful rose gardens.
Open 25 Mar to 31 Oct, daily, 10.30am–5pm (last entrance 4.30pm). Admission: House, Costume Galleries, Gardens £2.60 adults, £2.10 OAPs, £1.30 children, £2.10 parties, by appt; Gardens only £1.20 adults, 60p children.
☎ *Coneysthorpe (065 384) 333.* &

Constable Burton Hall Gardens
nr Leyburn, North Yorkshire
Large garden with something of interest all spring and summer. Splendid display of daffodils; rockery with wide variety of alpines; extensive shrubs and roses; small lake with wildfowl; woodland walks.
Open 1 Apr to 12 Aug, daily, 9am–6pm. Admission 50p adults, 25p children/students; parties by arangement.
☎ *Bedale (0677) 50428.*

Cusworth Hall
nr Doncaster, South Yorkshire
Imposing country house museum, with 'Pleasure Grounds' laid out by Richard Woods in 1763 with groves and plantations of ornamental trees and shrubs. Lakes.
Open all year, daily, 7.30am–sunset. Museum daily exc Fri; Mar to Oct, Mon to Thur, Sat 11am–5pm, Sun 1pm–5pm; Nov to Feb, Mon to Thur, Sat 11am–4pm, Sun 1pm–4pm. Admission free.
☎ *(0302) 785732 (park) or 782342 (museum).* &

Ebberston Hall
Scarborough, North Yorkshire
Water gardens attributed to William Benson and Switzer. Palladian villa 1718 designed by Colen Campbell. Elaborate woodwork and cornices comparable to Castle Howard and Beningbrough.
Open 28 Mar to 1 Nov, daily, 10am–6pm. Admission £1 adults, children free.
☎ *(0723) 85516.* & *(garden only).*

Elsham Country Park
nr Brigg, South Humberside
Magnificent park with lakes and wild gardens. Butterfly garden, bird garden. Arboretum; walled garden. Waterfowl, poultry and domestic animals. Nature trails; tearoom; adventure playground.
Open 24 Mar to 28 Sept, Mon to Sat, 11am–5.30pm, Sun 11am–6pm. Admission (1985 prices) summer £1.20 adults, 60p children; winter £1 adults, 50p children. Parties and coach tours by prior arrangement. No dogs.
☎ *Barnetby (0652) 688698.* &

Fountains Abbey and Studley Royal
Ripon, North Yorkshire
18th-century water gardens, river walks, temples, statues and ponds. 400-acre deer park; lake; Victorian church; ruins of 12th-century Cistercian abbey.
Open all year, exc 24 & 25 Dec, Apr to Sept 10am–7pm; Oct to Mar 10am–4pm. Admission £1.50 adults, 70p children; reduced rates for parties.
☎ *Sawley (076 85) 333 or 639. NT* ※ &

Gilling Castle
Gilling East, North Yorkshire
House dating from 14th century (preparatory school for Ampleforth College), set in fine gardens. Elizabethan Great Chamber and hall shown.
Open all year, daily exc 25 & 26 Dec, 10am–12 noon, 2pm–4pm. Admission 50p adults.
☎ *Ampleforth (043 93) 238.*

Golden Acre Park
Bramhope, Leeds, West Yorkshire
Approx. 137 acres of mature woodland and gardens; lakes and ponds with an interesting collection of wildfowl; variety of trees, shrubs, herbaceous and aquatic plants; limestone and sandstone rock gardens, alpine house, demonstration garden, arboretum and pinetum with wildflowers. Information centre; shops; Bakery Coffee House; restaurant.
Open all year, daily. Admission free. &

Harewood House
Harewood, nr Leeds, West Yorkshire
'Capability' Brown landscape surrounding 18th-century house; terraces, woodland walks, water garden and lakeside Bird Garden.
Open Apr to Oct, daily; Feb, Mar, Nov, Sun only; from 10am (House opens 11am). Admission (1985 prices) £3 adults, £2.20 OAPs, £1.20 children; Gardens only £1 adults, 50p children; special party rates.
☎ *(0532) 886225.* &

THE MAJESTIC — Harrogate
A 4 star hotel set in extensive well kept gardens offering superb accommodation, excellent food, free parking and leisure facilities including heated indoor pool, squash, tennis, snooker and Children's Adventure Playground.

Close to the town centre, Harrogate's renowned Public Gardens and the ornamental and trial gardens at Harlow Car.

For details of rates and leisure breaks contact:
The Majestic, Ripon Road, Harrogate, N. Yorks. 0423 68972

Burton Agnes Hall, Humberside

Harlow Car Gardens
Harrogate, North Yorkshire
Interesting ornamental and botanic gardens; arboretum and superb rhododendron woods. Established centre for North of England horticultural trials.
Open all year, daily, 9.30am–dusk. Admission £1.50 adults, £1 OAPs, accompanied children free; £1 parties 20+. No dogs.
☎ *(0423) 65418.* &

Kiplin Hall
nr Catterick, North Yorkshire
Fine Jacobean house with period gardens, including herb garden. Home-made teas on Sun.
Open 21 May to 31 Aug, Wed, Sun, Bank Hols, 2pm–5pm. Admission 80p adults, 50p OAPs, 40p children.
☎ *Richmond (0748) 818178.* &

Lotherton Hall
nr Aberford, West Yorkshire
Edwardian country house in attractive gardens set amid pleasant countryside. Large Bird Garden with over 400 exotic birds; Norman Chapel; deer park.
Open: Gardens & grounds all year, daily, dawn to dusk; Bird Garden Easter to Oct, daily exc Mon, 11am–5pm; House all year, daily exc Mon, 10.30am–6.15pm or dusk; also Thur, May to Sept, 10.30am–8.30pm. Admission to Gardens free; House extra.
☎ *Leeds (0532) 645535.* &

Newby Hall
Ripon, North Yorkshire
Attractive 25-acre gardens sloping to banks of river; unusual garden ornaments; plant stall selling rare and unusual plants.
Open Easter to 30 Sept, daily exc Mon (but open Bank Hol Mons), 11am–5pm.
Admission (1985 prices) £1.40 adults, 90p children; parties £1.20 & 80p. No dogs.
☎ *Boroughbridge (090 12) 2583.* &

Normanby Hall Country Park
Scunthorpe, South Humberside
350 acres of gardens and parkland surrounding a Regency mansion, with rhododendron walks, ornamental duckpond, aviary, deer park, fishing lake and nature trails.
Open all year, daily, during daylight hours. Admission free to gardens; 50p adults, 20p children & OAPs (house).
☎ *(0724) 720215 (hall); 720588 (information centre); 862141 ext. 297 (parks dept.).* &

Norton Conyers
Wath, nr Ripon, North Yorkshire
Jacobean house, belonging to the same family since 1624. Said to be the original of Thornfield House in Jane Eyre. Large 18th-century walled garden with orangery and fine borders. Hardy plants, alpines, herbs and dried flowers for sale.
Garden open all year, Mon to Fri, 9am–5pm; also Sat & Sun Apr to 1 Oct, 2pm–5pm. House open 1 June to 7 Sept, Suns & Bank Hol Mon, 2pm–5.30pm. Admission Garden free, House £1.20 adults.
☎ *Melmerby (076 584) 333.* &

Parcevall Hall Gardens
Appletreewick, nr Pateley Bridge, North Yorkshire
Beautiful woodland and terrace garden in hillside setting, 3 miles from Burnsall in Wharfedale. Garden plants for sale. Old orchard picnic area.
Open Easter to 31 Oct, daily, 10am–6pm. Admission 50p adults, 25p children; parties by arrangement.
☎ *Burnsall (075 672) 311 or 214.*

Rievaulx Terrace
Helmsley, North Yorkshire
Beautiful half-mile grass terrace with 18th-century temples overlooking Rievaulx Abbey. Permanent exhibition on English landscape design in the 18th century.
Open 29 Apr to 31 Oct, daily, 10.30am–6pm (last admission 5.30pm). Admission £1.20 adults, 60p children; parties £1 adults, 50p children.
☎ *Bilsdale (043 96) 340. NT* ❧ &
Wheelchairs available.

Ripley Castle
Ripley, nr Harrogate, North Yorkshire
Dates back to early 14th century. Pleasure grounds and gardens laid out by 'Capability' Brown. Specimen trees from many parts of the world.
Open 28 Apr to 12 Oct, daily, 11am–6pm, gardens only. Admission 80p adults, 60p OAPs/unemployed, 50p children; parties on application.
☎ *Harrogate (0423) 770152.* &

Roundhay Park
Leeds 8, West Yorkshire
Large park with tropical plant house. Coronation House—glasshouse full of flowers, Canal Gardens with 80ft fountain; aquarium, rose garden, boating lakes, sports and recreational facilities and events.
Open all year, daily, 9am–dusk. Admission free.
☎ *(0532) 661850.* &

NOTES ON GARDEN VISITING

These entries have been compiled from information supplied by the gardens and were correct at the time of going to press (November 1985). However, opening times can be subject to sudden change, often because of uncontrollable factors such as the weather. We advise you to telephone the garden to check before setting out – check the admission charges, too. Those given in the entries do not always include admission to the house or other facilities in addition to the garden. Some of the gardens are willing to allow visitors by prior appointment at other times apart from their normal opening days. Where dogs are allowed in a garden, they should always be kept on a lead. NT ❧ denotes gardens belonging to the National Trust – see also pages 8–9. The & symbol shows which gardens are accessible to physically handicapped visitors – see also page 97.

Rievaulx Terrace, North Yorkshire

Rudding Park
*Follifoot, nr Harrogate,
North Yorkshire*
Romantic garden with magnificent views across Vale of York. Woodland garden introducing a considerable degree of formality. Landscaped by Repton, and noted for its rhododendrons and azaleas.
Open 1 Apr to 30 June, daily 11am–5pm. Admission £1 per car, occupants free.
☎ *(0423) 870439.*

St Nicholas
Richmond, North Yorkshire
Garden laid out in 1910, with Tibetan rhododendrons; topiary, shrub roses.
Open Apr to Oct, daily, all day. Admission 30p adults, 15p children.
☎ *(0748) 2328.*

Sewerby Hall
Bridlington, Humberside
Fascinating gardens of botanical interest set in parkland. Zoo; Museum and art gallery.
Open all year, daily, 9am to dusk. Hall open 28 Mar to 28 Sept. Admission (1985 prices) Park & Zoo from Spring Bank Hol to mid-Sept 60p adults, 30p children; Hall free.
☎ *(0262) 678255.* &

Sheffield Botanic Garden
Sheffield, South Yorkshire
Victorian heather and rock gardens; trial grounds; garden for disabled and education centre.
Open all year, Mon to Sat 7.30am–dusk, Sun 10am–dusk. Admission free.
☎ *(0742) 663115.* &

Sledmere House
Driffield, Humberside
Fine Georgian house in beautiful park and grounds designed by 'Capability' Brown. Rose gardens.

*Open 28 Mar to end Sept, daily exc Mon & Fri (open Bank Hol Mon);
1.30pm–5.30pm (last entry 5pm). Admission (1985 prices) £1.40 adults, £1.20 OAPs/parties, 80p children.*
☎ *(0377) 86208.* &

Sutton Park
*Sutton-on-the-Forest,
North Yorkshire*
Early Georgian House with attractive, terraced garden; herbaceous borders and roses; landscaped setting designed by 'Capability' Brown.
Gardens open daily exc Sat in Apr; House & Gardens open 4 May to 5 Oct, Sun & Tue; 1.30pm–5.30pm. Admission £1.60 adults, £1.25 OAPs/students, 60p children, £1.25 parties. Gardens only half-price. No dogs.
☎ *Easingwold (0347) 810249.* &

Temple Newsam Estate
Leeds, West Yorkshire
900-acre estate with extensive mature gardens with herb, formal, spring and bog gardens, rhododendrons, rose garden and conservatory. Park, landscaped by 'Capability' Brown, has woodland walks, sports facilities, adventure playground and working farm. House, birthplace of Lord Darnley, houses fine Museum of Decorative Art.
Gardens open all year, daily, dawn to dusk. House open all year, Tue to Sun, Bank Hol Mon, 10.30am–6.15pm or dusk; also Wed, May to Sept, 10.30am–8.30pm. Admission to Gardens & Park free; House extra.
☎ *(0532) 645535.* &

Thorpe Perrow Arboretum
Bedale, North Yorkshire
65 acres of landscaped grounds, containing over 2,000 species of trees and shrubs, including some of the largest and rarest in England. (Entrance on Well-Bedale road, 2½ miles from Bedale.)
Open 1 Mar to 2nd week Nov, daily, 9.30am–dusk. Admission £1 adults, 50p children/OAPs.
☎ *(0677) 22480.* &

Valley Gardens
Harrogate, North Yorkshire
Formal gardens with lawns, woods, walkways and colonnade. Wide variety of flowering plants, with something to see at all times of the year.
Open all year, daily. Admission free.
☎ *(0423) 68966.* &

Wilberforce House
Hull, Humberside
17th-century mansion, birthplace of William Wilberforce, now a museum. Large, secluded gardens reaching down to the river.
Open all year, daily exc Good Fri & 24–26 Dec, Mon to Sat 10am–5pm, Sun 1.30pm–4pm. Admission free. No dogs.
☎ *(0482) 222737.* &

Yorkshire Museum and Botanical Gardens
York, North Yorkshire
Botanical gardens including ruins of St Mary's Abbey, Multangular Tower and Observatory.
Open all year, daily, Mon to Fri 7.30am–dusk, Sat 8am–dusk, Sun 10am–dusk. Observatory normally open Apr to Sept, Wed to Sun, 1pm–4.30pm. Museum open all year, Mon to Sat 10am–5pm, Sun 1pm–5pm. Admission (1985 prices): Gardens free; Observatory 15p adults, 10p children; Museum 80p adults, 40p children/OAPs.
☎ *(0904) 29745/6.* &

GARDENS *for* DISABLED PEOPLE

More and more gardens are making a special point of looking after the needs of disabled or visually handicapped visitors. Throughout this guide, the familiar ♿ symbol is used to indicate those gardens that are suitable for the physically handicapped. Since the particular facilities available may vary from garden to garden – some may provide wheelchairs, for instance, while others have installed special ramps and toilets – it's a good idea to ring the garden concerned in advance to see what arrangements have been made. In some cases, the symbol simply means that the design of the garden is such that it is easily accessible to those in wheelchairs. It does not always mean that the house or other buildings are accessible however, so again, we would advise you to check to avoid disappointment.

Listed here are those gardens which are of particular interest to disabled people. Some are there to be enjoyed for their own sake, others can give handicapped visitors useful ideas which can be adapted for their own gardens – growing plants in raised beds or containers, for instance, so they can be tended without too much exertion, or designing the layout of the garden so that it is easy and safe to move around in. For further information about opening times, garden features, historical background etc, please see the garden's main reference entry on the page indicated at the end of each entry.

Many of these gardens hold a special attraction for visually handicapped people. Of all the characteristics of plants, that of scent can be the most evocative, and a perfumed garden is a marvellous place to visit. The true skill of this aspect of gardening lies in grouping the plants so that we can enjoy them all individually – the strong scent of some plants is carried upon the air for considerable distances, and unless careful thought is given to the arrangement of the perfumed garden they can easily swamp more delicate fragrances and lead to a confusion of the senses.

But scent in plants is not there merely for our pleasure – its function is an ecological one. The aromatic oils of rosemary and lavender, for instance, evolved as a defence against browsing animals which do not share our enjoyment of their scent. Other fragrances developed as a means of attracting the birds and insects upon which such plants depend for pollination. An interesting aspect of many perfumed gardens is that here we can enjoy flowers in their original, old-fashioned forms, before the process of hybridization robbed many of them of their distinctive scents in the pursuit of better shape and colour.

Most foliage plants, on the other hand, release their scent only when touched – in some gardens, therefore, visitors are encouraged to handle them, thus adding the tactile enjoyment of texture to the delicacies of scent. This is something we can enjoy with many non-aromatic plants as well, of course. Walking on a chamomile lawn or path has a pleasure all of its own, as the long, pointed leaves of this herb release a most attractive aroma when crushed. There is also much to be gained from the sound of running water – again a feature of some of these gardens, from the gentle murmur of a slow-flowing stream to the bubbling and splashing of a cascade – and this too is something which the visitor can learn from and apply at home. Classical Japanese gardens exploited to the full the various sound effects produced by water, a feature which Western gardeners have only recently come to appreciate.

Blind visitors and their guide dogs will be admitted to most of the gardens listed in this guide, but they are advised to bring along a sighted companion who can help them with stairs, overhanging branches, slippery paths and so on. And it's probably best to visit on weekdays, when visitors are fewer and access is easier.

A Guide to English Gardens

Gardens for Disabled People

CUMBRIA

Lake District National Park Visitor Centre
Brockhole, Windermere, Cumbria.
Batricar and two wheelchairs available for hire. Audio-visual presentation for groups of disabled visitors; also special guidebook with map. Scented herbs and plants. *See page 33.*

Mirehouse
Keswick, Cumbria.
Part of the lakeside walk has wire guideline for the partially sighted. *See page 33.*

EAST ANGLIA

Cambridge University Botanic Gardens
Cambridge, Cambridgeshire.
Scented garden. *See page 36.*

Clare College
Cambridge, Cambridgeshire.
Scented garden. *See page 36.*

Hyde Hall Garden
Rettendon, Essex.
Two wheelchairs available. *See page 37.*

Ickworth
nr Bury St Edmunds, Suffolk.
Braille guide available. *See page 37.*

Mannington Hall Gardens
Saxthorpe, Norfolk.
Scented garden. *See page 37.*

Mark Hall Gardens
Harlow, Essex.
Scented herb borders and rose gardens. *See page 37.*

Netherfield Herbs
Rougham, nr Bury St Edmunds, Suffolk.
Scented herb garden. *See page 37.*

River Cam Farm House
Wimpole, Cambridgeshire.
Scented gardens: chamomile collar garden, herb garden. *See page 38.*

Sprowston Garden Centre
Sprowston, Norwich, Norfolk.
Wheelchair for public use. *See page 38.*

Thornham Herb Garden
Thornham Magna, nr Eye, Suffolk.
Scented herbs. *See page 38.*

EAST MIDLANDS

Abington Park
Northampton, Northamptonshire.
Garden for the blind containing features of sound, touch and smell; raised pond and fountain; chamomile aromatic lawn; braille labels. *See page 41.*

Clumber Park
Worksop, Nottinghamshire.
Free wheelchairs available, also powered 'outrider' bike for hire.

Fishing platforms for wheelchairs. Guided walks can be arranged for visually handicapped. *See page 41.*

Gunby Hall
Gunby, nr Spilsby, Lincolnshire.
Scented herb garden. *See page 42.*

Hardwick Hall
nr Chesterfield, Derbyshire.
Herb garden with wide pathways for wheelchairs. *See page 42.*

Harrington Hall
Spilsby, Lincolnshire.
Scented garden. *See page 42.*

Rufford
nr Ollerton, Nottinghamshire.
Scented garden and herb garden. *See page 43.*

HEART OF ENGLAND

Attingham Park
Shrewsbury, Shropshire.
Braille leaflet available. *See page 46.*

Berrington Hall
nr Leominster, Herefordshire.
Wheelchair available. *See page 46.*

The Commandery
Worcester, Worcestershire.
Herb garden with raised beds for the disabled and thermoformed labels for the poor sighted. *See page 47.*

Croft Castle
Croft, nr Leominster, Herefordshire.
Wheelchair available. *See page 47.*

Hidcote Manor Garden
Mickleton, Gloucestershire.
Wheelchairs available. *See page 48.*

Jephson Gardens
Leamington Spa, Warwickshire.
Scented garden. *See page 48.*

Jubilee Maze
Symonds Yat West, Herefordshire.
Maze suitable for blind – rope guides. *See page 48.*

Queens Park
Harborne, Birmingham, West Midlands.
Garden for blind visitors, with braille notices. *See page 49.*

Shugborough
Great Haywood, Staffordshire.
Scented rose garden. *See page 49.*

LONDON

Battersea Park
Albert Bridge Road, London SW11
Garden for the disabled run by Horticultural Therapy Unit. *See page 53.*

The Chelsea Physic Garden
Chelsea, London SW3.
Scented garden: 'Perfumery border'. *See page 53.*

Dulwich Park
College Road, London SE21.
Braille maps. Garden for the disabled (opens late 1986). *See page 53.*

Hall Place Gardens
Bexley, Kent.
Herb garden for the blind with plant identification in braille. *See page 53.*

Hampton Court
East Molesey, Surrey.
Audio tapes for hire in summer. Wheelchairs available. *See page 53.*

Royal Botanic Gardens, Kew
Kew, Richmond, Surrey.
Wheelchairs for hire. *See page 54*

Syon Park Garden
Brentford, Middlesex.
Disabled Living Foundation Garden. *See page 54.*

Trent Park
Cockfosters, Hertfordshire.
Braille notices on woodland trail. *See page 55.*

NORTHUMBRIA

Wallington House, Walled Garden and Grounds
Cambo, Northumberland.
Wheelchairs available. *See page 59.*

NORTH WEST

Arley Hall and Gardens
Between Northwich and Knutsford, Cheshire.
Scented garden and herb garden. *See page 62.*

Chester Zoo
Chester, Cheshire.
Wheelchairs available. *See page 62.*

City of Liverpool Botanic Gardens
Calderstones Park, Liverpool, Merseyside.
Gardens for blind and disabled people; raised beds planted for texture and scent. Cassette tapes available. Activity Garden for physically handicapped visitors to 'do their own thing'. *See page 62.*

Hornsea Pottery
Lancaster, Lancashire.
Scented garden. *See page 62.*

Liverpool University Botanic Gardens
Ness, Wirral, Cheshire.
Scented garden with braille labels on rail. Wheelchair available. *See page 64.*

SOUTH

Barton Manor
Whippingham, Cowes, Isle of Wight.
Scented 'secret' garden. *See page 67.*

Highbury
West Moors, nr Wimborne, Dorset.
Conducted tour available for blind visitors if requested in advance. *See page 68.*

Houghton Lodge
Stockbridge, Hampshire.
Herb garden, rose garden.
See page 68.

Merley Bird Gardens
nr Wimborne Minster, Dorset.
Scented garden. Wheelchairs available (no charge). See page 68.

Old Smithy Complex
Godshill, Isle of Wight.
Scented herb garden. See page 69.

Seafront Gardens
Southsea, Hampshire.
Scented rose garden. See page 69.

Tudor House Garden
Southampton, Hampshire.
Scented garden. Cassette recorded tour to hire. See page 69.

Gilbert White Museum
Selborne, nr Alton, Hampshire.
Old-fashioned scented rose garden (July). Visually handicapped can crush and smell herbs. See page 69.

SOUTH EAST

Bedgebury National Pinetum
nr Goudhurst, Kent.
Scent/touch tree trail for the blind. See page 72.

Fishbourne Roman Palace
nr Chichester, West Sussex.
Tactile maps and taped guides for visually handicapped visitors. See page 73.

Goodnestone Park
nr Canterbury, Kent.
Scented, old-fashioned roses, lavender, pinks etc. See page 73.

Hannah Peschar Gallery Garden
Ockley, Surrey.
Sculpture exhibits in garden can be touched and felt. See page 73.

Iden Croft Herbs
Staplehurst, Kent.
Aromatic garden. See page 73.

Leeds Castle
nr Maidstone, Kent.
Culpeper Garden – an oasis of scent and colour designed by Russell Page in the International Year of the Disabled 1980. See page 73.

Polesden Lacey
nr Dorking, Surrey.
Scented lavender and rose gardens. See page 74.

Preston Manor
Brighton, East Sussex.
Garden for the blind: 2 acres of scented shrubs and plants to touch. See page 75.

Sheffield Park Garden
Uckfield, East Sussex.
Wheelchairs available. See page 75.

Wisley
nr Ripley, Surrey.
Small model garden for the disabled. Wheelchairs available. Signposted wheelchair route. See page 76.

THAMES AND CHILTERNS

Capel Manor Horticultural and Environmental Centre
Waltham Cross, Hertfordshire.
New garden opens 1986, specially designed for disabled gardeners. See page 79.

The Gardens of the Rose
Chiswell Green, St Albans, Hertfordshire.
New scented rose border with all the best scented rose varieties. See page 80.

Greys Court
nr Henley-on-Thames, Oxfordshire.
Wheelchairs available for loan. See page 80.

WEST COUNTRY

Abbotsbury Sub-Tropical Gardens
Abbotsbury, nr Weymouth, Dorset.
Wheelchairs available (free of charge). See page 85.

County Demonstration Garden
Probus, nr St. Austell, Cornwall.
Garden for the disabled with raised beds, special tools etc; includes aromatic plants for the blind. See page 87.

Gaulden Manor
Tolland, Lydeard St Lawrence, Somerset.
Scented garden. See page 88.

Middle Hill
Washfield, nr Tiverton, Devon.
Many scented plants. See page 89.

Powderham Castle
Kenton, Exeter, Devon.
Scented rose garden. See page 90.

Stourhead
Stourton, nr Mere, Wiltshire.
Wheelchairs available. See page 90.

Trelissick Gardens
nr Truro, Cornwall.
Fragrant walled garden. See page 90.

Tregwainton Gardens
nr Penzance, Cornwall.
Scented flowers along drive and in walled gardens – especially April, May, June. See page 90.

Wilton House
nr Salisbury, Wiltshire.
Scented rose garden. See page 91.

YORKSHIRE AND HUMBERSIDE

Burnby Hall and Gardens
Pocklington, Humberside.
Scented garden. See page 94.

Fountains Abbey and Studley Royal
Ripon, North Yorkshire.
Wheelchairs available. See page 94.

Harlow Car Gardens
Harrogate, North Yorkshire.
Disabled route for handicapped visitors. See page 95.

Rievaulx Terrace
Helmsley, North Yorkshire.
Wheelchairs available. See page 95.

Sewerby Hall
Bridlington, Humberside.
Small scented garden with braille name plates. See page 96.

Sheffield Botanic Garden
Sheffield, South Yorkshire.
Garden for disabled, with raised beds. Wheelchair available. See page 96.

Stourhead, Wiltshire

GARDEN CENTRES & NURSERIES

If you're inspired by your visits to the great English gardens in this guide, visit one of the garden centres or nurseries listed below. Here you'll find all the plants, advice and equipment you'll need to recreate in your own garden (however humble) some of your favourite features. These entries have been paid for by the establishments, and it is advisable to check important details before setting out.

CUMBRIA

Dalemain Garden
Dacre, Penrith, Cumbria CA11 0HB.
☎ *Pooley Bridge (085 36) 450.*
Herbaceous plants and bedding plants available all year from garden featured on BBC2's 'Gardener's World'. Old-fashioned roses and Himalayan Poppy are specialities. Licensed restaurant.
Open 30 Mar to mid-Oct, Sun to Thur, 11.15am to 5pm.

Hayes Garden World
Lake District Nurseries, Ambleside, Cumbria LA22 0DW.
☎ *(0966) 33434.*
One of Britain's finest garden centres, situated in one of her finest landscapes.
Open all year, daily, 9am (10am Sun) to 6pm or dusk. Closed 25 & 26 Dec, 1 Jan.

EAST ANGLIA

The Beth Chatto Gardens
Elmstead Market, Colchester, Essex CO7 7DB.
☎ *Wivenhoe (0206 22) 2007.*
The Nursery stocks one of the largest collections of unusual hardy plants in the country, suited for all conditions. Fully-descriptive catalogue, price £1.28 inc. postage.
Open all year, Mon to Sat, 9am–5pm. Closed Sun, Bank Hols; & Sat mid-Nov to 1 Feb.

Bypass Nurseries
Ipswich Road, Colchester, Essex.
☎ *(0206) 865500.*
Capel, St. Mary, A12 nr Ipswich, Suffolk.
☎ *(0473) 310604.*
East Anglia's finest selection of house plants, shrubs, trees, seeds and bulbs. Swimming pools, conservatories, greenhouses and everything else for the garden. Ample free parking.
Open all year, daily, Mon to Sat, 9am–5.30pm, Sun, Bank Hols, 10am–5pm.

Clippesby Garden Centre and Nurseries
Clippesby, nr Great Yarmouth, Norfolk NR29 3BJ.
☎ *Fleggburgh (049 377) 367.*
A plant nursery with display greenhouses. Ornamental walks beneath cascading fuchsias and other tender plants. Home-made teas and other simple meals.
Open Mar to Oct, daily, 10am–5pm.

EAST MIDLANDS

Baytree Nurseries Garden Centre
High Road, Weston, nr Spalding, Lincolnshire PE12 6JU.
☎ *Holbeach (0406) 370242.*
Bulbs, plants, trees, shrubs, indoor plant house. Shop, display gardens, aquatic area. Adventure playground, kiddies' corner. Licensed self-service restaurant.
Open all year, daily, 9am–7pm (summer), 9am–6pm (winter).

Harrington Hall Garden Centre
Harrington Hall, Spilsby, Lincolnshire PE23 4NH.
☎ *(0790) 52281.*
Interesting and unusual shrubs and plants raised in garden. 18th-century walled garden; Jacobean terrace. Tours by arrangement with Head Gardener.
Open Easter to end Oct, Wed & Thur, 12 noon–8pm.

Springfields Gardens
Springfields, Spalding, Lincolnshire PE12 6ET.
☎ *(0775) 4843.*
25-acre gardens, together with a woodland area, sunken garden, paved walks, lake. Glasshouses with hundreds of varieties of tulips in the spring to various displays of summer flowering plants, shrubs and trees.
Open 29 Mar to 30 Sept, daily, 10am–6pm.

HEART OF ENGLAND

Bernhard's Rugby Garden and Leisure Centre
Bilton Road, Rugby, Warwickshire CV22 7DT.
☎ *(0788) 811500.*
The Midlands No. 1 garden centre. Huge selection of top-quality indoor and outdoor plants. Gift department, speciality foods. Fine Art gallery.
Open all year, daily, winter 9am–6pm, summer 9am–6.30pm.

Lechlade Garden and Fuchsia Centre
Fairford Road, Lechlade, Gloucestershire GL7 3DP.
☎ *Faringdon (0367) 52372.*
Indoor fuchsia garden displaying over 800 varieties.
Garden centre open all year, daily, Mon to Sat 9am–5.30pm, Sun & Bank Hols 10am–5pm.

Stone House Cottage Nursery (Arbuthnotts)
Stone, nr Kidderminster, Worcestershire DY10 4BP.
☎ *(0562) 69902*
On A448. Plantsman's nursery attached to walled garden where all plants may be seen growing. Unusual wall shrubs, climbers and herbaceous plants.
Open Mar to Dec, Wed to Sat, 10am–6pm.

Treasures of Tenbury Ltd
Burford House Gardens, Tenbury Wells, Worcestershire WR15 8HQ.
☎ *(0584) 810777.*
Holders of National Clematis Collection. Large range of clematis for sale, also rare and unusual herbaceous plants, shrubs, trees.
Open all year, Mon to Sat 9am–5pm, Sun 2pm–5pm, except in winter when the Nursery closes at dusk.

Webbs Garden Centres Ltd
Wychbold, Droitwich, Worcestershire.
☎ *(052 786) 245. Wordsley, Stourbridge, W. Midlands.*
☎ *(0384) 78834.*
Select from the finest houseplants, seeds, bulbs, shrubs, trees, dried/silk flowers plus all the garden sundries you could need.
Open all year, daily, summer 9am–5.45pm, winter 9am–5pm; Suns 10am–5pm.

LONDON

Chelsea Gardener
125 Sydney Street, Kings Road, Chelsea, London SW3.
☎ *01-352 5656.*
The source of imaginative plants and gardens.
Open all year, daily, Mon 10.30am–6pm, Tue, Thurs, Fri, Sat 10am–6pm, Sun, Bank Hols 10am–5pm, Wed 10am–7.30pm.

Clifton Nurseries
Clifton Villas, London W9 2PH.
☎ *01-289 6851.*
Very wide range of interior and exterior plants, garden antiques and statuary, furniture, vases and all garden services.
Open all year, daily, Mon to Sat 8.30am–5.30pm, Sun 9.30am–1.30pm.

Squire's Garden Centres
Sixth Cross Road, Twickenham, Middlesex TW2 5PA.
☎ *01-977 9241.*
One of West London's largest garden centres, stocking every type of garden requirement with experts to advise in all departments.
Open all year, daily, 9am–6pm.

NORTHUMBRIA

Gateshead Metropolitan Borough Council Central Nursery
Whickham Highway, Lobley Hill, Gateshead, Tyne & Wear NE11.
☎ *(091) 4873311/4600331.*
¾-acre of productive glasshouses and ¼-acre Show House; landscaped interior. Over 100 varieties of indoor plants; pools and fish. Rose garden, herb garden, heather garden, tree and shrub areas. Total site 20 acres.
Open Apr to Sept, Mon to Fri, 10am–7.30pm; Oct to Mar, Sat & Sun, 10am–3pm.

Rookhope Nurseries
Rookhope, nr Stanhope, Upper Weardale, Co. Durham DL13 2DD.
☎ *(0388) 517272.*
Small but attractive nursery and garden situated high in the North Pennines, growing a surprisingly wide range of hardy plants.
Open all year, daily, summer 9am–7pm, winter 9am–5pm; Tea Room 10am–6pm (summer only).

NORTH WEST

Caldwell & Sons Ltd
Nurseries & Garden Centre, Chelford Road, Knutsford, Cheshire WA16 8LX.
☎ *(0565) 4281.*
A tree and shrub nursery dating back to 1780; now also an international garden centre.
Open all year, daily, Mon to Sat 8.30am–5pm, Sun 10am–5pm.

Grosvenor Garden Leisure
Wrexham Road, Belgrave, Chester, Cheshire CH4 9EB.
☎ *(0244) 672856.*
Display gardens; tea-house; play area; pet/aquatic centre; large range of buildings; landscaping/planting advice; machinery; D.I.Y.
Open all year, daily; April to Sept, Mon to Fri & Bank Hols 9am–5.45pm, Sat & Sun 10am–5.45pm; Oct to Mar, Mon to Fri & Bank Hols 9am–5.45pm, Sat & Sun 10am–5pm.

Stapeley Water Gardens
London Road, Stapeley, Nantwich, Cheshire CW5 7LH.
☎ *Crewe (0270) 623868.*
Water garden specialists; aquatic plants, pool equipment. Full range of garden accessories, trees, shrubs, furniture etc.
Open all year, daily; Easter–1 Sept, Mon to Fri 9am–6pm, Sat & Sun 10am–7pm; Winter, Mon–Fri 9am–5pm, Sat & Sun 10am–5pm.

Woodford Park Garden Centre
Chester Road, Woodford, Cheshire SK7 1QS.
☎ *061-439 4955.*
Home and garden improvement centre on 10-acre, landscaped site. Restaurant, cold water and tropical fish, display gardens, pools and chalets. Large range of indoor and outdoor plants.
Open all year, Mon to Sat 8am–6pm; Sun 9am–6pm.

SOUTH

Deacon's Nursery
Dept ETB, Moor View, Godshill, Isle of Wight PO38 3HW.
☎ *(0983) 840750.*
Fruit tree specialists. Apples (over 120 varieties), pears, plums, nectarines, peaches, figs, soft fruit etc. Free catalogue (stamp appreciated).
Open all year, daily (mail orders) 8am–10.30pm, Mon to Fri (callers) 9am–5pm.

Exbury Gardens Plant Centre
Exbury, nr Southampton, Hampshire SO4 1AZ.
☎ *Fawley (0703) 891203.*
A wide range of rhododendrons including garden and hardy hybrids, evergreen and deciduous azaleas, camellias and pieris.
Open Mar to Nov, daily; Mar, Aug to Nov, 1pm–5pm, Apr to July 10am–5.30pm.

BEACON GARDEN CENTRES LIMITED

ANDOVER GARDEN CENTRE
Salisbury Road
Andover
Hants
SP11 7DN
Tel: 0264 710551

AYLESBURY GARDEN CENTRE
(Next to Smith's Do It All)
Gatehouse Road
Aylesbury
Bucks
Tel: 0296 29551

BEACONSFIELD GARDEN CENTRE
London Road
Beaconsfield
Bucks
Tel: 04946 2522

CHICHESTER GARDEN CENTRE
Bognor Road
Merston
Chichester
Sussex
PO20 6EG
Tel: 0243 789276

HANDCROSS GARDEN CENTRE
London Road
Handcross
Sussex
RH17 6BA
Tel: 0444 400725

HASTINGS GARDEN CENTRE
Bexhill Road
St Leonards on Sea
East Sussex
TN38 8AR
Tel: 0424 443414

WORTHING GARDEN CENTRE
Littlehampton Road
Ferring
Worthing
Sussex
BN12 6PG
Tel: 0903 42003

DORKING GARDEN CENTRE
Reigate Road
Dorking
Surrey
Tel: 0306 884845

BUTCHERS' GARDEN CENTRE
Wickham Road
Shirley
Croydon
Surrey
CR9 8AG
Tel: 01 654 3720

A Guide to English Gardens

Garden Centres & Nurseries

Blenheim Palace, Oxfordshire

SOUTH EAST

Savill Garden Plant Centre
Wick Lane, Englefield Green, Egham, Surrey TW20 0UU.
☎ *(0784) 35544.*
We offer a wide range of choice and rare plants, all propagated in the adjoining world-famous Savill and Valley Gardens; also well-stocked gift/book shop.
Open all year, daily, 10am–6pm or sunset when earlier.

West Dean Gardens
Apple House Nursery, West Dean, nr Chichester, West Sussex PO18 0RB.
☎ *Singleton (024 363) 301.*
Plants grown by gardeners. Specialities: Old roses, herbaceous plants. Extensive range of trees, shrubs, climbers. Quality, price, service our priorities.
Open Apr to Sept, daily, 11am–5pm; Oct to Mar, Mon to Fri, 9am–4pm.

THAMES AND CHILTERNS

Lathbury Park Herb Gardens
Lathbury Park, Newport Pagnell, Buckinghamshire MK16 8LD.
☎ *(0908) 610316/612373.*
On B526 north of Newport Pagnell. Wide range of herb plants and cut herbs for sale in walled garden of old house. Display border. Historic church with wall paintings.
Open Mar to Oct, Mon to Fri (closed Bank Hols), 9am–4.30pm.

Waterperry Gardens
Waterperry Horticultural Centre, nr Wheatley, Oxon OX9 1JZ.
☎ *Ickford (084 47) 226.*
Ornamental gardens, herbaceous and alpine nurseries, soft fruit section and orchards, glasshouses; all-year-round interest. Garden shop; tea shop. Saxon church.
Open all year, daily, summer 10am–6pm, winter 10am–4pm.

WEST COUNTRY

Bowood Garden Centre
Bowood Estate, Calne, Wiltshire SN11 0LZ.
☎ *(0249) 816828.*
Entrance off A4 in Derry Hill village. Rare and unusual plants, aromatics, old-fashioned roses, herbaceous, trees and shrubs. Large garden and gift shop, books. Stately home and grounds.
Open all year, daily, 9am–5pm.

Brackenwood Nursery and Garden Centre
131 Nore Road, Portishead, nr Bristol, Avon BS20 8DU.
☎ *(0272) 843484.*
Rare and unusual plants, trees and shrubs of all types; garden sundries; garden centre in unique setting overlooking Bristol Channel.
Open all year, daily, 9am–5.30pm.

Burnloose and South Down Nurseries
Gwennap, Redruth, Cornwall TR16 6BJ.
☎ *Stithians (0209) 861112.*
30-acre woodland garden, on main Redruth–Falmouth road. Widest range of ornamental plants in the South West.
Open all year, daily, Mon to Sat 9.30am–5pm, Sun 2pm–5pm.

Clapton Court Gardens and Plant Centre
Crewkerne, Somerset TA18 8PT.
☎ *(0460) 73220.*
Unusual plants, shrubs and trees, including herbaceous, pelargoniums, fuchsias.
Open all year, Mon to Fri 10am–5pm, Sun 2pm–5pm; Easter Sat & Sun in May only, 2pm–5pm.

The Margery Fish Nursery
East Lambrook Manor, South Petherton, Somerset TA13 5HL.
☎ *(0460) 40328.*
Range of rare and unusual plants propagated from East Lambrook Manor Garden, originally planted by the late Margery Fish.
Open all year, daily, 9am–5pm.

Otter Nurseries Garden Centre
Gosford Road, Ottery St. Mary, Devon EX11 1LZ.
☎ *(040 481) 3341.*
One of the largest and most popular garden centres in Devon. Fine selection of house plants, shrubs, sundries. Coffee shop.
Open all year, daily, Mon to Sat 8am–5pm, Sun 9am–5pm.

Trewithen Nurseries
Grampound Road, nr Truro, Cornwall TR22 4DD.
☎ *St. Austell (0726) 882764.*
On A390 between Truro and St. Austell. Camellias, rhododendrons, magnolias, azaleas and pieris, plus a wide range of ornamental shrubs at exceptional prices (retail and wholesale). Expert advice always available. Collect from Nursery point of sale when Gardens are closed. Delivery of large orders by arrangement.
Open Mar to Sept, daily exc Sun, 2pm–4.30pm.

Triscombe Nurseries and Garden Centre
Bagborough, Taunton, Somerset TA4 3HG.
☎ *Crowcombe (098 48) 267.*
Noted for our wide selection of unusual plants. A comprehensive stock of trees, shrubs, hard and soft fruit, conifers, perennials, rock plants.
Open all year, Mon to Sat 9am–1pm, 2pm–5.30pm; Sun 2.30pm–5.30pm.

YORKSHIRE AND HUMBERSIDE

Castle Howard Plant Centre
The Gardens, Castle Howard, York YO6 7BY.
☎ *Coneysthorpe (065 384) 333 & 312.*
Herbaceous, alpines, old roses, dwarf conifers and heathers, trees and shrubs for all purposes; ericaceous plants, clematis, herbs and seeds.
Open Mar to Oct, daily, 10am–5pm.

HOTELS

Whilst there are certain to be many lovely gardens within reach of your home on a day's excursion, you might like to venture further afield and spend a weekend or longer break visiting gardens in a different area. Besides providing a perfect base for touring, many of the hotels listed here are set in their own exquisite gardens or landscaped grounds, worth visiting in their own right.

It should be noted that the entries are paid advertisements, and all the details and descriptions have been supplied by the proprietors. The English Tourist Board cannot accept responsibility for any inaccuracy in the information or for any consequence arising from reliance on it. However, all the hotels are registered with the English Tourist Board and have agreed to abide by a seven-point Code of Conduct. This code is explained in the English Tourist Board's *Where to Stay* accommodation guides.

CUMBRIA

Coniston Sun Hotel
Coniston, Cumbria LA21 8HQ.
☎ *(0966) 41248.*
Located in spectacular scenery under 'Old Man' of Coniston. Attached to 16th-century inn. Restaurant. All bedrooms with *en suite* bathrooms. **Garden:** Natural woodland garden in mountain location. Fine displays of rhododendrons, azaleas, magnolias. Mountain stream. **Gardens to visit:** Brantwood; Levens Hall; Holker Hall; Stagshaw Garden; Holehird. **Price range:** B.

The Gretna Chase Hotel
Gretna, Carlisle, Cumbria CA6 5JB.
☎ *(0461) 37517.*
Excellent menu, first class accommodation, Honeymoon Suite. Ideal centre for touring. Bargain weekend breaks November–May. Full colour brochure. **Garden:** National Winner of the Benson & Hedges UK Pub Garden of the Year Competition, 1984. **Gardens to visit:** Corby Castle.
Price range: B.

The **Price Range** given is per person sharing a room per night for bed, breakfast and evening meal and the range is as follows.
A Less than £25 **B** £25-£35
C More than £35.
Do check all details with the individual hotel before booking.

Langdale Chase Hotel
Windermere, Cumbria LA23 1LW.
☎ *Ambleside (0966) 32201.*
35-bedroom Country-House Hotel bordering Lake Windermere. Panoramic restaurant; cocktail bar. Bedrooms with colour TV, telephones; most have private facilities. **Garden:** 5-acre landscaped gardens. Wide terraces and lawns; flowering shrubs, rose and heather gardens, herbaceous borders. **Gardens to visit:** Stagshaw; Holehird; Holker Hall; Levens Hall; Brockhole.
Price range: C.

Lindeth Fell Country House Hotel
Bowness-on-Windermere, Cumbria LA23 3JP.
☎ *Windermere (096 62) 3286.*
One of Lakeland's loveliest houses in private grounds overlooking Lake Windermere and the Coniston range. Offers elegance, tranquillity, superb food. Private bathrooms.
Garden: Daffodils, azaleas, rhododendrons, maple and specimen trees in landscaped grounds, with majestic lakeland views. **Gardens to visit:** Brantwood; Brockhole; Dalemain; Graythwaite; Holker Hall; Holehird; Levens Hall; Rydal Mount; Sizer Castle; Hayes Lake District Nurseries and others.
Price range: B.

Rickerby Grange
Portinscale, Keswick, Cumbria CA12 5RH.
☎ *(0596) 72344.*
Country house in quiet village on outskirts of Keswick. Home cooking, cosy bar, TV lounge, *en suite* facilities. Relaxed atmosphere. **Garden:** Pretty country garden with attractive rose border along front lawn; conifer tree-shaded rear lawn. **Gardens to visit:** Lingholm Gardens; Portinscale.
Price range: A.

EAST ANGLIA

Hotel Norwich
121–131 Boundary Road, Norwich, Norfolk NR3 2BA.
☎ *(0603) 410431.*
102-bedroom hotel, all with private bath, colour TV, radio, early morning call, baby monitoring system, tea and coffee-making facilities.
Gardens to visit: Blickling Hall; Bressingham; Somerleyton; Sandringham.
Price range: B.

Oaksmere Country House Hotel
Brome, Eye, Suffolk IP23 8AJ.
☎ *(0379) 870326.*
Restored Tudor/Victorian country house. Tastefully decorated with period furnishings and paintings. Modern *en suite* bathrooms. Romantic restaurant, historic beamed bar.
Garden: Majestic lime avenue leads to ancient box and yew topiary gardens; spacious lawns, mature trees.
Gardens to visit: Bressingham Gardens; Thornham Herb Garden; Helmingham Hall Gardens.
Price range: B.

EAST MIDLANDS

Buckingham Hotel
1 Burlington Road, Buxton, Derbyshire SK17 9AS.
☎ *(0298) 70481.*
Traditional owner-managed hotel overlooking the Pavilion Gardens, offering excellent cuisine and comfort. All bedrooms have TV, radio, tea/coffee-making facilities, and most have bathrooms en suite.
Garden: Town centre hotel overlooking the Pavilion Gardens. **Gardens to visit:** Ideally situated for the 1986 Garden Festival; Chatsworth; Gawsworth; Haddon and others.
Price range: A.

The Peacock Hotel
Rowsley, nr Matlock, Derbyshire DE4 2EB.
☎ *(0629) 733518.*
20 bedrooms beautifully styled, blending antique furnishings with modern amenities. Hotel renowned for its superb restaurant and extensive wine-cellar. Ideally situated for touring. **Garden:** Charmingly set in peaceful riverside gardens. **Gardens to visit:** Chatsworth; Haddon Hall; Hardwick Hall; Lea Rhododendron Gardens; Ednaston Manor.
Price range: C.

Petwood
Stixwould Road, Woodhall Spa, Lincolnshire LN10 6QF.
☎ *(0526) 52411.*
Elegant Edwardian country house refurbished in 1985, set in 40 acres of woodland and gardens. Restaurant, bars, 30 bedrooms. **Garden:** Designed by H. Petto. It is abundant in rhododendrons, azaleas and roses. Landscaped lawns and unusual trees.
Gardens to visit: Harrington Hall; Springfields.
Price range: B.

HOTELS

Washingborough Hall Hotel
Church Hill, Washingborough, Lincolnshire LN4 1BE.
☎ *Lincoln (0522) 790340.*
Old manor house in quiet surroundings, 2 miles from Lincoln. Comfortable rooms, excellent food. Pleasant lounge bar, real ales. Outdoor swimming pool (summer). **Garden:** 3½ acres, lawns, mature trees, shrubs, flower-beds, roses, geraniums, perennials, large collection fuchsias grown by proprietors. **Gardens to visit:** Lincoln Castle grounds; Gunby Hall; Belton House; Doddington Hall.
Price range: A.

HEART OF ENGLAND

Bibury Court
Bibury, Cirencester, Gloucestershire GL7 5NT.
☎ *(028 574) 337.*
A Jacobean mansion with 16 bedrooms, 15 with private bath, and many with four poster beds. Informal surroundings. **Garden:** 'Capability' Brown-style landscape setting with lawns running down to the River Coln. **Gardens to visit:** Barnsley House; Hidcote.
Price range: B.

Clifford Manor
Clifford Chambers, Stratford-upon-Avon, Warwickshire CV37 8HU.
☎ *(0789) 292616.*
A fine Queen Anne manor house restored by Edwin Lutyens, 2 miles from Stratford-upon-Avon in a quiet and peaceful setting. **Garden:** 10 acres of moated, woodland and terraced gardens, designed by Gertrude Jekyll. **Gardens to visit:** Hidcote; Kiftsgate; Charlecote; Shakespeare Gardens; Upton House.
Price range: C.

The Croft Country Guest House
Vowchurch, Golden Valley, Hereford, Herefordshire HR2 0QE.
☎ *Peterchurch (098 16) 226.*
Small, personally run, elegant Edwardian country house with magnificent views to Welsh borders. Excellent cooking using home produce. Licensed. **Garden:** 2 acres attractively landscaped of much interest. Mature specimen trees. Shrubberies. Herbaceous beds. Orchard. Tennis lawn. **Gardens to visit:** Abbey Dore Court; The Weir; Hergest Croft; Burford House; Berrington Hall; Dinmore Manor; Stoke Lacy; Lydney Park, and others.
Price range: C.

Goldstone Hall
Goldstone, Market Drayton, Shropshire TF9 2NA.
☎ *Cheswardine (063 086) 202.*
Lovely country house in beautiful Shropshire. Well-appointed *en suite* bedrooms. First class English food. Owned and managed by a welcoming family. **Garden:** A country garden with mature trees, rose and herbaceous borders, scree garden, sheltered, with lovely views. **Gardens to visit:** Hodnet Hall; Dorothy Clive Garden; Willoughbridge; Weston Park; Stoke-on-Trent National Garden Festival; Bridgemere Nurseries.
Price range: B.

The Grange
Ellesmere, Shropshire SY12 9DE.
☎ *(069 171) 3495.*
Magnificent Georgian country house. 14 bedrooms all with private bath/shower, tea/coffee, colour TV. Licensed bar. Conservatory dining room. Verandas. **Garden:** 4 acres of established gardens; many mature trees, large vegetable garden with greenhouses and vinery. **Gardens to visit:** Erdigg; Hodnet Hall; Percy Thrower's 'Magnolias'; Nesscliffe Herb Garden; Cholmondeley Castle; Chirk Castle.
Price range: A.

Hawkstone Park Hotel
Weston-under-Redcastle, Shrewsbury, Shropshire SY4 5UY.
☎ *Lee Brockhurst (093 924) 611.*
Delightful, sporting country house hotel in beautiful 300-acre estate. Two golf courses, where Sandy Lyle, Open champion, learnt his game. **Garden:** Exquisite historical antiquities in own estate with guided tours and relaxing hotel gardens. **Gardens to visit:** Hodnet Hall.
Price range: B.

Lords of the Manor
Upper Slaughter, Bourton-on-the-Water, nr Cheltenham, Gloucestershire GL54 2JD.
☎ *Cotswold (0451) 20243.*
17th-century manor managed by the family whose home it has been for over 200 years. 15 rooms, all with bath. Non-residents welcome. **Garden:** 7 acres, including the River Eye and artificial lake, water garden and walled kitchen garden. **Gardens to visit:** Hidcote; Kiftsgate; Barnsley; Upton; Pewsey; Oxford Botanical; Westonbirt; Burford House and others.
Price range: B.

Old Farmhouse Hotel
Lower Swell, Stow-on-the-Wold, Gloucestershire GL54 1LF.
☎ *Cotswold (0451) 30232.*
A traditional Cotswold farmhouse sympathetically converted to a small and very comfortable hotel, privately owned and run. **Garden:** A small, walled and peaceful garden in the course of restoration. **Gardens to visit:** Hidcote; Kiftsgate; Barnsley; Sezincote; Priory; Upton; Misarden; Westonbirt; Batsford and others.
Price range: A.

Pengethley Hotel
nr Ross-on-Wye, Herefordshire HR9 6LL.
☎ *Harewood End (098 987) 211.*
Exquisite Georgian country house in 15 acres of gardens and grounds. Historic suites, including library. Superb restaurant using home grown produce. **Garden:** Rose and sunken gardens. Walled fruit and vegetable gardens, herb borders. Adjoining Pengethley Park and Grove. **Gardens to visit:** Abbeydore Court; Dinmore Manor; Hergest Croft; Lydney Park.
Price range: C.

Prince Rupert Hotel
Butcher Row, Shrewsbury, Shropshire SY1 1UQ.
☎ *(0743) 52461.*
Combines character of 15th-century with modern accommodation in centre of historic Shrewsbury. International reputation for fine cuisine. 70 well-appointed bedrooms. **Gardens to visit:** Hodnet; Powis Castle; Weston Park; Shrewsbury Quarry; Percy Thrower's Garden Centre.
Price range: B.

The Redesdale Arms Hotel
Moreton-in-Marsh, Gloucestershire GL56 0AW.
☎ *(0608) 50308.*
Former 18th-century coaching inn – one of the best preserved inns in Gloucestershire. Charmingly restored. In the centre of the Cotswolds. **Gardens to visit:** Hidcote Manor; Batsford Arboretum; Sezincote Gardens.
Price range: B.

White Bear Hotel
High Street, Shipston on Stour, Warwickshire.
☎ *(0608) 61558.*
Garden: Window boxes, hanging baskets and tubs. Winner of Shipston in Bloom '85. **Gardens to visit:** Hidcote; Kiftsgate; Farnborough Hall; Paxford Arboretum; Packwood House and others.
Price range: B.

NORTHUMBRIA

St Aidan's College (University of Durham)
Windmill Hill, Durham DH1 3LJ.
☎ *(0385) 65011.*
Modern, spacious college, operated as hotel. Excellent catering; bar, friendly service; single and twin-bedded rooms. Very low rates. **Garden:** Extensive attractively-landscaped garden with trees, shrub and herbaceous beds and 2 tennis courts. **Gardens to visit:** Raby Castle; South Park; Ormesby Hall.
Price range: A.

HOTELS

NORTH WEST

The Dene Hotel
Hoole Road, Chester, Cheshire CH2 3ND.
☎ *(0244) 21165.*
Family-owned, conveniently situated on the A56 approach to city centre, adjacent to Alexandra Park. Ample parking. **Garden:** 1½ acres, mainly lawns and mature trees. **Gardens to visit:** Stoke Garden Festival; Ness Gardens; Erddig; Bodnant; Tatton Park; Chirk Castle; Norton Priory; Cholmondeley Castle Gardens; Arley Hall.
Price range: A.

The Inn at Whitewell
Forest of Bowland, nr Clitheroe, Lancashire BB7 3AT.
☎ *Dunsop Bridge (020 08) 222.*
11 bedrooms, antique furnishings, log fires. Home-made lunches, suppers and dinners. **Garden:** Lawns on the bank of the River Hodder offer breath-taking views of a beautiful untouched valley. **Gardens to visit:** Whalley Abbey; Hoghton Tower.
Price range: B.

SOUTH

Careys Manor
Brockenhurst, New Forest, Hampshire SO4 7RH.
☎ *Lymington (0590) 23551.*
Attractive old manor with modern garden wing, 57 luxury rooms. Indoor heated pool. Excellent restaurant. **Garden:** 5 acres of grounds including walled garden with very old mulberry. Croquet and putting lawns.
Gardens to visit: Exbury; Compton Acres; Stourhead; Rhinefield Ornamental Drive.
Price range: B/C.

Fairlight Hotel
1 Golf Links Road, Broadstone, Dorset BH18 8BE.
☎ *(0202) 694316.*
Quiet, comfortable, private licensed hotel with bridlepath from grounds to woodlands. Close to countryside, coast and rivers. **Garden:** Large lawn bordered by a variety of shrubs and trees offering a sheltered sun trap. **Gardens to visit:** Kingston Lacey; Spinners; Mompesson; Stourhead; Stourton House; Heale House; Mottisfont Abbey; Compton Acres; Athelhampton; Cranbourne; Exbury; Furzey.
Price range: A.

SOUTH EAST

Black Mill House Hotel
Princess Avenue, Bognor Regis, West Sussex PO21 2QU.
☎ *(0243) 821945.*
26-room hotel in quiet avenue leading to Marine Gardens and sea, 300 yards from beach. Two lounges, games room, cocktail bar. Car park. Mini-breaks available.

Garden: Traditional enclosed garden with fine lawns, roses and shrubs, hanging baskets and a rockery.
Gardens to visit: Leonardslee; Nymans; Parham Park; West Dean.
Price range: A/B.

Croft Hotel
18 Prideaux Road, Eastbourne, East Sussex BN21 2NB.
☎ *(0323) 642291.*
Set back from the sea, with fine views of Pevensey Bay, in select residential area. 10 bedrooms, including 5 ground floor garden bedrooms; all rooms have TV and tea/coffee making facilities. Two restaurants.
Garden: 1-acre garden with pathways round lily ponds, shrubbery, fruit trees. Outdoor heated pool, tennis court. **Gardens to visit:** Charleston Manor; Michelham Priory.
Price range: B.

Flackley Ash Hotel and Restaurant
Peasmarsh, nr Rye, East Sussex TN31 6YH.
☎ *(079 721) 381.*
Georgian country house hotel in 5 acres. Quiet village 4m NW of Rye. Scotch beef, fresh vegetables and fresh fish from our own trawler.
Garden: Informal rambling gardens but with spectacular early rhododendrons and azaleas.
Gardens to visit: Sissinghurst; Great Dixter; Sheffield Park; Fletching Gardens; Balcombe Gardens.
Price range: B.

Halland Forge Hotel
Halland, nr Lewes, East Sussex BN8 6PW.
☎ *(082 584) 456.*
Charming, family-run hotel with oak-beamed, fully licensed restaurant, lounge bar and coffee shop. All bedrooms have private bath or shower. **Garden:** The hotel is set in lawns and flower beds, adjacent to woodland. **Gardens to visit:** Sheffield Park; Scotney Castle; Sissinghurst; Wakehurst Place; Emmetts; Charleston Manor.
Price range: B.

Highley Manor Hotel
Crawley Lane, Balcombe, West Sussex RH17 6LA.
☎ *(0444) 811711.*
Old country house hotel. 20 bedrooms with *en suite* bathrooms, dining room with à la carte menu. Wedding and conference facilities. **Garden:** 8 acres of landscaped garden with far-reaching views of the South Downs. **Gardens to visit:** Borde Hill; Nymans; Wakehurst Place.
Price range: B.

Hilton Park Hotel
Cuckfield, Haywards Heath, West Sussex RH17 5EG.
☎ *(0444) 454455.*
Country house hotel situated in the heart of Sussex. Garden Vinery bar. Most bedrooms with private bathroom, colour TV. **Garden:** Own landscaped gardens of 4 acres command panoramic views of the South Downs. **Gardens to visit:** Heaselands; Sheffield Park; Nymans; Leonardslee; Wakehurst Place; Borde Hill.
Price range: B.

Russell Hotel
80 London Road, Tunbridge Wells, Kent TW1 1DZ.
☎ *(0892) 44833.*
Large Victorian house facing common. Excellent restaurant serving all freshly prepared foods. All bedrooms have bathrooms *en suite*, colour TV, telephone, tea-making facilities. **Gardens to visit:** Sissinghurst; Scotney Castle; Owl House; Great Comp; Great Dixter; Hall Place; Leonardslee; Ruerhill House; Emmetts; Crittenden House; Sheffield Park; Borde Hill; Cobblers.
Price range: B.

Spa Hotel
Mount Ephraim, Tunbridge Wells, Kent TN4 8XJ.
☎ *(0892) 20331.*
Country mansion built in 1766, the hotel combines old-world charm with modern facilities. Luxury health complex, tennis, golf, playground. **Garden:** 6 landscaped acres of lawns, rhododendrons, fine specimen trees and lake with wildfowl reserve.
Gardens to visit: Penshurst Place; Chiddingstone Castle; Hever Castle; Owl House Garden; Scotney Castle.
Price range: B.

Spindlewood Country House Hotel and Restaurant
Wallcrouch, Wadhurst, East Sussex TN5 7JG.
☎ *Ticehurst (0580) 200430.*
Family-run country house hotel renowned for its food and comfort; nine individually decorated bedrooms with bathroom, TV, radio, telephone, tea-making facilities.
Garden: Thousands of spring bulbs and interesting plants in five acres of gardens, ponds and woodland.
Gardens to visit: Sissinghurst; Sheffield Park; Scotney Castle; Borde Hill; Great Comp; Great Dixter; Leonardslee; Nymans; Wakehurst Place; Sprivers; Riverhill House and many others open on an irregular basis.
Price range: C.

BEFORE SETTING OUT it's always best to 'phone and check garden details. Opening times and prices may be subject to change at short notice!

A GUIDE TO ENGLISH GARDENS

HOTELS

Thatchers Hotel
*Epsom Road, East Horsley,
nr Guildford, Surrey KT24 6TB.*
☎ *(04865) 4291.*
Half-timbered hotel, beautifully restored in 1984/85, fine restaurant, elegant modern bedrooms, many around swimming pool.
Garden: English country garden setting, beautiful trees, terraced lawns. **Gardens to visit:** RHS Wisley; Polesdon Lacey; Bookham.
Price range: B/C.

THAMES AND CHILTERNS

Briggens Hotel
Stanstead Road, Stanstead Abbotts, Ware, Hertfordshire SG12 8LD.
☎ *(027979) 2416.*
Magnificent country house hotel set in 45 acres of parkland. Luxurious individually decorated bedrooms. Excellent cuisine, friendly attentive service. **Garden:** Picturesque gardens landscaped by Charles Bridgeman with rare trees and shrubs from around the world. **Gardens to visit:** Audley End; Hatfield House.
Price range: B.

The Spread Eagle Hotel
Cornmarket, Thame, Oxfordshire OX9 2BW.
☎ *(084 421) 3661.*
Converted 300-year-old coaching inn with renowned restaurant, bars and comfortable lounges. **Gardens to visit:** Blenheim Palace; Hughenden Manor; Waddesdon Manor; Waterperry; Mattocks Roses and others participating in the National Gardens Scheme.
Price range: C.

West Lodge Park
Cockfosters Road, Hadley Wood, nr Barnet, Hertfordshire EN4 0PY.
☎ *01-440 8311.*
Country house hotel in 34 acres of grounds. All rooms have country views, yet only 12 miles from Piccadilly Circus. **Garden:** Lovely country estate with outstanding beauty of lawns and trees, including the famous Beale Arboretum.
Gardens to visit: Trent Park.
Price range: B.

WEST COUNTRY

The Berribridge
Thorverton, nr Exeter, Devon EX5 5JR.
☎ *(0392) 860259.*
17th-century thatched hotel, 6 miles from Exeter in country setting. Beamed restaurant with good food. Personal attention and service.
Garden: 1½ acres of rambling, country garden with shrubbery, ponds, orchard and interesting flowers. **Gardens to visit:** Cadhay, Bicton Park, Fursdon.
Price range: B.

Carnarvon Arms Hotel
Dulverton, Somerset TA22 9AE.
☎ *(0398) 23302.*
A privately-owned hotel set on the edge of Exmoor National Park. Renowned for fine food and hospitality. **Garden:** Large sheltered gardens of lawns surrounded by trees, shrubs and roses. **Gardens to visit:** Knightshayes Court; Bicton; Rosemoor; Killerton; Combe Sydenham.
Price range: B.

Castle Hotel
Castle Green, Taunton, Somerset TA1 1NF.
☎ *(0823) 72671.*
Originally part of an old Norman fortress and with many historical links, this 35-bedroom luxurious hotel offers top quality comfort and cuisine.
Garden: Beautiful 12th-century Norman garden with an ancient moat wall, castle keep and square well.
Gardens to visit: Stourhead; Knightshayes; Montacute; Killerton; Clapton Court; Barrington Court; Gaulden Manor.
Price range: C.

Chedington Court
Chedington, Beaminster, Dorset DT8 3HY.
☎ *Corscombe (093 589) 265.*
Magnificently situated manor house hotel with reputation for good food, fine wines. Eight bedrooms all with bathroom, TV and telephone.
Garden: Mature garden of 10 acres. Fine old trees. Water garden, ponds and source of River Parrett. Putting, croquet. **Gardens to visit:** Clapton Court; Montacute; Barrington Court; Mapperton; Abbotsbury; Minterne; Tintinhull.
Price range: C.

Cliff Hotel
Cheddar Gorge, Cheddar, Somerset BS27 3QE.
☎ *(0934) 742346.*
Small, family-owned hotel at foot of Cheddar Gorge. Tudor restaurant and carvery, wine and lounge bars, TV lounge with peaceful view across lake. Four-poster bed available.
Garden: Tropical waterfall gardens with meandering mill streams, tropical birds and animals. Abundance of wildlife. **Gardens to visit:** Ashton Court, Clevedon Court, Oakhill Manor.
Price range: A.

Corisande Manor Hotel
Riverside Avenue, Pentire, Newquay, Cornwall TR7 1PL.
☎ *(0637) 872042.*
Hotel with residential licence, 19 bedrooms – many with *en suite* facilities. Putting green, solarium. Dogs accepted. Ample parking.

Garden: 3 acres of peaceful, landscaped, southerly-facing grounds, leading to private foreshore on the Gannel Estuary. **Gardens to visit:** Trerice; Trewithen; Trelissick; Probus Demonstration Garden.
Price range: A.

Fairwater Head Hotel
Hawkchurch, nr Axminster, Devon EX13 5TX.
☎ *(029 77) 349.*
Welcoming country house noted for peace, tranquillity, excellent food, comfortable lounges, *en suite* bedrooms. **Garden:** Well-stocked gardens with specimen trees, shrubs, flowers, ponds and panoramic views across Axe Valley. **Gardens to visit:** Clapton Court; Bicton Park; Killerton; Knightshayes; Montacute House; Barrington Court; Forde Abbey; Abbotsbury and Wild Life Park.
Price range: B.

Green Lawns Hotel
Western Terrace, Falmouth, Cornwall TR11 4QJ.
☎ *(0326) 312734.*
Chateau-style hotel with 43 bedrooms, *à la carte* restaurant, new indoor leisure complex; tennis, squash and golf nearby. **Garden:** The garden is adorned with flowering shrubs and trees, well-maintained flower beds and patio. **Gardens to visit:** Trelissick Gardens; Lanhydrock; Trerice; Foxhill Gardens; Queen Mary Gardens; Fox's Gardens.
Price range: B.

Ivy House Hotel and Garden Restaurant
High Street, Marlborough, Wiltshire SN8 1HJ.
☎ *(0672) 53188.*
Former coaching inn; all rooms with *en suite* bathroom. The Garden Restaurant serves quality English fare and overlooks the garden. ETB Category 6.
Garden: Mature ¼-acre walled garden with herbaceous borders and copper beach tree. **Gardens to visit:** Bowood; Stourhead; Montpesson.
Price range: B.

Lanscombe House Hotel
Cockington Lane, Cockington Village, Torquay, Devon TQ2 6XD.
☎ *(0803) 607556.*
200-year-old detached, family-run, licensed hotel of much charm and character set in a beautiful, peaceful and unique situation.
Garden: Grounds extending to 3½ acres comprise lawns, ponds, relaxation areas, with many fine trees and plants. **Gardens to visit:** Cockington Hall Gardens with own right of way.
Price range: A.

HOTELS

Marsh Hall Country House
South Molton, North Devon EX36 3HQ.
☎ *(07695) 2666.*
Luxuriously appointed, seven bedroomed hotel, set in its own secluded grounds – style and elegance of an almost forgotten era.
Garden: Two lawned terraces with flower borders. Small wood with unusual trees – Planes, Tulip trees, very large horsechestnut. Rhododendrons, ornamental pond, bamboo canes, weeping tree.
Gardens to visit: Knightshayes Court; Arlington Court; Killerton; Marwood.
Price range: B.

Melville Hotel
Sea View Road, Falmouth, Cornwall TR11 4NL.
☎ *(0326) 312134.*
Charming house set in 2 acres of sub-tropical gardens. Elegant lounges, magnificent views. Barbecue from late spring to late autumn. Croquet lawn, putting green. **Garden:** A profusion of rhododendrons, camellias, rare South American flax, banana trees, Eucryphia. Several varieties of palm trees. **Gardens to visit:** Trelissick; Ylenduryan; Fox's; Rosehill.
Price range: A.

Moonfleet Manor Hotel
nr Weymouth, Dorset DT3 4ED.
☎ *(0305) 78948.*
38 rooms, most with private bath. Conference room. Large indoor swimming pool, gym, sauna, 3 squash courts, tennis, snooker. Planned 1986 indoor bowls.
Garden: Set in 5 acres, lawns, borders, small arboretum, alongside Chesil Beach and The Fleet.
Gardens to visit: Abbotsbury; local mature area and bird sanctuary.
Price range: B.

Nansidwell Country House Hotel
Mawnan, nr Falmouth, Cornwall TR11 5HU.
☎ *(0326) 250340.*
Family-run country mansion set in magnificent grounds sloping to the sea, between Falmouth and Helford River. Excellent food and wine.
Garden: 5 acres of rare and tropical shrubs. Mimosa, datura, davidia, bananas, camellias, azaleas, rhododendrons, magnolia. **Gardens to visit:** Glendurgan, Trelissick; Penjerrick; Trewithen; Probus Demonstration Garden.
Price range: B.

The Old Rectory
Martinhoe, Parracombe, Barnstaple, Devon EX31 4QT.
☎ *(059 83) 368.*
Georgian country house hotel, well-appointed and tastefully decorated, offering peace and quiet. Traditional English cooking, ground and 1st floor *en suite* bedrooms.
Garden: Very mature rectory garden with lake, stream, small waterfalls, maze and sundial. **Gardens to visit:** Marwood; Arlington Court; Rosemoor; Tapeley Park; Chambercombe Manor.
Price range: B.

Old Ship Hotel
Mere, Wiltshire BA12 6JE.
☎ *(0744) 860258.*
Period hotel with 25 bedrooms, colour TV. Two bars, fine food and cheer. Central heating and log fires.
Gardens to visit: Stourhead; Stourton.
Price range: B.

Garden Lovers Weekends

- **England's finest gardens**
- **Illustrated talks on seasonal topics**
- **Expert instruction and demonstrations**
- **Yorkshire Gardens with Alan Titchmarsh**

Join us for a unique weekend and enjoy some of England's finest gardens in the company of experts who will bring them all to life for you.

Southern Garden Weekends from Ladbroke Seven Hills Hotel, Cobham, visiting RHS Wisley Garden, Savill Garden, Hampton Court Garden and Claremont Landscape Garden.

National Garden Festival Weekends from Ladbroke Hotels at Warwick and Birmingham with visits to the Stoke Garden Festival and Packwood House with its beautiful gardens and Shugborough.

Yorkshire Garden Weekends with Alan Titchmarsh from Ladbroke Hotels at Garforth and Wetherby including guided tours of Temple Newsam, Roundhay Park, Golden Acre Park and Harlow Car Gardens.

These weekends are excellent value **from £70** (inc VAT) per person. Prices include cocktail reception, 2 nights' dinner, bed and breakfast, Sunday lunch, admissions and guided visits with coach travel.

For a full colour brochure ring our instant **Holiday Hotline** on: **0923 38777** or write to: **Garden Lovers Weekends, Ladbroke Hotels, P.O. Box 137, Watford, Herts WD1 1DN**

Ladbroke Hotels

HOTELS

Orestone House Hotel
Rockhouse Lane, Maidencombe, Torquay, Devon TQ1 4SX.
☎ *(0803) 38099.*
Gracious County House situated in beautiful rural location overlooking Lyme Bay. Luxuriously appointed bedrooms. Elegant lounge and restaurant. Swimming pool.
Garden: Two acres of landscaped elevated gardens with mature trees. Some interesting and unusual species of shrubs and plants. **Gardens to visit:** Cotehele House; Coleton Fishacre; Killerton; Knightshayes.
Price range: B.

Portledge
Fairy Cross, nr Bideford, Devon EX39 5PB.
☎ *Horns Cross (023 75) 262.*
Quiet, 17th-century country house in own 2,000-acre estate of farmland and beach. Heated pool, tennis, croquet, mini-golf, walking. **Garden:** Wild flowers, trees, herbs, roses, young azaleas. Mid-week in spring and autumn: lectures, videos and other garden tours. **Gardens to visit:** Rosemore; Tapeley; Dr Smart and others.
Price range: A/B.

St Elmo Hotel
Sandhills Road, North Sands, Salcombe, Devon TQ8 8JR.
☎ *(054 884) 2233.*
Delightfully situated Edwardian country house hotel, 400 yards from the beach. All rooms *en suite*, tea-makers, TV, radio. Heated outdoor pool. **Garden:** Interesting variety of tropical plants in a tranquil setting with magnificent views of Salcombe Estuary. **Gardens to visit:** Sharpitor; Saltram House.
Price range: B.

St Quinton Hotel
Bridgwater Hotel, Taunton, Somerset TA2 8BG.
☎ *(0823) 59171.*
10-bedroom country hotel in own grounds adjacent to inland waterway. TV, radio, tea/coffee facilities in all bedrooms; some private bathrooms. **Garden:** Half-acre of lawns and rockery beside unspoilt canal scene; rowing boats available. **Gardens to visit:** Hestercombe House; Gauldon Manor; Barrington Court; Clapton Court; Montacute; Dunster Castle plus many private and local authority gardens – information leaflet on request.
Price range: A.

Ston Easton Park
Ston Easton, Bath, Somerset BA3 4DF.
☎ *Chewton Mendip (076 121) 631.*
18th-century Palladian mansion, grade I listed. 20 bedrooms with private bath, direct dial telephone. Restaurant offering English and French cuisine, fine wine cellar.
Garden: House set within a Humphry Repton 150-acre parkland, with water garden and cascades, fine mature trees. Good walks. **Gardens to visit:** Stourhead; East Lambrook Manor; Brympton d'Evercy; Sheldon Manor; Bowood House.
Price range: C.

Swan Hotel
Sadler Street, Wells, Somerset BA5 2RX.
☎ *(0749) 78877.*
15th-century inn facing magnificent West Front of Wells Cathedral. Original four-poster beds and cheerful log fires. Ideally situated for touring. **Gardens to visit:** Stourhead; Oakhill Manor; Longleat.
Price range: C.

Teignworthy Country House Hotel
Frenchbeer, nr Chagford, Devon TQ13 8EX.
☎ *(064 73) 3355/6/7/8/9.*
Nine double bedrooms with own bathroom, TV and telephone. One of the West Country's best restaurants. Featured in all major guides.
Garden: 14 acres of natural garden laid out in the 1930s, 1,000ft up on Dartmoor. **Gardens to visit:** Castle Drogo; Killerton; Knightshayes; Cotehele.
Price range: C.

Tiverton Hotel
Blundells Road, Tiverton, Devon EX16 4DB.
☎ *(0884) 256120.*
Modern 29-bedroom hotel, spacious *en suite* bedrooms all with colour TV and free beverage facilities. Excellent cuisine. All-inclusive breaks.
Gardens to visit: Knightshayes; Killerton; Bicton Park; Arlington Court; Castle Drogo and others.
Price range: A.

Tregarthen Country Cottage Hotel
Mount Hawke, nr Truro, Cornwall TR4 8DS.
☎ *Porthtowan (0209) 890399.*
Small cottage hotel retaining old-world atmosphere in rural surroundings near coast. Nine comfortable bedrooms with private facilities, two lounges, bar.
Garden: Pretty, well-kept garden set with shrubs, shrubs, lawns and flowers in 1 acre. Seats to enjoy peace and tranquillity. **Gardens to visit:** Glendurgan; Lanhydrock; Trelissick; Trengwainton; Trerice; Probus Demonstration Garden.
Price range: A.

Wenn Manor Hotel
St Wenn, nr Bodmin, Cornwall PL30 5PS.
☎ *Roche (0726) 890240.*
Country house with *en suite* bedrooms, central heating, licensed bar, TV lounge, heated outdoor pool, car park, snooker and other games. 4-acres of natural gardens of woodlands, rhododendrons, azaleas, grotto. Croquet and putting.
Gardens to visit: Trewithen; Pencarrow House; Probus Demonstration Garden and others.
Price range: A.

YORKSHIRE AND HUMBERSIDE

Cavendish Hotel
3 Valley Drive, Harrogate, North Yorkshire HG2 0JJ.
☎ *(0423) 509637.*
Small, friendly hotel, overlooking Valley Gardens, with 11 bedrooms all with colour TV, radio, tea/coffee facilities; most with bathrooms *en suite*. Good food; licensed.
Garden: Town centre hotel overlooking the famous Valley Gardens. **Gardens to visit:** Harlow Car Gardens; Ripley Castle; Rudding Park; Valley Gardens.
Price range: A.

Lastingham Grange Country House Hotel
Lastingham, York, North Yorkshire YO6 6TH.
☎ *(075 15) 345.*
Family-run hotel set in 10 acres of fields and gardens on the edge of the moors; a peaceful backwater.
Garden: South-facing terrace with sunken rose garden; lawns, pergola, beautiful mature shrubs and trees. **Gardens to visit:** Castle Howard, Pennyholme and many others open only on special days.
Price range: B.

Old Swan Hotel
Swan Road, Harrogate, North Yorkshire HG1 2SR.
☎ *(0423) 500055.*
A traditional luxury 4-star hotel with Victorian features skilfully blended with modern amenities. Excellent cuisine and personal service.
Garden: Eight acres of lawns, picturesque flower beds, pinewoods, flowering shrubs. Tennis, Croquet, Putting. **Gardens to visit:** Valley Gardens; Harlow Car Gardens; Montpelier Gardens; Crescent Gardens; The Stray parkland.
Price range: C.

Whitwell Hall Country House Hotel
Whitwell-on-the-Hill, York, North Yorkshire YO6 7JJ.
☎ *(065 381) 551.*
Genuine country house, magnificent views, in Howardian Hills, an area of outstanding natural beauty. Indoor swimming pool, tennis court, games room. **Garden:** 18 acres of woodlands and formal gardens, with orchard, kitchen garden, exceptionally fine trees and shrubs. **Gardens to visit:** Sutton Park; Castle Howard; Newby Hall; Sledmere House; Beningbrough Hall.
Price range: C.

GARDEN HOLIDAYS & TOURS

These companies offer a range of garden tours and special interest holidays on a garden theme. Some include guided visits to a variety of gardens, while others offer talks and demonstrations by experts. The entries were paid for by the holiday operators, and were correct at the time of going to press, but all details should be carefully checked before making a booking.

The Eastern National Omnibus Company Ltd
New Writtle Street, Chelmsford, Essex CM2 0SD.
☎ *(0245) 56151.*
Day excursions to many famous gardens.
Departure Points: Towns in Essex.
Gardens Visited: Alton Towers, Audley End, Beaulieu, Belton House, Bressingham, Compton Acres, Hampton Court, Hever Castle, Kew Gardens, Luton Hoo, Nymans, Sandringham, The Savill Garden, Sheffield Park, Springfields, Syon Park, Wisley Garden.

Galleon World Travel Ltd
Galleon House, 52 High Street, Sevenoaks, Kent TN13 1JG.
☎ *01-859 0111.*
Five-day 'English Country Gardens Tour' departing from London, visiting Blenheim Palace, Sudeley Castle, Hidcote Manor Gardens and Warwick Castle. All entrance fees included in tour price from £214 per person.

H F Holidays Ltd
142 Great North Way, London NW4 1EG.
☎ *01-203 3381.*
Visiting gardens, gardening and many nature holidays are among the vast range of titles offered. Expert leadership, friendly company and traditional country house accommodation in over 30 locations. Full board and excursions from around £155 weekly.

Hawkstone Park Hotel
Weston under Redcastle, Shrewsbury, Shropshire SY4 5UY.
☎ *Lee Brockhurst (093 924) 611.*
Percy Thrower speciality gardening weekends: 2-night Autumn/Winter break with relaxed programmes with TV's most famous gardener.

Hotel St Michaels
Gyllyngvase Beach, Seafront, Falmouth, Cornwall TR11 4NB.
☎ *(0326) 312707.*
Cornish gardens at their loveliest – Spring Garden Holidays available weekly from 29 March to 10 May; Autumn Holidays 20 & 27 Sept, 4 Oct; from £185 inc VAT, including coach travel and entrance fees to gardens.

Ladbroke Hotels
Garden Lovers Weekends based at the Seven Hills Hotel, Cobham and Ladbroke Hotel, Garforth, nr Leeds; also Stoke Garden Festival Weekends at Ladbroke Hotel, Warwick and Ladbroke International Hotel, Birmingham.
From £70 per person from Friday dinner to Sunday lunch (excluding Saturday lunch), see advertisement on page 107 for more details. For full details on all Garden Lovers Weekends contact: Ladbroke Hotels, Garden Lovers Weekends, PO Box 137, Watford, Herts WD1 1DN.
☎ *(0923) 38877.*

Pavilion Hotel
Bath Road, Bournemouth, Dorset.
☎ *(0202) 291266.*
Centrally-situated hotel offering 'Garden Lovers Holiday': two nights half-board accommodation, picnic lunch for two, flowers in your room on arrival, admission to Compton Acres and Furzey Gardens, free list of all gardens in the area, £5 voucher between two for a local garden centre. Price per person from £54.

Peak National Park Centre
Losehill Hall, Castleton, Derbyshire.
☎ *(0433) 20373.*
Great Houses and Gardens: a 7-day summer holiday with expert guides, including visits to Chatsworth and the National Garden Festival. £134 + VAT per person.
Chris Baines' Wildlife Gardening Weekend – June 1986. Learn how to make your own wildlife garden. £60 per person.

Spring Garden Holidays in Cornwall and Autumn Country Houses & Gardens Holidays
Dept EG, 7 Polventon Close, Falmouth, Cornwall TR11 4AS.
☎ *(0326) 314744.*
Special fully-inclusive, one-week holidays in April, May and September. Visits to many of the beautiful gardens and houses of Cornwall. Accommodation in any of nine recommended Falmouth hotels, £115–£197 per person depending on hotel.

Thatchers Hotel
Epsom Road, East Horsley, nr Guildford, Surrey KT24 6TB.
☎ *(04865) 4291.*
Weekend garden breaks, inclusive of free admission to Royal Horticultural Society Gardens, Wisley. Full details from hotel.

The Gilbert White Museum
'The Wakes', Selborne, Alton, Hampshire GU34 3JH.
☎ *(042 050) 275.*
Historic home and museum of Gilbert White, author of *The National History of Selborne*, and 5-acre garden that was cultivated by White, a keen 18th-century gardener. Adult education day courses run at The Wakes.
Open Mar to Oct, daily exc Mon, 12 noon–5.30pm (last entrance 5pm). Tickets valid all day.

> BEFORE SETTING OUT it's always best to 'phone and check garden details. Opening times and prices may be subject to change at short notice!

KENT GARDEN LOVERS WEEKENDS 1986

A CHANCE TO VISIT HOUSES AND GARDENS SELDOM OPEN TO THE PUBLIC

2 and 3 night breaks including quality hotel accommodation, welcome reception and introductory talk, fully escorted tours by luxury coach to famous and less well known gardens and the option of coach travel from your home town.
PLUS a range of other special interest holidays.

For a brochure, write or phone:
KENT CRUSADER, Dept. GEG. Hill Place, London Road, Southborough, Kent. TN4 0PX   Tel: (0892) 37617

INDEX to GARDENS

Abbey Dore Court Garden	46
Abbey Park	41
Abington Park	41
Abbotsbury Sub-Tropical Gardens	85
Acorn Bank	32
Adlington Hall	62
Akenfield	36
Alton Towers	46
Ambleside Water Gardens	85
Anglesey Abbey	36
Antony House	85
Arbury Hall	46
Arkley Manor Farm & Gardens	79
Arley Hall & Gardens	62
Arlington Court	85
Ascott Gardens	79
Ashridge House Gardens	79
Ashton Court Mansion & Estate	85
Athelhampton	85
Attingham Park	46
Audley End House	36
Jane Austen's House	67
David Austin Roses	46
Avebury Manor	85
Ayscoughfee Gardens	41
Barford Park	85
Barnsley House Garden	46
Barrington Court	85
Barton Manor	67
Batemans	72
Batsford Park Arboretum	46
Battersea Park	53
Beaulieu	67
Bedgebury National Pinetum	72
Beeches Farm	72
Beeston Hall	36
Bekonscot Model Village	79
Belgrave Hall	41
Belle Isle	32
Belsay Gardens	58
Belton House	41
Belvoir Castle	41
Beningbrough Hall	94
Benington Lordship Gardens	79
Bennetts' Water Lily & Fish Gardens	85
Benthall Hall	46
Bentley Wildfowl	72
Berkeley Castle	46
Berrington Hall	46
Bickham House	85
Bickleigh Castle	86
Bicton Park	86
Birdworld Park & Gardens	72
Birmingham Botanical Gardens	46
Blackgang Chine Fantasy Theme Park	67
Blake Hall Gardens	36
Blenheim Palace	79
Blickling Hall	36
Bohunt Manor	67
Borde Hill Garden	72
Borough of Brighton	72
Boughton House	41
Boughton Monchelsea Place	72
Bowes Museum Formal Gardens	58
Bowood House & Gardens	86
Brackenhall Nurseries	58
Bramham Park	94
Brantwood	32
Bredon Springs	47
Bressingham Gardens	36
Bridge End Gardens	36
Bridgemere Garden World	62
Bristol Zoological Gardens	86
Broadlands	67
Broadleas	86
Broughton Castle	79
Brympton d'Evercy	86
Buckland Abbey	86
Burford House Gardens	47
Burnby Hall Gardens	94
Burrow Farm Garden	86
Burton Agnes Hall	94
Burton Constable	94
Buscot Park	79
Cadhay	86
Callally Castle	58
Cambridge University Botanic Gardens	36
Cannon Hall	94
Cannon Hill Park	47
Capel Manor Horticultural and Environmental Centre	79
Capesthorne Hall	62
Castle Ashby	41
Castle Drogo	86
Castle Howard	94
Caversham Court Gardens	79
Central & Lower Gardens, Bournemouth	67
Charlecote Park	47
Chartwell	72
Chase Park	58
Chatsworth	41
Beth Chatto Gardens	36
Chelsea Physic Garden	53
Chenies Manor	79
Cheslyn Gardens	79
Chester Zoo	62
Chiddingstone Castle	72
Chilham Castle Gardens	72
Chillington Hall	47
Chiswick House Grounds	53
Cholmondeley Castle Gardens	62
Christchurch Park	36
City of Bath Botanical Gardens	86
City of Liverpool Botanic Gardens	62
Clack's Farm	47
Clapton Court Gardens	86
Clare College	36
Claremont Landscape Garden	73
Claverton Manor	86
Clevedon Court	86
Cliveden	79
Dorothy Clive Garden	47
Clumber Park	41
Cogges Farm Museum	79
Coleton Fishacre Garden	86
Combe Sydenham Hall	87
The Commandery	47
Compton Acres	67
Constable Burton Hall Gardens	94
Corby Castle	32
Corfe Castle Model Village & Gardens	67
Corsham Court	87
Cotehele House	87
Coton Manor Gardens	41
Cotswold Wild Life Park	80
County Demonstration Garden	87
The Courts	87
Cragside	58
Croft Castle	47
Crossing House	36
Crosspark	87
Crowder's Nurseries & Garden Centre	41
Croxteth Hall & Country Park	62
Cusworth Hall	94
Dalemain	32
Dartington Hall & Gardens	87
Deans Court	67
Deene Park	41
Delapre Abbey Gardens	41
Denmans	73
Dinmore Manor	47
Docwra's Manor	36
Doddington Hall	41
Dorfold Hall	62
Dorney Court	80
Dorsington Manor Gardens	47
Dove Cottage	32
Dudmaston Hall	47
Dulwich Park	53
Dunham Massey	62
Dunster Castle	87
Dyrham Park	87
East Bergholt Lodge	36
East Lambrook Manor	87
Eastnor Castle	47
Ebberston Hall	94
Ednaston Manor	41
Elsham Country Park	94
Elvaston Castle Country Park	42
Emmetts Garden	73
Exbury Gardens	67
Eyhorne Manor	73
Fairhaven Garden Trust	36
Farnborough Hall	80
Felbrigg Hall	36
Ferndene Park	58
Fernwood	87
Fishbourne Roman Palace	73
Fitz House Garden	87
Fletcher Moss Botanical Gardens	62
Forbury Gardens	80
Forde Abbey	87
Fritton Lake	37
Fursdon House	87
Furzey Gardens	67
Fyne Court	87
The Garden House	88
The Gardens of the Rose	80
Gaulden Manor	88
Gawsworth Hall	62
Gilling Castle	94
Glendurgan Gardens	88
The Gnome Reserve	88
Godinton Park	73
Golden Acre Park	94
Golders Hill	53
Gooderstone Water Gardens	37
Goodnestone Park	73
Goodwood House	73
Graythwaite Hall	32
Great Comp	73
Great Dixter	73
Greatham Mill	68
Greenwich Park	53
Greys Court	80
Gunby Hall	42
Haddon Hall	42
Hadspen House	88
Hales Hall	37
Hall Place Gardens	53
Ham House	53
Hampton Court Palace & Gardens	53
Hannah Peschar Gallery	73
Hardwick Hall	42
Hardy's Cottage	88
Hare Hill	62
Haremere Hall	73
Harewood House	94
Harlow Car Gardens	95
Harrington Hall	42
Haseley Manor	68
Hatfield House	80
Haughley Park	37
Heale House Gardens	88
Heaton Park	62
Helmingham Hall Gardens	37
Hergest Croft Gardens	47
Herterton House	58
Hestercombe House	88
Hever Castle	73
Hidcote Manor Garden	48
Highbury	68
Highdown	73
High Peak Garden Centre	42
Hillier Arboretum	68
Himley Hall Park	48
Hoar Cross Hall	48
Hodnet Hall Gardens	48
Hoghton Tower	62
Holdenby House Gardens	42
Holehird	32
Holker Hall & Gardens	32
Holkham Hall	37
Holland Park	53
Hollycombe Garden & Steam Collection	68
Holme Pierrepont Hall	42
Horniman Gardens	53
Hornsea Pottery	62
Houghton Lodge	68
Howick Gardens	58
Hunts Court	48
Hutton-in-the-Forest	32
Hyde Hall Garden	37
Ickworth	37
Iden Croft Herbs	73
Ilford Manor Gardens	88
Isabella Plantation	54
Iveagh Bequest, Kenwood	54
Ivy Cottage Garden	68
Jarrow Hall & Herb Garden	58
Jephson Gardens	48
Jesmond Dene	58
Jodrell Bank Visitor Centre Gardens	62
Jubilee Maze & Museum	48
Kedleston Hall	42
Kelling Park	37
Kensington Gardens	54
Kensington Roof Gardens	54
Kidbrooke Park	73
Kiftsgate Court	48
Killerton	88
Kingston House	80
Kingston Lisle Park & Gardens	80
Kiplin Hall	95
Knebworth House	80
Knightshayes Court	88
Lake District National Park Visitor Centre	33
Lamport Hall	42
Lanhydrock	88
Layer Marney Tower	37
Lea Gardens	42
Lechlade Garden & Fuchsia Centre	48
Leeds Castle	73
Leigh Park Gardens & Sir George Staunton Estate	68
Leith Hill Rhododendron Wood	73
Leonardslee Gardens	74
Lesnes Abbey Woods	54
Levens Hall	33
Lindisfarne Castle Walled Garden	59
Lingholm	33

110

Haddon Hall, Derbyshire

Linton Zoological Gardens	37	Netherfield Herbs	37	Preston Manor	75	Sheffield Botanic Garden	96
Little Moreton Hall	62	Nether Winchendon House	81	The Priory	49	Sheffield Park Garden	75
Liverpool Festival Gardens	64	Newby Hall	95	Pusey House Gardens	81	Sheldon Manor	90
Liverpool University Botanic Gardens	64	New Forest Butterfly Farm	69			Sherborne Castle	90
		Newick Park	74	Quarry Park	49	Sheringham Hall Park	38
Long Cross Victorian Gardens	88	Newstead Abbey	43	Queen Elizabeth Gardens	90	Shinfield Grange	81
		Norfolk Lavender	37	Queen Mary's Rose Garden	54	Shipton Hall	49
Longleat House	88	Normanby Hall Country Park	95	Queens Park	49	Shugborough	49
Loseley House & Park	74			Quex House & the Powell-Cotton Museum	75	Sizergh Castle	33
Lotherton Hall	95	Northbourne Court	74			Sledmere House	96
Luckington Court	88	Norton Bird Gardens	37	Raby Castle	59	Snowshill Manor	50
Luton Hoo	80	Norton Conyers	95	Ragley Hall	49	Somerleyton Hall	38
Lydney Park Gardens	48	Norton Priory Gardens	64	Rainthorpe Hall & Gardens	38	Southover Grange Gardens	76
Lyme Park	64	Nunwell House	69	Red House Museum	69	South Park	59
Lytes Cary Manor	88	Nymans	74	Rievaulx Terrace	95	Spains Hall	38
				Ripley Castle	95	Speke Hall	64
Macpenny's	68	Oakhill Manor	89	River Cam Farm House	38	Spetchley Park	50
Mannington Hall Gardens	37	Old Rectory Herb Garden	74	Riverhill House	75	Spinners	69
The Manor House	88	Old Smithy Complex	69	Rockingham Castle	43	Springfields	43
The Manor House Gardens, Cranborne	68	Ormesby Hall	59	The Rosarium	38	Spring Hill Wildfowl Park	76
		Overbecks	89	Rosemoor Garden Trust	90	Sprivers Gardens	76
Mapperton	88	The Owl House Gardens	74	Roundhay Park	95	Sprowston Garden Centre	38
Mark Hall Gardens	37	Oxburgh Hall	38	Rousham	81	Squerryes Court	76
Marle Place	74			Royal Botanic Gardens, Kew	54	Stagsden Bird Gardens	81
Marwood Hill Gardens	89	Packwood House	48	Rudding Park	96	Stagshaw Gardens	33
John Mattock Rose Nurseries	80	Padstow Tropical Bird & Butterfly Garden	89	Rufford, Notts	43	Standen	76
				Rufford Old Hall, Lancs	64	Stansted Park	69
Mayfield Park	68	Parade Gardens	90	Rusland Hall	33	Stapeley Water Gardens	64
Melbourne Hall	42	Paradise Centre	38	Rydal Hall	33	Stoke Lacy Herb Garden	50
Meldon Park	59	Parcevall Hall Gardens	95	Rydal Mount	33	Stoneacre	76
Merley Bird Gardens	68	Parham Park Gardens	74			Stone House Cottage Gardens	50
Michelham Priory	74	Parnham	90	St Aidan's College	59		
Middle Hill	89	Paultons Country Park & Bird Gardens	69	St James's Park	54	Stonor House & Park	82
Midelney Manor	89			St John's Jerusalem Garden	75	Stour Gardens	38
Milton's Cottage	80	Pavilion Gardens	43	St Nicholas	96	Stourhead	90
Minster Lovell Hall	81	Peakirk Waterfowl Gardens	38	Saling Hall Garden	38	Stourton House Garden	90
Minterne	89	Peckover House	38	Saltram	90	Stowe School Gardens	82
Mirehouse	33	Pencarrow	90	Saltwell Park	59	Stratfield Saye House	69
Misarden Park	48	Penjerrick Gardens	90	Sandford Orcas Manor House	90	Sudbury Hall	43
Moccas Court	48	Penshurst Place	74			Sudeley Castle & Gardens	50
Model Village Gardens	89	Peover Hall & Gardens	64	Sandringham Gardens	38	Sutton Park	96
Montacute House	89	Petworth House & Park	74	Savill/Valley Gardens	81	Swallowfield Park	82
Morton Manor Gardens	68	The Pines Garden	74	Scotney Castle Garden	75	Swanton Mill	76
Moseley Old Hall	48	Pittville Park	49	Seafront Gardens & Canoe Lake, Southsea	69	The Swiss Garden	82
Mottisfont Abbey	68	Polesden Lacey	74			Syon Park Garden	54
Mount Edgcumbe Country Park	89	Port Lympne Zoo Park, Mansion & Gardens	75	Selsley Herb & Goat Farm	59	Tapeley Park	90
				Sewerby Hall	96	Tatton Park	64
Mount Ephraim Garden	74	Poundisford Park	90	Sezincote Garden	49	Temple Newsam Estate	96
Muncaster Castle	33	Powderham Castle	90	Shakespeare Gardens	49		

111

A GUIDE TO ENGLISH GARDENS

ADVERTISERS' INDEX

Tenterden Vineyard Herb Garden	76	University of Bristol Botanic Garden	91	Wallington House, Walled Garden & Grounds	59	Wilberforce House	96
Thoresby Hall	43	University of Durham Botanic Garden	59	Izaak Walton Cottage	50	Wilton House	91
Thornham Herb Garden	38			Walton Hall	64	Wimpole Hall	38
Thorpe Perrow Arboretum	96	University of Leicester Botanic Garden	43	Warwick Castle	50	Winkworth Arboretum	76
Tintinhill House Garden	90			Washington Old Hall	59	Winslow Hall	82
Tradescant Garden	55	University of Oxford Botanic Garden	82	Waterlow Park	55	Winter Gardens, Avery Hill Park	55
Trelissick Gardens	90			Waterperry Gardens	82	Wisley	76
Tremeer Gardens	90	Unwins Seeds Ltd	38	The Weir	50	Wollaton Hall	43
Trengwainton Gardens	90	Upton House	50	Westbury Court Garden	50	Wolterton Hall Gardens	38
Trentham Gardens	50	Upton Country Park	69	West Dean Gardens	76	Woodland Gardens, Bushy Park	55
Trent Park	55			West Green Garden	69		
Tresco Abbey Gardens	90	Vale Royal Abbey	64	Westonbirt Arboretum	50	Wordsworth House	33
Trewithen	91	Valley Gardens	96	Weston Park	50	Wrest Park	82
Tropical Bird Gardens	91	Ventnor Botanic Garden	46	West Wycombe Park	82	Wroxton Abbey	82
Tudor House Garden	69	The Vyne	69	Whalley Abbey	64	Wythenshawe Park & Horticultural Centre	64
		Waddesdon Manor	82	Whatton Gardens	43		
Ugbrooke House	91	Wakehurst Place	76	Gilbert White Museum	69	Yorkshire Museum & Botanical Gardens	96
				Wightwick Manor	50		

ADVERTISERS' INDEX

Alton Towers	19	Festival Gardens	63	Merseyside Development Corporation	63	The Royal National Rose Society	80
Antony Woodland Gardens	85	Granada Motorway Services	22	National Garden Festival, Stoke-on-Trent	23	Savill Garden	81
Bargain Breakaways (National Express)	26	Great Dixter	18			County of Stafford	26
		The Hillier Arboretum	68			Staffordshire Moorlands	25
		Hodnet Hall Gardens	48	National Trust	17	Stoke-on-Trent	27
Batsford Arboretum & Garden Centre	46	The Imperial Hotel, Torquay	89	Ness Gardens	21	Stowe School	82
Beacon Garden Centres Inside Front Cover & 101		Kent Crusader (Kent C.C.)	109	Newby Hall & Studley Royal Inside Back Cover		Sutton Place	72
						Syon Park	55
Brackenwood Nurseries	21	Knebworth House, Gardens & Park	80	North Stafford Hotel, (THF) Stoke-on-Trent	28	Tatton Park	20
Bypass Nurseries	37					The Tradescant Trust	54
Castle Ashby	41	Ladbroke Hotels	107	Painswick House Gardens	48	Trewithen Gardens	20
Chatsworth	42	Leeds Castle	112	Parham Park, House & Gardens	74	Trusthouse Forte Hotels	28
The Chelsea Gardener	53	Levens Hall	18			Tudor House Museum	69
Cheltenham Spa	49	Losehill Hall	43	The Polurrian Hotel, Helston	91	Wakehurst Place	76
County Demonstration Garden, Cornwall	87	Lyme Park	64			Waterperry Gardens	82
		The Majestic Hotel, Harrogate	94	Port Lympne	75	Wisley Garden, (The Royal Horticultural Society's Garden)	76
Dormy House Hotel, Broadway	47			Post House (THF), Newcastle-under-Lyme	28		
Exbury Gardens	67	Mersey River Festival	63				

Once upon a time it was only the loveliest castle in the world.

Set on two islands in the middle of a lake and surrounded by 500 acres of magnificent parkland, Leeds Castle has always been a jewel in the garden of England.

But now it's more.

You can explore the enchanted woodland garden and the Culpeper Flower Garden. Wander through collections of rare wildfowl and exotic tropical birds. See the castle greenhouses, and a vineyard recorded in the Domesday Book. Even play a nine-hole golf course.

The castle itself dates from AD 857 and was converted into a royal palace by Henry VIII. On display are fine paintings, antiques and medieval Flemish tapestries. There's also a museum of ornamental dog collars from the Middle Ages.

When it's time for refreshment there's a choice of restaurants, and several picnic sites. Every Saturday traditional Kentish evenings are held.

Open every day from April to October, 11am to 5pm. Open Saturdays and Sundays only November to March, 12-4pm.

Leeds Castle, nr. Maidstone. Kent. Tel: (0622) 65400.